Praise for Denise Duffield-Thomas

'Denise Duffield-Thomas [is] one of the foremost financial advisors for females.'
ENTREPRENEUR.COM

'Denise Duffield-Thomas is a much-needed voice of practical wisdom for women looking to build a financially thriving future. She's also a shining example of what it means to create a business and life you love while also serving the world.'
MARIE FORLEO, FOUNDER OF MARIETV, B-SCHOOL, AND MARIEFORLEO.COM

'Denise has helped her growing community of 120,000+ business owners overcome their money blocks and build successful companies.'
FORBES.COM

'Denise is one of the most honest, transparent, unapologetic voices out there leading women to prosperity. Her work is so important.'
KATE NORTHRUP, AUTHOR OF MONEY, A LOVE STORY

'Denise offers… so much value and openly and honestly shares what has worked well for her business – and what has not.'
HUFFPOST

'Every single one of us has the ability to create so much success, and what I love about Denise is her ability to show people the way. She's empowered so many women to create the business and life they dreamed of – everyone needs to listen up.'
CARRIE GREEN, FOUNDER OF THE FEMALE ENTREPRENEUR ASSOCIATION AND AUTHOR OF SHE MEANS BUSINESS

'What I love about Denise is her ability to demonstrate that it doesn't have to be all about hustle and grind! [Chill and Prosper] shows that you can make money doing what you love and take great care of yourself and your family along the way, without the stress or burnout. Her authenticity and expertise has inspired me since the very beginning of my journey into business, mindset, and abundance.'
MEL WELLS, AUTHOR OF THE GODDESS REVOLUTION AND HUNGRY FOR MORE

'[Chill and Prosper] *offers a reassuring, practical yet revolutionary take on entrepreneurship. Trade in the hassle of hustle for strategic flow. And get richer to boot!*'

SUSAN HYATT, AUTHOR AND MASTER LIFE COACH

'*Denise is the leading voice in building a highly profitable business with ease and grace. The guidance this book provides will absolutely change your outlook and mindset on not only business, but life itself. I am forever grateful for the work Denise is putting into the world!*'

MAGGIE BERGHOFF, CELEBRITY HEALTH EXPERT

'*Denise is one of the world's best teachers on the Law of Attraction. Every day she impresses me with her wisdom, business savvy, integrity, and teachings.*'

LEONIE DAWSON, AUTHOR OF *LESSONS EVERY GODDESS MUST KNOW* AND THE *MY SHINING YEAR* WORKBOOKS

'*Denise is the ultimate money mindset mentor. With her systems, tools, and tricks to open up your heart and mind to receive the abundance that is your birthright, you can't fail. Everybody needs some Denise in their life.*'

SUSIE MOORE, AUTHOR OF *WHAT IF IT DOES WORK OUT?*

'*I am a massive fan of Denise, her books, and her courses. Down to earth, honest, and at times hilarious, she shows us how to create a truly exceptional life.*'

REBECCA CAMPBELL, AUTHOR OF *LIGHT IS THE NEW BLACK* AND *RISE SISTER RISE*

'*I am constantly referring people to Denise's work on money mindset so they can break through their money blocks and step into their highest potential. She is a fresh and powerful voice in business, finance, and lifestyle design.*'

DIANA HOUSE, REAL ESTATE DEVELOPER AND PRIVATE LENDER

'*Denise is a refreshing voice on money mindset. She writes in a way that is easeful and humorous, and you'll feel like she's right there with you as you put her lessons to work and create a more abundant business and life.*'

NATALIE MACNEIL, AUTHOR OF *SHE TAKES ON THE WORLD* AND *THE CONQUER KIT*

'In a world that traditionally celebrates "busy" as a badge of honor, Denise is leading the way with a fresh (and much-needed) approach to entrepreneurship. With easy-to-follow steps and her signature down-to-earth style, we can all put our feet up and breathe a sigh of relief that running our own business no longer has to lead to burnout.'

AMANDA JANE DALEY, BUSINESS MENTOR TO WELLNESS ENTREPRENEURS

'[Chill and Prosper] is a much-needed antidote to today's busy-worshipping culture, and a complete breath of fresh air for over-hustled women in business everywhere. In true Denise style, this book is full of no-BS, practical advice for creating success without the stress.'

KATE MCKIBBIN, FUNNEL AND MARKETING MENTOR

'Denise's approach to business is smart, funny, HONEST, and delightfully practical. In her books, her programs, her LIFE... she's walking her [Chill and Prosper] talk, holding up the mirror to remind us that when in doubt (or stuck in overwhelm, perfectionism, or shoulds), "there are easier ways to make money."'

NIKKI ELLEDGE BROWN, AUTHOR AND CREATOR OF A COURSE ABOUT COPY® AND NAPTIME EMPIRES™

'[Chill and Prosper] almost sounds too good to be true, especially living in a world where the word "hustle" seems like the only prescription for a successful business. Denise offers an alternative that intersects intentional manifesting and mindful actions which keeps you and your business in receiving mode, while giving you more energy, time, and money as you grow in your entrepreneurship'

JENNIFER KEM, FOUNDER OF THE MASTER BRAND METHOD

'Denise and I are so on the same page when it comes to designing your business around what you love most. [Chill and Prosper] makes it crystal clear that you simply don't need to overcomplicate anything. By being a Chillpreneur you commit to simplifying everything, focusing on your strengths, appreciating what you already have, and then sitting back to watch the abundance and joy you've manifested into your life as a result! In a world where too many people are stressed out, burned out, anxious, and hustling like crazy, Denise's book is a breath of fresh air to do the exact opposite. It's a must read!'

NATALIE SISSON, FREEDOMIST AND AUTHOR OF THE FREEDOM PLAN AND THE SUITCASE ENTREPRENEUR

'Denise Duffield-Thomas is authentic, real, and inspiring. In [Chill and Prosper], she redefines entrepreneurial culture from the perspective of balance and conscious integration. This is a must-read book for attracting abundance into your life.'

SARAH PROUT, AUTHOR OF *DEAR UNIVERSE* AND HOST OF THE JOURNEY TO MANIFESTING PODCAST

'If you're exhausted, sick of being told you have to "crush it," and over the mindset that you need to work like a maniac to be successful in business, this book will be the balm to your burnout. You don't have to sacrifice your sanity or your soul to run a successful business. There is a more aligned path to abundance and Denise has written the roadmap.'

MEGAN DALLA-CAMINA, FOUNDER OF WOMEN RISING AND AUTHOR OF *SIMPLE SOULFUL SACRED*

'Who said we had to work harder to live larger? Not true. Denise reminds us that income can be elegant when we align with our divine design. A wonderful read and long overdue permission slip!'

MARSHAWN EVANS DANIELS, GODFIDENCE COACH® AND FOUNDER OF SHEPROFITS.COM

'[Denise] offers her unique take on how to work less, earn more and leave the daily grind behind so you can enjoy what many of us value most: our time.'

ELAINE POFELDT, SENIOR CONTRIBUTOR, *FORBES*

Chill

and

PROSPER

Also by Denise Duffield-Thomas

Lucky Bitch: A Guide for Exceptional Women
to Create Outrageous Success

Get Rich, Lucky Bitch!: Release Your Money
Blocks and Live a First-Class Life

DENISE DUFFIELD-THOMAS

Chill and PROSPER

The New Way to **Grow** Your Business, **Make** Millions, and **Change** the World

Previously published as *Chillpreneur*

HAY HOUSE

Carlsbad, California • New York City
London • Sydney • New Delhi

Published in the United Kingdom by:
Hay House UK Ltd, The Sixth Floor, Watson House
54 Baker Street, London W1U 7BU
Tel: +44 (0)20 3927 7290; www.hayhouse.co.uk

Published in the United States of America by:
Hay House Inc., PO Box 5100, Carlsbad, CA 92018-5100
Tel: (1) 760 431 7695 or (800) 654 5126; www.hayhouse.com

Published in Australia by:
Hay House Australia Ltd, 18/36 Ralph St, Alexandria NSW 2015
Tel: (61) 2 9669 4299; www.hayhouse.com.au

Published in India by:
Hay House Publishers India, Muskaan Complex, Plot No.3, B-2,
Vasant Kunj, New Delhi 110 070. Tel: (91) 11 4176 1620; www.hayhouse.co.in

Text © Denise Duffield-Thomas, 2019, 2022

Previously published as *Chillpreneur* (hardback ISBN: 978-1-78817-203-5;
tradepaper ISBN: 978-1-78817-139-7).

A catalogue record for this book is available from the British Library.

Tradepaper ISBN: 978-1-4019-6830-4
E-book ISBN: 978-1-78817-803-7
Audiobook ISBN: 978-1-78817-799-3

Interior images: 1, 63, 135, 217: Shutterstock.com; author photo 303: Michelle
Swan

This book was written on the traditional lands of the Awabakal people.
We pay our respect to Elders past, present, and future.

11 10 9 8 7 6 5 4 3 2

Printed in the United States of America

This book is dedicated to my family.
Thanks for supporting my work
(even on my not-so-chilled days)
so that together, we can create a life of freedom,
adventure, abundance, and JOY.

Contents

Introduction

*Y*ou've heard of resting bitch face, right? Well, apparently, I have resting chill face. Everyone assumes that I'm calm, collected, and never stressed about anything. 'Denise, you're so *relaxed!*' they say. 'What's your secret?'

Maybe it's because I'm Australian: as a nation, we're notoriously laid-back, and our unofficial motto is: 'She'll be right, mate.' But the truth is, I wasn't born with a happy-go-lucky personality: I've *consciously* learned how to cultivate that attitude. Remember the book *Don't Sweat the Small Stuff... and It's All Small Stuff?* Well, I used to sweat *everything*. Literally. Anxiety often made me a sweaty, stinky mess. And then I'd get worried about *that* too.

In my early days as an employee and a fledgling entrepreneur, I was riddled with insecurity. I worried about everything, but especially about making mistakes. I second-guessed every word I spoke or wrote, and constantly thought:

- Am I good enough to make it?

- Was that really a good session with my client? Or is she regretting working with me? She'll probably ask for a refund, won't she?

- Did I say that in the right tone of voice? Did I apologize too much? Was I too demanding?

I was terrified of opening my email inbox because I was sure I'd find bad news, like a complaint, a refund request, or hate mail. In snail mail, I just expected bills, parking fines, or speeding tickets. I was afraid of getting things wrong, like which system to use, which book to write first (I've always had a million ideas floating around my head), or whether a specific coach was right for me. I was in analysis paralysis because I second-guessed myself at every turn, and the consequences of making the wrong decision seemed catastrophic.

I even worried about what would happen if I *did* become wildly successful. I had a recurring nightmare about being a regular on Oprah's show and having to wake up at 4:30 a.m. every day for hair and makeup. I'd lie awake and stress: 'But I like my sleep! How do I say no to *Oprah*?' I barely had a business, but I had tons of future worries about it!

Personal development helped a lot. Through it all, I had an underlying belief that, one day, I would be successful, even though I was so often anxious. I always had big dreams and just knew I'd be a millionaire one day.

I always wanted to run my own business. Even as a kid, I was the 'go-to' girl for others. I had a knack for breaking down people's problems and helping them, even if all I did was reassure them that, somehow, we'd figure it out together. When my friends' parents thought I was dealing drugs to their teenagers, I was just selling self-help! 'Don't worry, let's journal it out,' I'd tell my friends. Or I'd parrot Oprah advice I'd heard on TV.

My academic advisor at university laughed at my A+ grades in marketing and my Fs in economics, statistics, and accounting. 'Denise, you're so creative, but your assignments are full of BS,' he said. 'In 10 years' time, you'll either be a millionaire or in jail for fraud.' Well, here I am, free as a bird, a self-made millionaire using my powers for good! Rather than learning to be a better statistician or economist, I doubled down on my creativity and became an entrepreneur!

When I started teaching my first personal development workshops (at age 19), I was surprised that people listened to what I had to say. Even though I was just regurgitating the words of the male self-help gurus of the time, people *believed* in the borrowed confidence that helped me believe in myself.

Slowly, slowly, I got more traction in my business, until I became one of those 20-years-in-the-making 'overnight successes' and could legitimately call myself a millionaire. Along the way, I got more chill about making mistakes (I still make them all the time), and I stopped caring (as much) about whether everyone liked me. I finally learned not to sweat the proverbial small stuff.

The idea of being a Type A personality never quite resonated with me – although I'm hardworking and ambitious, I've never been about winning for the sake of winning. I'm not really competitive, even though I have high standards for myself; Type B seemed more my style. But I realized there's a third category that's even more my style: Type C – a chilled, ambitious-but-lazy, wants-to-change-the-world-but-also-thinks-there's-an-easier-way person.

That's what this book is about. I'm not going to teach you how to hustle or tell you to get up earlier (the older I get, the more I realize how important sleep is). I'm actually going to teach you the opposite – business really doesn't have to be that hard! You can get to a place where your business supports your dreams but doesn't burn you out. Where you feel 'enoughness' at the end of the day, but you're excited to achieve your next big goal.

I know the future is uncertain but there's never been a better time to be in business for yourself, and the opportunities before us are mind-blowing. Freedom and independence can be yours with just a little bit of upfront work. I don't understand, technically, how the internet works, but the tools we have available to us are magical and life-changing.

When I count my blessings and write my gratitude list, you'd better believe that techy geeks are on it, because they helped me change my life, and in turn, the lives of thousands of other women. All hail those Silicon Valley dudes (let's face it, most of them are men). They might not be the most feminist people, but they've created opportunities for people like us to gain an unprecedented level of economic independence, and for that, I'm grateful.

Being an entrepreneur once required a lot of upfront capital for machines and stock, or techy know-how. It felt official and serious, like a title that was bestowed upon you (maybe even by a business school). An entrepreneur was either an eccentric inventor or a door-to-door salesman. You were restricted by where you lived, so too bad if that was some crappy little town in the middle of nowhere.

Hey, but not now! Today, anyone can start a business, good or bad. As long as you have internet access, you can sell glitter penis-grams from your tiny house in Nebraska. You can design websites from the beach in Tulum, Mexico. Or you can run a global coaching business from a small town in Australia (even with crappy internet), which is exactly how I got started.

There's no limit to what you can do. Not everyone will succeed the first (or 40th) time, but while failure used to mean bankruptcy or piles of unwanted stuff in your garage, now you can just close up your virtual shop and try something else. No big deal: there are plenty more ideas in the sea! People like us are succeeding more than ever and are finally seeing entrepreneurship as a viable vehicle for supporting their families, for creating wealth for themselves and others, and for changing the world.

But it's not all sunshine and roses. Even though women (especially women of color) are the fastest-growing group of entrepreneurs, there's a lot of built-in obstacles if you don't fit the mold of traditional business. Being an entrepreneur used to mean men in suits, and now it's bro-dudes in hoodies. Small (to Silicon Valley's eyes) businesses aren't always considered 'real enterprises' or respected by mainstream entrepreneurial publications. There's a very real wage gap in the entrepreneurial world, too, and a real lack of diverse role models. But nobody can work harder than an entrepreneur with a dream, and most people I meet are *more than* smart and creative enough. The biggest problem is that we're all still trying to fit our businesses into an old, outdated model. And that's exhausting! Throw in global uncertainty, political division, and community groups imploding with in-fighting, and I can imagine you could be feeling less-than-chill right now.

What Inspired This Book?

I love business books, but at some point I noticed the usual ones stopped resonating with me. So much so that, one day, I briefly considered throwing the book I was reading across the room. I may even have sworn at it.

It was a bestselling title about how world-class performers live and work, and the case study I'd just read featured a 'successful' entrepreneur who got up every day at 4:30 a.m. to work on his blog and podcast until 1 a.m., slept on the couch, and woke the next morning to do it all again – on three hours' sleep.

I actually wrote 'WTF!' in the margin. My first thought was, *He has a kid? And a wife?* My second thought was, *Wait. This is success?* These business books were full of talk about 'crushing your goals' and 'killing your competition.' It was the old, hustle-at-all-costs nonsense that still permeates entrepreneurial culture. It's exhausting.

I realized that many of the people I was taking business advice from had no clue how hard it was to juggle a business and young kids, because often it didn't impact them.

Not everyone reading this book has kids (or wants them), but maybe you're sick of the hustle culture and how it messes with your wellbeing or other life obligations. Equally, many traditional non-fiction authors have never experienced running a business when faced with systemic inequality, racism, homophobia, transphobia, a chronic illness, discrimination, or other realities of life.

Your story matters too. You deserve business success too.

> *'I am endlessly fascinated that playing*
> *football is considered a training ground for*
> *leadership, but raising children isn't.'*
>
> DEE DEE MYERS

At the beginning of my business, I didn't know any better either. I regularly woke at 4:30 a.m. to work with international clients. I worked day and night. I dreamed about clients and spreadsheets in my sleep. I never had time for friends, let alone decent meals. I was obsessed with 'making it' at all costs, and it wasn't healthy.

Everyone's version of success is different, but most people I talk with these days have lost a certain amount of *richness* in their lives. They feel like they're working harder than ever for diminishing returns, both in a financial sense and in satisfaction with their work. They are missing the *joy*.

Hustling for cash is exhausting. Many of us are juggling our business dreams with partners, kids, family obligations, school, waxing appointments, and just *life*. You don't want to work all day and night. You want time to go to the beach, get to that yoga class, see your friends and family, and be a more present partner, caregiver, sibling, and friend. And you can. But it's really common to get sucked into the trap of: 'If I want more money, I have to work *harder*.' Most of the methods we use in our work, and those in the books we read, have been created and governed by outdated models of success. I never questioned that until I burned myself out.

*'Entrepreneurs are the only people who will
work 80 hours a week to avoid working
40 hours a week for someone else.'*

LORI GREINER

Why was I waking up at 4:30 a.m. when I started my business? Well, I had clients on the other side of the world, and I felt bad about asking them to work with me outside their normal hours. (Oh boy, we're going to have an honest conversation about boundaries later in this book.) Why did I often pull all-nighters? I once worked on a sales page all night, followed by three straight hours of coaching calls, and then delivered a live webinar – all on no sleep. I did this because I felt terrible about the idea of hiring someone and asking for help. If you suck at this, too, don't worry: I have some tips for you later.

Back then, my friend James told me, 'Denise, you can't get to six figures by doing it all yourself.' My answer? 'Watch me.' Yeah, that's stupid. But when I *did* hit six figures, I felt a massive wave of discouragement instead of celebration. I was a 'success story,' but not really. My success didn't feel sustainable (in truth, it felt like a massive fluke), and there was no obvious way to increase my income without working harder. I was already stressed and tired.

In my early days in business, I met a fellow coach who told me she saw 100 clients a week. My first thought was, *When do you pee?* My second was, *Oh my God – I energetically max out at 15 clients a week.* I probably made the same amount of money as she did, and I instantly felt guilty for working fewer hours than I 'should.' *Maybe I should see 100 clients?* I thought. *What's wrong with me?*

I honestly believed that taking any shortcut was lazy, instead of smart. But the truth is that we've all started our business for the freedom and flexibility it gives us, not to replicate our old jobs, and definitely not to do *more* work for less lifestyle. I wanted a business that helped others, was wildly profitable, but didn't suck all my energy and time or leave me a husk of a person attached to my computer screen. It was time for a new breed of entrepreneur. It was time for the Chillpreneur. It was time to chill and prosper.

I know, I know. Everyone is some type of '-preneur' these days; it's *beyond* cheesy. But most of the heart-centered entrepreneurs I know don't want to hustle anymore. We don't want to 'crush' anything, especially not the competition. We want to *collaborate* with other women, not *kill* them! We want *everyone* to succeed. And we'd also love to have the time to create a garden, have a hobby, or get our hair and nails done occasionally.

Is that too much to ask? No.

What's a Chillpreneur Anyway?

> *'My guiding principle is that prosperity can be shared. We can create wealth together. The global economy is not a zero-sum game.'*
>
> JULIA GILLARD, FORMER PRIME MINISTER OF AUSTRALIA

As you'll discover, being a Chillpreneur isn't about working from a hammock in Bali (I've been in a hammock twice in my life, and I fell out of it the first time). Instead, it's about finding a new way of doing business: one that works for your bank account and supports your wellbeing; one that works for you and everyone else on the planet.

A Chillpreneur:

- Believes in abundance for everyone and builds equity and equality into business

- Finds the path of least resistance and doesn't reinvent the wheel

- Practices kindness and self-acceptance, knowing perfection is impossible

- Gives themselves permission to succeed precisely as they are

- Wants to make the world a better place

Being a Chillpreneur is a practice. I'm no Jedi Master of business, even though I've made tens of millions of dollars. I'm still in my 'chillprenticeship,' and I have to practice being a Chillpreneur every day because the 'hustle and grind' culture is embedded as the norm.

How to Read This Book 'Perfectly'

Do you want to know how to *crush* this book and *win* at reading it? Yeah... no. There's no badge for finishing it in record time, and no prizes for perfection. Some people tell me they love to have multiple versions – the audiobook for the car and a paper copy to take notes. Whatever works!

There are four parts to the book:

- **Mindset** (how to get your head in the game)

- **Business Models** (how to structure your business for success)

- **Money** (how to set prices and deal with awkward money conversations)

- **Marketing** (how to get clients by using the most uncomplicated two-step marketing strategy ever)

I've created a bonus online 'Action Guide' that summarizes each chapter and has all the exercises in one handy place, plus some extra resources and bonuses. Download it at www.denisedt.com/chill (do this now, before you forget).

Why a New Edition?

First up, a big thank you to everyone who read and shared the first edition, titled *Chillpreneur*; it got to #1 on multiple Amazon Best Seller lists.

Since handing in the manuscript while heavily pregnant with baby #3, a lot has changed in my life. We built our dream house by the ocean and bought a rose farm property as a second business and holiday home. We've got two dogs now, too. So I have an even bigger appreciation for business simplification.

I was also recently diagnosed with ADHD, something that, in hindsight, I've had all my life. Many people pointed out that *Chillpreneur* was a manual for those who struggle with executive dysfunction (hello, #keylesslife). A lot of my business tips are obvious ADHD hacks – so that was a fun realization.

I wrote the first edition of this book during one of the most challenging years of my entrepreneurial journey, and now I've written this new edition during a global pandemic where life has changed for all of us.

During stressful times, we forget that life is allowed to be easy and that you don't have to put literal blood, sweat, and tears (ew) into your business. You don't have to sacrifice your adrenals, relationship, or sleep to create success in your life.

Hear this from a recovering perfectionist workaholic who is now a pretty chilled-out multimillionaire with young kids: it's possible, and this book will show you how.

I've received so many emails and social media messages from people about how *Chillpreneur* has inspired business simplification, pivots, and fresh, new ideas to get them through hard times. In many cases, it's helped them achieve their best revenue ever.

In this new edition, retitled *Chill and Prosper*, I wanted to showcase some of these success stories, so you can see it's possible for YOU too. No matter what's happening in the world, I want you to know you can still thrive and, yes, prosper.

Keep this secret between us, okay? I've made $20 million (Australian dollars) with the advice I'm going to give you in this book, yet I feel like I've half-assed everything in my business. I've simply shown up and told people how I can help them.

My favorite affirmation of all time is: 'It's my time, and I'm ready for the next step.'

I can show you the path, but you have to decide on your own that you're ready to walk it. You won't have to make big, dramatic changes; just take a teeny baby step forward, and the following action will become clear. Someone has already invented every conceivable tool you'll need to support your business (and think how many more are to come!) Your ideas might not yet be fully formed, but you have everything you need to birth them.

It's your time, and you're ready for the next step.

You're ready to chill and prosper.

xx Denise

P.S. I'm sorry in advance, but there are so many cheesy chill-related puns in this book. Feel free to DM me if you think of any I missed. I'm always happy to hear from you regardless!

Keep in touch while you're reading this book; I'm here for you and rooting for your success:

Instagram: @denisedt
Facebook: facebook.com/denisedt
Twitter: @denisedt
Download your book bonuses here: www.denisedt.com/chill

— PART I —

Mindset

CHAPTER 1

Playing the Game of Business

*'Most people consider life a battle, but
it is not a battle, it is a game.'*

FLORENCE SCOVEL SHINN

*H*aving created a multimillion-dollar business without taking outside investment or working my guts out (while also raising young kids), I'm often asked my number-one secret to success. The answer is: *mindset*. Constantly working on your mindset is honestly the most important – if not the only – thing you have to master. Everything else, you can just Google. Really. Business isn't that complicated.

Unfortunately, entrepreneurs often think they need more qualifications, a new funnel, or a different website, instead of working on their fears, beliefs, and other mindset issues. (Seriously, stop worrying about your funnels; you'll figure it out.) Of course, you need a product or service that people want to buy, you need to market yourself, and there are a million logistical things to do, but without the right mindset, everything else will fall apart.

Basically, being in business is like playing a giant, real-life game of snakes and ladders (AKA chutes and ladders). The board-game version is a game of chance. If you roll the dice and happen to land on a snake (chute), you fall behind. Bad luck. And if you land on a ladder, you get to skip ahead. There's no skill involved at all – your fortune is totally determined by the luck of the dice.

In reality, the rules aren't so clear-cut or the same for everyone. Even so, I believe we can make our own luck. In the world of entrepreneurship, each time you encounter an obstacle, you can choose how you engage with it. You can't avoid obstacles, but fortunately, you don't need to do that to 'win' the game. The weird thing is that, when normal, inevitable challenges come up – like a refund request – some people not only fall down, they launch themselves down a snake/chute and refuse to play the game again, convinced they're a failure. They quit, or remain paralyzed for years by fear, shame, and indecision.

Your life and business are never going to be perfect. But as a Chillpreneur, you see the silver lining in everything.

Failed launch? *We can learn so much from this for next time!*

Tech screw-up? *Sweet, this is a juicy chapter for my next book!*

Everything is useful and nothing is wasted. In fact, failures are great fodder for podcasts, blog posts, and future Oprah interviews.

I call these 'chilltastrophes' – when shit happens, but it doesn't ruin your life anymore. Remember, perfection isn't the goal. Perfection doesn't make you money. You can play the game lightly. It doesn't have to weigh down on you and be super-serious.

Knowing ahead of time about these inevitable rites of passage gives you the opportunity to be reasonably chill about things you can't avoid. It's unlikely that you'll have zero refund requests for your services; so, if you know that they're inevitable, you can stop 'pre-worrying' about them, and they won't bother you as much when they happen (and they will).

You have a choice: throw yourself down a snake/chute and stop playing the game, or shrug, pick yourself up, and roll the dice to see what's next in your entrepreneurial adventure. Being an entrepreneur isn't life-or-death. In the grand scheme of things, it's not that serious or hard. As scary as it is some days, it's still better than doing a job you hate or wasting your potential. Working on a good money mindset is like finding the cheat codes or a bonus power-up.

I'm not that amazing at business, but I know how to play the game. I've become successful because I choose to see obstacles as inevitable rites of passage along the path to my destiny. I've experienced the same challenges as any other entrepreneur, but I've always found a way to reframe them instead of letting them derail me.

Seriously, I've celebrated every 'bad' thing that has happened because I know it brings me one step closer to success. My first one-star book review on Amazon? I celebrated! My first refund request? I felt like I'd made it! It's not that these things felt good (far from it): I just knew that it was a mark of success, like making it through to the next level of a challenging video game. I made it through and I didn't die! Whoo-hoo! See the difference?

How many people do you know who have experienced an ordinary setback like this and just quit in shame and fear? I've seen people quit after a single refund request, convinced they must be terrible at their business. I've seen entrepreneurs give up after a less-than-spectacular launch, not realizing that anyone who has created a thriving business had crappy launches too.

Everyone starts from zero – *everyone*! The journey is inescapable. You have to be willing to get through everything on your way to your chillionaire life. Playing the game doesn't mean you won't get scared. In fact, the biggest obstacle you'll face is fear.

Do You Really Have What It Takes?

You might be thinking *I'm not brave enough to do this*. Or *I'm not competitive enough to make it in business*. I understand. I don't even like playing Monopoly, and I'm not at all cut-throat. Plus, I'm the biggest introvert in the world. But the belief that you have to be a certain way or a particular personality type comes from a place of scarcity. There's more than enough business to go around, but we've been taught from a young age that there are only a few slots available for success, and they go to the most competitive, deserving, or ambitious.

I call this the 'Highlander Myth.' *Highlander* is the cult 1986 movie, starring Christopher Lambert and Sean Connery, whose premise is that some immortal Highlander warriors have to defeat each other for the ultimate prize: the power to rule the world. There's no amicable sharing of power. It's a fight to the death, and the winner absorbs the other's life-force after basically decapitating him for no reason other than to win. On its release, the movie's tagline was: 'There can be only One.'

I don't know about you, but I don't want to rule the world: I just want to contribute to making it a better place. I don't want to kill my competitors – I actually like them. I'm just not that competitive or ruthless; I want everyone to win! Before you beat yourself up for not having the right 'edge' to make it in business, think about the messages you've been absorbing your whole life: success is a zero-sum game. This age-old story leads to all sorts of screwed-up business beliefs, including:

- There can be only one person like me in my industry or niche.

- There's only one guru of the gurus.

- There can be only one success story in my peer group.

How many times have you come up with a great idea, but thought it was already taken? Or believed you have to be the Oprah of your industry, and therefore didn't even try? Think of the 'cool kid' in your industry. Do you compare yourself (unfavorably) to them? Are they your benchmark of success because they seem to be the popular one who everyone wants to work with?

Good news: you don't have to decapitate anyone to be successful in business! Whew, right? They're probably no more special than you are; there's room for you, too. You just have to release some of your old programming about competition. There's only one Oprah, and there's only one you. You have just as much right to be here as anyone else. So, every time you think you're not unique enough to make it, remember: you don't have to kill everyone else in your industry and absorb their power. There's more than enough to go around!

It's not just *Highlander*. Pretty much every movie perpetuates this 'there can be only one' myth, especially when there's room for only one primary female character. She's usually of royal birth (Princess Leia, Snow White, Wonder Woman), The Smart One (Hermione Granger), or the token minority character (where there's definitely only one).

Back in 1991, Katha Pollitt of *New York* magazine coined a term for token female characters: the 'Smurfette Principle.' She says: 'The message is clear. Boys are the norm, girls the variation; boys are central, girls peripheral; boys are individuals, girls types. Boys define the group, its story and its code of values. Girls exist only in relation to boys.'[1]

In the Smurfs cartoon, there was Brainy Smurf, Clumsy Smurf, Greedy Smurf, Hefty Smurf, Jokey Smurf, and... Vagina Smurf. Sorry, I mean Smurfette: the only female Smurf in the whole village. Smurfette didn't have any defining attributes or personality traits – she was special because she was the Only.

But that's the message all around us. Most reality shows follow the same concept: there can be only one winner. Participants have to compete and be eliminated each week until there's only one contestant left. Most of the time, there isn't even a prize for the runner-up! Everyone else must lose, which sucks, because most people don't want to win at the expense of someone else. It feels mean and bitchy, especially if you've ever been excluded from the 'cool group' yourself.

Beyond the Smurfette/Princess trope, there's rarely more than one Black main character, or a LGBTQ2+ main character, or a disabled character with their own agency and personality beyond their disability.

Do you see yourself represented on the bookshelves or winning entrepreneurial awards? The rallying cry of this decade is 'representation matters,' and in a world where you may still face inequality, you have to deem yourself eligible to play the game and make your own rules. There can be more than one winner.

As my friend Rachel Rodgers says in her book *We Should All Be Millionaires*, 'To earn millions, you first have to stop believing what the world says you are capable of as a Black woman, lesbian woman, disabled woman, fat woman, trans woman, loud woman, bossy woman, or filthy-mouthed woman.'[2]

Choosing Yourself

The great news is that you don't have to be the best or the smartest to succeed in business. It's not a popularity contest, and there's more than enough room for everyone. *But you do have to choose yourself.* And that's one of the hardest mindset lessons to master: *I deserve success. I'm good enough. I'm ready. I believe in myself.*

It feels presumptuous to choose yourself, or to be too confident about your accomplishments. It feels audacious to say that you like and believe in yourself, let alone believe in your business success.

> *'I had to make my own living and my own opportunity!*
> *But I made it! Don't sit down and wait for the*
> *opportunities to come. Get up and make them.'*
> MADAM C.J. WALKER

I once had a dude at a barbecue ask my husband how my business was doing, and when Mark said, 'Great, actually!' the guy responded, 'Well, some people will buy any old shit, won't they?' I couldn't believe it! Obviously if I was successful without working hard, I must be somehow scamming people.

Sometimes I forget that my business success isn't the norm. I chose myself. I self-published my first books, built my first website myself, and had the audacity to run my own workshops before anyone else thought I was worthy enough. No way was I going to wait until the dice rolled a lucky number. I decided I was enough to get started and to build success, despite what other people thought.

Here's the thing: nobody is going to give you permission to be successful, so stop waiting for external validation. I know – waiting for someone to pick you can be excruciating. Remember at school when you had to line up and wait for the team captains to pick those they wanted on their side? It can feel that way in business, too – like someone else has to deem you ready for the big stage.

The truth is that you'll never feel ready enough, and chances are that nobody is going to 'choose' you. You have to choose yourself. When I first started teaching personal development, I didn't exactly look and feel like a success story, especially when I drove up in my dodgy 20-year-old car with the saggy roof hanging around my ears. But I started small, and most importantly, I *showed up* and declared myself ready. My first few goal-setting workshops had four people on average. Then 10, then 20, and now, we regularly get hundreds to a seminar. Maybe one day, thousands.

I declared myself an author way before anyone else believed I was one. I wasn't waiting for someone else to choose me, and I wasn't waiting until I felt 'anointed' by the universe. I decided that there was room for me, and yes, there's room for you too. There's room for:

- The introverts and extroverts

- The natural leaders and the more quiet followers

- The confident and the sensitive

- All ages, sizes, and backgrounds

You don't have to be the best, and you don't have to compete against anyone to be successful. Why not you, too?

> *— Lesson —*
>
> **You'll never feel ready enough, and chances are that nobody is going to 'choose' you. You don't have to wait to be anointed by someone. You can choose yourself.**

CASE STUDY: PLAYING THE GAME

Name: *Olga Bochareva, Texas, USA (born and raised in Russia)*
Business: *Real estate law*

My husband and I run our business together, and we were particularly helped by the 'snakes and ladders' concept. You roll the dice, and sometimes you win, sometimes you lose. It doesn't mean you should stop playing the game.

We were embarking on some new marketing projects, and our first big attempt, cold-calling large complexes, was pretty much a lost cause. We didn't enjoy it, and it didn't work. But thanks to Chill and Prosper, we didn't make it mean that we couldn't do marketing. We rolled the dice again, this time opening a Facebook group for Texas landlords. The group was a hit; we grew to 1,500 members quickly and we now have new clients finding us every week.

We've since taken more of a game-like approach to our marketing, and it's a fun experiment to see what works. We recently started playing with Instagram, and we're excited to see if it's a snake or a ladder for us. Now we know that some of our marketing efforts won't work, and that's okay. Through consistently implementing small changes in our business and playing the game of snakes and ladders, we have generated a multiple six-figure income in the last year.

— *Lesson* —

You don't have to quit. You can roll the dice and play again.

Be a Contributor, Not a Guru

One of the most popular posts on my blog was '37 Lessons from Becoming a Self-Made Millionaire,' and lesson number 35 was: 'I'm a contributor, not a guru.' As soon as I gave myself permission to *contribute* to the conversation about money and mindset, and not have to be a guru or expert on it, my business became fun. If you truly and deeply care about a topic or cause, be a contributor. Who cares if you don't know everything? You don't have to be the best to make a difference to someone.

I didn't expect the response I got to that 'lesson.' People took screenshots of it and messaged me to say how powerful it was and how relieved they were to hear that they don't have to be a guru to be successful. It resonated so deeply with people that I decided to include it in this book. And it's central to the Chillpreneur philosophy. To me, it meant that I didn't have to try so hard. Suddenly, success in business seemed attainable. I could just show up and teach what I knew, and that was enough. I didn't have to be super-special! I could be one of many voices.

When I really 'got' this, everything changed in my business. I gave myself permission to show up exactly as I am. It helped me to feel excited about offering my work to the world, to make offers to potential clients, and to extend invitations to people to join my Money Bootcamp – even though I wasn't Oprah.

I also became a lot less precious about my work because I knew it didn't have to be completely groundbreaking or unique to make a difference to the people who needed to hear it from *me*. I worried less about competitors because I cared so much about the overall mission: that heart-centered entrepreneurs change the way they feel about money. How can I begrudge anyone talking about money, too, when we're all striving to achieve the same outcome?

I was so passionate about the topic that I didn't care about being the 'One' anymore. In fact, I realized that my voice was needed to tip the overall mission into the mainstream. The more money conversations, the better, and I didn't need the ego trip of being the gatekeeper of information.

Why *not* you, too? You're allowed to add your voice and perspective. Who's going to stop you? There's no 'cool kid' deciding who's in and who's out. Only *you* can decide if you're 'worthy' enough. And you are – but only if you choose to be.

I no longer get hugely nervous when speaking on stage, and I don't feel overwhelmed by meeting hundreds of people at events, because I know they aren't showing up to see 'me.' They want to see a representation of themselves. They want to see an example of an imperfect person choosing herself. It's attractive, compelling, and inspiring.

In his book *The War of Art*, Steven Pressfield says that 'Madonna does not identify with "Madonna." Madonna employs "Madonna."' I feel the same about 'Lucky Bitch/Chillpreneur/DDT Denise.' She works for me: the actual human Denise, who makes mistakes all the time, farts out loud without shame, and is sometimes a very unchill, cranky bitch.

It helps me play the game when I think this way and take things way less personally. I don't mind if 'Denise Duffield-Thomas' gets criticized. I hate stuff too. No big deal. She's my game piece on the Monopoly board, not the *me* me. Does that make sense?

I'm happy to be an example and symbol for people who need to hear from me. Some like me because I'm Australian. Others like the fact that I'm not a perfect body shape. Some relate to me because I have kids. Others like my sense of humor. Whatever the reason, someone in that audience will be thinking, *If she can do it, so can I. Why not me?*

Gurus want people to follow their particular brand of 'religion,' forsaking all others. That's not what you're looking for, because it's a lot of pressure. You don't need *all the followers*, just the people who want to see and hear from *you*. Lots of people will be happy to tell you why you can't play the game. They'll say you're too young, too old, too inexperienced, too shy, too sensitive, too loud, too… *something*. But we need *all* types of leader, not just the obvious ones. Show up and fill that gap.

Why not you?

CASE STUDY: I DON'T HAVE TO BE THE EXPERT OF EVERYTHING

Name: *Star Khechara, England, UK*
Business: *Beauty nutrition and Nutridermatology™*

My knowledge in skin nutrition is particularly niche, but I fell into the trap of needing to be 'the world-class expert' in everything skin-related. As a result, I was running around like a headless chicken, trying to research 'all the answers.' It was exhausting!

Denise's advice to be a contributor, not a guru, was the permission slip I needed. I was creating unnecessary stress when I could choose to focus and take the easier route for myself.

Although (thanks to my ADHD and perfectionism) I still 'feel' the need to be the know-it-all in beauty nutrition, I no longer act on it. I'm much more comfortable saying, 'That's outside my scope of research,' with clients or during interviews and podcasts.

I also cut my workload by over half. Instead of creating separate courses to cover every sub-niche, I create a single video masterclass and it's done.

While I was already successful financially, Chill and Prosper helped me significantly shift my perfectionism, over-delivering, and over-working.

— *Lesson* —

You don't have to solve all the problems

The Witch Wound, Fear, and Imposter Syndrome

> *'Fearlessness is not the absence of fear. It's about getting up one more time than we fall down.'*
>
> ARIANNA HUFFINGTON

Joan of Arc is reported to have said, 'I am not afraid… I was born to do this.' You might not be fighting an army, but being in business is still scary! Just because you feel like it's your destiny, doesn't mean it will be smooth sailing. I'm happy for you, Joan, but some days I'm terrified! How about you?

A friend who was relatively new to online business sent me a text saying, 'I'm hosting a live webinar today, and I'm so scared! Tell me the fear goes away?' Um, I'm sorry, but no, it doesn't. Not entirely. But here's the good news: what scares you today won't scare you tomorrow. I can now host webinars with little stress, even though the first dozen were terrifying. Paying a six-figure tax bill isn't scary now, though I worried about paying my very first (tiny) tax bill when I started out.

At some point, with practice, everything you do in business will feel like second nature. But the first time you refuse a discount request or have to chase down a client who defaults on a payment, it's going to feel horrible, like you might actually die of fear. But you won't, and soon it will be no big deal.

And here's the bad news: there's always something new to be afraid of. Sorry! No matter how often I do it, public speaking still scares me, though it depends on the audience. Speaking to a small group is on the lower end of my fear spectrum, but people are asking me to speak to increasingly larger audiences, and that pushes me toward the middle of the spectrum. On the higher end is the idea of doing live TV interviews, which is kinda scary to me. Soon, that will be no big deal.

Why does something that seems so simple, like 'just publish a blog post' or 'just ask for the sale,' make us feel like we're literally going to *die*? I've found some good theories.

The Witch Wound

Have you ever heard of the 'Witch Wound' or the 'feminine wound?' I hadn't, until I read Lisa Lister's amazing book *Witch*; it helped me understand the fear that I and many others experience when we start out in entrepreneurship. You don't have to be a woman (or a witch) to understand how that feels.

According to spiritual teacher Kimberley Jones, the Witch Wound is 'the psychic scar in the collective consciousness that (mostly) women start to awaken to and feel deeply in their bodies as soon as they consider stepping into their power.'[3]

Think of your own experiences. Have you ever felt irrational terror or reluctance over something quite simple? Well, no wonder: it's never really been safe to speak up against the status quo, display power, or create our reality without fear of persecution or conflict.

Millions of people throughout history have been burned, drowned, hanged, tortured and enslaved for their beliefs, or for simply being born in the 'wrong' body. The advice I teach in my books and courses would be enough proof for me to be called a witch.

Times have changed in most countries, but this stuff runs *deep*. Even though we're unlikely to be literally burned at the stake, it still feels dangerous to step into our power. You don't have to go very far back to see how people have been treated when they speak up. Your ancestors faced a very different world than we do – one in which they had fewer rights and protections, and less respect in the workplace. And it still happens. Female politicians are called witches and bitches, and online trolls often target successful, outspoken entrepreneurs and activists.

Kimberley Jones says, 'When your throat closes over when you stand up to speak or face up to authority, that's the Witch Wound closing your throat chakra. It's the shared memory of thousands of spiritual brothers and sisters being hanged and persecuted for generations of going against the grain.'[4]

Heavy, I know, but it makes sense, right? Studies are starting to reveal that we can inherit trauma from previous generations of our family,[5] and when you think about it, that makes sense, too. Passing down information about potential dangers from one generation to the next can help a species survive. Inherited trauma may be one of the reasons it feels so unsafe to make your voice heard by publishing a blog post or creating a simple video. Your body goes into fight-or-flight mode to keep you safe from centuries of dangerous conditions for outspoken changemakers like us.

Life coach Natalie Ann Taggart says: 'For the longest time I couldn't figure out *why* I and the spiritual, creative women I work with felt such massive, existential fear when it came to sharing our spiritual messages. It often bordered on the point of irrational, like the time I literally felt like I was dying after I posted on Facebook or the time a client sobbed and sobbed over creating her opt-in.'[6]

Natalie says that just knowing about the collective experience of the Witch Wound can help you heal it. 'Next time you feel that resistance, that inner tug that wants to keep you safe in the status quo, recognize it as your Witch Wound. Give it love – it is protecting you. And you can choose to not be beholden to it. You can choose to heal, and to rise into the powerful magic that your soul is calling you to.'[7]

Author Seren Bertrand says, 'As women rise into their power, we face all that once held us down. We meet everything that has shamed us, blamed us, judged us. We face the long shadow of "The Inquisitor" in all the forms he or she takes. It looms large in the dark of our nightmares, our anxiety, our self-doubt.'[8]

One of my earliest memories is sitting in the welfare office with my mother, feeling terrified of the stern, besuited man and the power he had over my family and our ability to eat that month. That one experience lived with me for decades. It kept me scared about getting into trouble with authority figures like the 'taxman,' which caused me to unconsciously hold back my income for years. Starting my business made me feel incredibly vulnerable and unsafe.

And you thought you were just procrastinating! Maybe you thought you weren't qualified enough or that you needed a different background color on your website? Nope. You're breaking cycles, kicking through glass ceilings, and smashing the patriarchy! Your lizard brain thinks you're going to die, so cut yourself some slack!

> *'We are the granddaughters of the witches*
> *you weren't able to burn.'*
>
> Tish Thawer

You might not have heard of the Witch Wound until today, but I'm sure you've experienced some other fears, like:

- Fear of failure, including disappointing clients or going bankrupt

- Fear of being found out as a fraud or an imposter

- Fear of being judged or criticized

I know I have. Let me tell you again, as a self-made millionaire: *the fear never truly goes away 100 percent*. No magical revenue number makes you immune to fear. And that's okay. The absence of fear is not the goal. This is just the game of business. The goal is to use the vehicle of entrepreneurship to create more freedom, abundance, and creativity in your life and to impact the lives of others positively. That's going to come with a healthy dose of fear. It's unavoidable, but it's survivable.

Have you ever bargained with the universe about your business? 'Give me a big following, but no unsubscribes!' 'Give me Oprah-level fame, but no haters or critics!' 'Send me lots of money, but no tax bills!' Yeah, it's not going to happen. But over time, you'll gain more experience, more resources, and more resilience, which will enable you to deal with anything that gets thrown at you, even a global pandemic. You'll learn to chill and prosper.

Fear of Failure

> *'A queen is not afraid to fail. Failure is*
> *another stepping stone to greatness.'*
>
> Oprah

You *will* fail in business. A lot. Some people won't like you or your work. You'll make mistakes – like sending out emails with broken links and typos. You'll f-ck up all the time, in big and little ways. When you accept that, you won't fear it, and you won't be surprised when it happens. In fact, you can plan for it.

I'm not psychic, but here are some predictions for how much you'll fail. Your sales will suck and 98 percent of people won't buy from you. (Actually, that's normal, as I'll explain later.) At least 75 percent of the customers you send newsletters to won't open them. Does that mean your emails stink? No: it has nothing to do with the quality of the content; that's just how the numbers play out. Track it over time and see – just don't think you're a failure because of it.

> *'You never lose in business. Either you win, or you learn.'*
>
> MELINDA EMERSON

People will complain. Whenever I create a course, I know that at least 3 percent of customers will need extra help, have complaints, or ask for a refund. It's inevitable and it has nothing to do with me. There's just no such thing as a 100 percent approval rating. That's not failure – it's statistics. Knowing that has helped me become way more chill. I know roughly how many customers will default on their payment plans and how many refund requests to expect when we do a big launch. As long as the numbers are within our predicted rates, I don't waste a minute worrying about it. You are going to have a lot of failures; it's part of doing business.

Imposter Syndrome

> *'I have written 11 books, but each time I think, "Uh-oh, they're going to find out now. I've run a game on everybody, and they're going to find me out."'*
>
> MAYA ANGELOU

Do me a favor: Google 'famous people with impostor syndrome.' You'll see that virtually everyone has it, including incredibly accomplished people.

In her book *Lean In: Women, Work, and the Will to Lead*, Sheryl Sandberg says: 'Every time I was called on in class, I was sure that I was about to embarrass myself. Every time I took a test, I was sure that it had gone badly. And every time I didn't embarrass myself – or even excelled – I believed that I had fooled everyone yet again. One day soon, the jig would be up.'[9]

In *The Secret Thoughts of Successful Women: Why Capable People Suffer from the Impostor Syndrome and How to Thrive in Spite of It*, author Valerie Young writes that Meryl Streep once told a reporter, 'You think, "Why would anyone want to see me again in a movie? And I don't know how to act anyway, so why am I doing this?"'[10] This wasn't baby Meryl speaking, either: it was after 17 Oscar nominations and 26 Golden Globe nominations!

Isn't it reassuring to know that accomplished and famous people feel the same way you do? The way I've overcome this particular fear is to forgive myself for not knowing everything, while at the same time realizing that what I *do* know can really help people. Being in business is simply sharing your gifts (knowledge and expertise) with others who don't have them. Your experiences are valuable; your opinions are useful; and someone out there needs what you have.

Entrepreneurs sabotage themselves by thinking they need to know everything about a topic before they teach it, or they'll be exposed as a fraud. When I started talking about money, I thought it would count only if I was as qualified as financial expert Suze Orman. Otherwise, what right did I have to teach anything to do with money? And who was I to talk about living your best life if I wasn't already as successful as Oprah?

But the world needed my unique take on money. I didn't have to worry about being exposed as a fraud because I wasn't pretending to be Suze. You don't have to lead the conversation to contribute to it and honestly share your experiences. When you realize that your opinions, thoughts, and voice not only matter but are also *needed*, you can give yourself a break and just show up.

Remember, you're an expert to someone. That realization has given me so much relief. The pressure was off to be Suze (I don't look good in a blazer anyway), and there's only one Oprah. And guess what: there's only one *you*, too. Someone needs to hear *your* voice.

If you show up with integrity and teach what you know with a lot of heart, you won't feel like an imposter.

CASE STUDY: TAKE A DEEP BREATH AND SELL!

Name: *Lee Chalmers, Scotland, UK*
Business: *Life coaching for midlife women*

I already had a successful six-figure corporate consulting business, but I wanted to serve a new audience and help midlife women gain the courage to pursue their secret ambitions.

I decided to do an online test pilot, right in the middle of the Covid-19 lockdown, to see if my audience was interested. I was completely struck by fear. Would I be good enough? Would they want to learn from me?

But then reading what Denise had to say about imposter syndrome really helped me to break free. I was stopping too early. What could happen if I went for it?

I took many deep breaths and pushed myself out of my comfort zone to advertise, and 720 amazing women signed up to help me test the idea. Additionally, creating the modules for my online offering got me over my imposter syndrome and the fear of failure.

At the end of the four weeks, my audience wanted to know the next step, so I offered them a three-month course and made my first-ever online business money – a whopping $33,000!

— *Lesson* —

**Everyone feels like an imposter. Take a
deep breath and do it anyway.**

Fear of Criticism

*'To people making mean comments about my GG
(Golden Globe) pics, I mos def cried about it on that
private jet on my way to my dream job last night.'*

ACTRESS GABOUREY SIDIBE

The fear of criticism or being 'cancelled' holds so many talented, creative people back. Being criticized hurts, but it's inevitable on some level, and therefore not a valid excuse to forfeit your business dreams. *Sorry!* Do I get criticized? Yes, I'm sure I do all the time. But I don't read much unsolicited feedback about my business because it's none of my business what other people think of me.

Being a Chillpreneur isn't about being dismissive of negative feedback. Chillpreneurs just realize that they can't do anything to avoid it, so they shrug it off. I have friends who take criticism personally – so much so that it paralyzes them and has driven some out of business. Negative feedback isn't personal, but it's entirely unavoidable. Criticism is another statistical problem because, no matter how much you try to please everyone, you won't.

If you disagree with something I've said, that's understandable. I can often be an intolerant, bossy know-it-all. I get it. But I'm not going to expend any energy trying to change your mind. I can only be myself. And honestly, it's a colossal waste of your time to read most feedback, comments or reasons why people unsubscribed from your newsletter – because it's usually about that person's personal preference.

I can guess exactly what my negative feedback will be:

- You swear too much!
- You send too many emails.
- I never signed up for this! (They did.)
- I don't like your face/hair/voice.

Again, I'm not psychic, it's just that business is very predictable and knowing this stuff helps you not freak out when it happens. When someone says you're 'too this' or 'too that,' there's nothing you can do about it. Should you change everything about your business to accommodate everyone's preferences? No: because it's impossible! You could shorten your newsletters, and you'll still be criticized. You could change your face, and someone won't like the new one.

What's the simplest solution to overcoming the fear of being criticized? Just be yourself: it's the only thing you can do. If people like that, great; if they don't, they can find someone else. It's no big deal. You're not a perfect match for everyone. It's not your job to fix every problem in the world. That's *so exhausting*. Stand steady in who you are and attract the people who not only accept that but *love* it.

> *'You cannot please everyone and the effort required to try shaves years off of your life and steals your joy.'*
> GAYNETÉ JONES

How to Handle Fear

So, how does a Chillpreneur deal with fear?

1. Recognize that it's an inevitable part of playing the game.

2. Love and accept yourself.

3. Roll the dice and play again.

You don't need to fight against the fear, completely change yourself, or find some way to protect yourself from it. It's going to happen. Period. Recognize that you're scared. Acknowledge that it's entirely normal. Accept that it's inevitable, predictable. Then, give yourself permission to be imperfect. Love and accept yourself, and move forward anyway.

EXERCISE: WHAT ARE YOU REALLY AFRAID OF?

Get out your journal and ponder the following questions until you get a juicy answer (or 10). Get specific: *what are you really afraid of?*

1. What do I worry about at 3 a.m.? (For example: getting kicked out of your community, embarrassing yourself on a global scale, attracting haters or stalkers?)

2. What's the worst thing that could happen if I moved forward in my business? (For example: are you worried about being called a fraud? About getting into trouble? Being sued? Going bankrupt? Get *specific*.)

Go deep and dirty. Get it all out. Better out than in.

Being in business is scary, but don't let fear derail you before you've even started. I hear newbie business owners say, 'Oh, I'm terrified of having a big tax bill when I'm a millionaire,' and I'm like, 'Chill out, just get your first client.' You'll deal with the million dollars later. You're smart and you can deal with it when it's a problem!

You might realize that some of your fears are so far in the future that you can 'park' them for a little while. It's like saying, 'Hey, Fear, you know that worry about dealing with a multimillion-dollar tax bill? Wanna come back when I'm actually a millionaire? Thanks, see you later.' And just let it go. You can't worry about everything at the same time; focus on baby steps right now.

Rather than obsess over worries (that might not even come true), use that energy to strengthen your vision for the future. The more time you spend connecting with your dreams, the less time you'll have to think about how terrified you are! Your vision only has to be a tiny bit bigger than your fear. That's the only thing that will keep you moving forward.

Remember: fear is normal, understandable, and totally inevitable. But it's not a good excuse to stop pursuing your dreams. If you're scared, welcome to the club! Now get on with it. You don't need to be the bravest to succeed. We're all scared, but it's our time and we've got a lot of work to do.

— *Lesson* —

The Chillpreneur approach to fear is to recognize that you're scared, acknowledge that it's entirely normal, and accept that it's inevitable, predictable, and totally figureoutable. Then, give yourself permission to be imperfect.

CHAPTER 2

Three Money Mindset Blocks That Will Derail Your Business Success

*C*hillpreneurs find the path of least resistance, which means they have to remove any obstacle that blocks their flow of abundance – otherwise known as a 'money block.' Your money blocks are the beliefs, habits, and stories that stop you from receiving money in the most natural way possible. How do you know if you have them? Everyone does: you're not the only one!

From years of working with thousands of entrepreneurs, I've acquired a pretty good sense of how these money blocks show up and how common they are. The truth is that most entrepreneurs have to work consistently at eliminating them. Including me. In business, your money blocks determine things like:

- **Your prices**: your ability to charge people appropriately and deal with requests for discounts.

- **Your money boundaries**: including how comfortable you feel chasing money that people owe you and how you deal with unreasonable refund requests.

- **How you spend and keep money**: this can manifest in extreme frugality or in spending every penny you make.

Dealing with your money blocks makes everything way easier, and we're Chillpreneurs, remember? The most laborious work is identifying your limiting beliefs in the first place. There are *many* types of money blocks, and you might have to do some digging to uncover yours, but I've found that those below are the most universal. You'll probably identify most strongly with one or two of them, but you might experience all three at some point.

1. You have to work really hard to make money.

2. You can help people *or* make money, but not both.

3. More money, more problems.

Let's look at these money blocks in turn:

Money Block #1:
You Have to Work Really Hard to Make Money

This block is probably the most common, and it's super-sneaky because hard work and busyness are culturally acceptable and, in some cases, admired and encouraged. It can help you create great success for a while, but the working 'hard' part becomes self-fulfilling. There's a more natural way – the Chillpreneur way – in which you find the path of least resistance, but it will require some counterprogramming.

There's less physical work required to run a business than ever before. I don't mean to sound all old-fashioned, but it was way harder when I started my business than it is now. There were no online payment systems, making a website was either crazy-expensive or incredibly complicated, and there was hardly any automation software. It was the dark ages! (I'm kinda joking.) The fact that we now have all these relatively cheap and easy systems can bring up weird feelings because the money we can earn by using them isn't always commensurate with the amount of physical labor involved. Ease goes against an established rule in our society: an honest day's work yields an honest day's pay.

Add the internet to the mix and, suddenly, making money becomes even less onerous. You could sell an e-book to someone in China while you're sleeping. You could have someone in Sydney pay for a consultation with you (and book it on your calendar) without any back-and-forth emails. Or you could have a piece of your artwork printed onto a phone case and shipped to Ohio without being physically involved at all! So many businesses had to pivot during the pandemic, and the tools are better than ever.

What a world we live in! And it's only going to get easier. But the downside is that all this ease and flow can bring up feelings of guilt for some people. It's as if it doesn't count if we don't work really hard for it. Why? Well, we may have been told things like this from a very young age:

- 'Money doesn't grow on trees.'

- 'You don't get something for nothing.'

- 'Another day, another dollar.'

Our parents might have worked long hours for their money (unlike us) or performed hard physical labor (instead of just sitting in front of a computer). It can feel unfair to earn money without trying hard – as if we're doing something terrible or disrespecting our elders. So we sabotage ourselves by procrastinating, or we paddle upstream and make everything harder than it needs to be. We want to prove that we've earned our money through struggle and hard work, even though that's no longer necessary. Chillpreneurship feels lazy.

Of course, I'm not saying entrepreneurship is easy. You still have to get over your resistance, fear, and procrastination. But there's nothing you can't figure out on the internet. Most entrepreneurs aren't suffering from a lack of 'how to': they just overcomplicate business and become too paralyzed to take action.

How Do You Know If You Have the 'Work Hard' Block?

Answer Never, Sometimes, or Always to the following:

- You find yourself reinventing the wheel or overcomplicating systems instead of following a proven plan.

- You procrastinate and end up doing things last-minute or having to pull all-nighters.

- You get bored and break stuff that works, just to prove you can start over from scratch.

- You resist delegating or outsourcing, preferring to do everything yourself because it's quicker or because nobody else can do it the way you do.

- You feel like you're cheating if things are too easy, or you write off your wins as flukes. You never feel proud of yourself, and move onto the next thing without celebrating or taking a break.

Overcoming the 'Work Hard' Block

For you, there may be a shadow side to easy money. Somewhere deep inside, you may think bad things will happen if money comes with ease. I've heard people express fears such as:

- 'If I didn't work hard for it, I'd feel like I didn't earn it.'

- 'I'll become lazy (and so will my kids) if things are too easy.'

- 'Struggling for money is part of who I am. Who would I be without that struggle?'

What comes up when you imagine money coming effortlessly? What could you do with your extra energy and resources if things *weren't* hard?

The Truth: Working Harder Doesn't Always Work

'We think, mistakenly, that success is the result of the amount of time we put in at work, instead of the quality of time we put in.'

Arianna Huffington

One of my early business mentors, Fabienne Fredrickson, told me an affirmation that she said completely changed her relationship to her business: 'I work half the time for twice as much money.' The first time I tried to say it, it came out backward: 'I work twice as hard for half the money.' Oops. Nope. Let the words soak in for a moment and then see how it feels to say aloud: 'I work half the time for twice as much money.' What comes up for you? Disbelief? Do you hear a voice in your head saying, 'That's cheating!' or 'That's impossible,' or 'But, Denise... how?'

Beliefs like these are why I see entrepreneurs earning $25,000 a year stressing about how they can crack six figures, thinking, *I have to work four times harder?* I did the same thing when I made $250,000. I couldn't do the math to figure out how to get to a million dollars. Surely I'd have to work harder, but there weren't enough hours in the day! I was already dangerously close to burnout, so four times as much work was impossible!

Here's the counterintuitive truth: you actually have to *work less* to earn more money. You have to work smarter, not harder, and you have to master the lessons of discernment. You get to let people support you in your business, and you have to give up control over doing everything yourself. Instead, you have to embrace elimination, automation, and delegation.

Too much focus on effort can have the opposite effect – we can get bogged down in procrastination, over-complication, or resistance to delegation. But what if it were allowed to be easier? What if you could create your business in a way that worked perfectly for you without feeling like you're paddling upstream? It's possible. It doesn't mean you'll never have to work; business isn't effort-*none*, but it can be effort-*less*.

It's okay for you to make money with ease and flow. Often people say to me, 'You must be so busy,' to which I respond, 'No, I'm not!' You'd think I'd said something outrageous: it's just so taboo to admit you're not that busy. It's actually the b-word I say the least! The truth is that I work a lot, but I just don't feel *busy*. It's because every part of my business and life is set up to help me thrive. I don't do things I hate. I don't work with people who annoy me, and I rarely feel stressed. It looks easy, but it took conscious effort to get here.

Now, let's talk about hustle. First, let me be super-clear on this – my business didn't happen by accident. As I explained in the introduction, in the early years I worked a *lot*. But that's not sustainable. I noticed how many entrepreneurial 'gurus' talk about 'grinding' every day until you drop. But a lot of these people lead incredibly unbalanced lives. Some of them crash and burn or wreck their health/marriages/businesses due to their hustle. They don't seem healthy, and when you look behind the scenes of their businesses, some aren't even that successful or making much profit.

If that's hustle, I want no part of it. I really like my sleep, and telling people to simply get up earlier – as if we don't have enough sleep deprivation in our lives already – isn't sustainable. I've seen some friends squeeze out all their energy for diminishing returns, or worse, serious health consequences. If you have caring responsibilities, or physical or mental health challenges, it's even harder to live that way. So please, don't feel like a loser if you can't figure out how those high-octane Insta-success-stories do it.

I personally don't want to live that way and, if you feel the same, I'm telling you there's an alternative: chustle (chilled hustle)! Just do the things that matter and leave everything else. If you want to make more money, you have a choice: work harder, or leverage everything in your life and make it easier.

— *Lesson* —

**It's counterintuitive, but you actually
have to work less to earn more.**

CASE STUDY: SHIFTING 'LAZY' INTO EASE

Name: *Caryna Khan, Queensland, Australia*
Business: *Cosmetic chemist, Private Label Skin Care*

I resisted the concept of Chill and Prosper. I grew up with a house full of hard workers who believed that you were lazy if you sat down for two seconds. There were so many mindset blocks to overcome about even wanting to have an easier life.

I was still very much attached to being in control, being deep inside the business, and doing too much myself. Then I became pregnant, and I was really sick. I had no choice but to let go. I was forced to consider the life I wanted to create for my family.

Why would I choose to do things the hard way? Why was I so attached to hard work? I could see that I had connected my desire to live my passions with a life of struggle.

It took a real minute for the lessons to actually sink in, but I started doing everything the book said, and the results started coming quickly. With that insight, I chose a new belief: I can live my passions and choose the path of least resistance.

Now I've embraced the Chill; there's no going back. It took time and having my hand forced, but I'm so grateful I can finally embrace ease.

— Lesson —

You have to break the cycle of hard work.

Money Block #2:
You Can Help People *or* Make Money, But Not Both (the 'Broke Healer')

You might be asking the universe for more time to devote to helping more people, yet somehow feel that making money through your talents is unspiritual. Or greedy. Or weirdly inappropriate. Often, people who want to help everybody can't because they get burned-out. If they allowed themselves to make money from their natural skills and talents, they could help a lot more people with ease and joy.

This is an insidious block for business success because we're conditioned to be helpful, kind, and giving, without expecting anything in return, let alone money. For many creative industries, charging people feels like exploiting customers instead of selflessly giving everything away.

It's easy to undervalue our gifts, especially if what we do is fun and easy for us. As in: 'Well, it only takes me a few hours to put up a website. I shouldn't charge too much for it.' But how awesome is making money from something that's easy? It should work that way! Have you ever said, 'I don't care about the money, I just want to help people?' That sends conflicting information out into the universe.

When you believe this one at a deep level, you'll continuously prove it by attracting people who'll mirror that belief back to you. You'll get broke clients turning up asking for your help, and you'll be compelled to do so. If you don't, you'll feel like a mean bitch. You'll get haters popping up who say, 'You're just in it for the money,' and you'll feel yourself shrinking away from marketing so people won't think you're greedy.

For example, I know lot a of healers working in different modalities, like Emotional Freedom Techniques (EFT), hypnotherapy, and Reiki, and they feel terrible about charging for their gifts. Sometimes their community reflects that back to them, saying things like, 'If you cared that much about people, this would be free,' or 'Your gift is God-given, you shouldn't charge for it.'

It's not nice to be shamed by your community. The most annoying thing is that, usually, these healers aren't charging a lot. Even when they ask for minimal contributions for things like meditations, e-books, or coaching, their audience reacts in a very unloving and outraged way. So the healer stays loving but broke. Or reverts to the centuries-old practice of bartering, but instead of receiving eggs and butter, she swaps services with a friend or gets some free bookkeeping in return for her talents.

You could even use this block to feel superior to others. You might tell yourself that your business nemesis may make more money than you do (or has a book deal, or is on *Oprah*), but *you* really care about your *clients*, and *she* doesn't. You're selfless and she's a greedy bitch!

Or you might tell yourself that you're staying 'affordable' for people and judge the 'outrageous prices' of others. That's why this block is so sneaky. Of course, it's not mutually exclusive to care for people and charge appropriately, but on the surface, it sounds entirely reasonable and kind-hearted to keep yourself small and broke.

The most annoying thing about this money block is that the very people who should have more money (the kind, caring, and generous ones) often have the least. The paradox, of course, is that when you're broke, overstretched, or over-giving, you can't help many people. You won't have the time or energy to write your book (which could potentially help millions), or create your course (which could make you millions while transforming lives) or, at the very least, quit your soul-sucking job so you can run your business and help people full-time.

How Do You Know If You Have the 'Broke Healer' Block?

Answer Never, Sometimes, or Always to the following:

- You feel it's exploitative to charge fees to help people transform their lives, particularly if they're struggling in some way.

- You feel so bad when people can't afford your fees that you work with them for free, at the expense of paying clients, or burn yourself out trying to help everyone.

- You feel guilty about making money, and feel like you should give it away to others.

- You secretly judge people in your industry who make a lot of money, or think they're doing something dodgy to be that successful.

Overcoming the 'Broke Healer' Block

Attending to the needs of others is much easier when your own needs are met. The same holds true for money. Imagine how much you could benefit the world if your own needs were met and you could give from your excess? You don't have to choose between helping people and making money.

In a *Forbes* magazine article titled 'The Rising Activism in Women's Philanthropy,' Abigail Disney – an award-winning filmmaker and philanthropist – says, 'Take the ownership of the money you have control of – stop apologizing for that; it's nothing to be ashamed of. Step into power. Ask for it. It's not going to just settle over you. This is about taking our fair share. We're half the population and we deserve half the power.'[1]

Imagine if women controlled half the money and had half the power? And obviously not just women; what if environmentally conscious, loving, kind people had more money? The world would be a very different place if we all embraced our ability to make more money doing things we loved that were good for the planet.

The best way to trick this block is by connecting deeply to the transformation you could make in others if you had more money, energy, and time to devote yourself full-time to your calling. If you allowed yourself to get paid for your talents, what could you create in the world? If you weren't so tired and burned out by the un(der)paying demands of others, what would be possible in your life?

I use a pattern-interrupting mantra for this purpose: 'I serve, I deserve.' It helps me remember that giving and receiving is a virtuous circle and that it's safe for me to make money by helping others. I remind myself of all the good I do with my wealth, and that nobody is served by my staying small and broke in the world.

Build Philanthropy into Your Business, Your Way

*'Abundance isn't just about money. It's about being
able to live in the overflow, where you've filled yourself
up so much that you have so much to give.'*

Dr. Ezzie Spencer

When you charge well for what you do, you're in a powerful position to help others. But that doesn't mean confusing running a business with becoming a charity. It's okay to embrace 'sustainable philanthropy,' AKA 'chillanthropy.'

It's okay to make sure that your bills and needs are taken care of before giving to others. You don't have to give away all your profits to 'deserve' success.

It's also okay to start where you are right now. Start with the idea of yourself as a wealthy philanthropist and act accordingly with what you have available. For example, you might decide to give away 10 percent of your profits to charity or build in a 'buy one, donate one' model, like Toms Shoes, Bombas socks, or Warby Parker glasses (companies that donate a product to someone in need for every purchase).

It's also okay to make money and give in other ways. Sometimes you have money to give, and other times you just have time. Sometimes all you can do is sign a petition, and other times you can sponsor others to be activists. Sometimes you have wisdom or a kind word to share. Other times you can be a kind boss, hire other people, or use ethical suppliers. You don't have to give in any particular way. You serve, you deserve, and that's enough.

*'What I learn from talking to so many women around
the world: if you can empower them with the right things,
the right tools, they can lift up their family. And that
ultimately lifts up their community and their society.'*

Melinda Gates

CASE STUDY:
CHARGING HELPS YOUR IMPACT

Name: *Frida Trönnberg, Sweden*
Business: *Pelvic floor yoga teacher*

I used to hold the belief that it was ugly to charge for women's health services. I thought that, because women truly need what I offer, it should be free or affordable for everyone. Helping women with pelvic floor pain become pain-free and feel pleasure again is so important to me.

The mindset change, that I can help more people if I charge more, was critical for me. I'd have the capacity to give away more freebies and run more free courses. I could write the book I never had the time or money to write. I adopted the affirmation: 'It's safe for me to make money by helping others.'

I increased my prices without feeling bad about it, allowing me to quit my job and outsource tasks in my business that weren't my zone of genius. As a result, I can now help more women and change more lives for the better.

I'm proud of my course these days, and I don't cringe when talking about my prices. I sold a record 75 spaces recently in a happy and easy-going launch, proving that when I Chill, I can absolutely Prosper.

— *Lesson* —

**Charging well helps you
serve a lot more people.**

Money Block #3: More Money, More Problems

People love stories about business owners or lottery winners who went broke, don't they? On the flipside, some people worry about the responsibility that would come with a windfall if they got one. For example, they fear that 'lost' family members might surface and hound them for money, or that they'll get a massive, unexpected tax bill.

The reality is that rich people have the same habits as everyone else, and often the same money problems – just on a different scale. You might judge someone who has a collection of 30 Hermès bags or a garage full of identical luxury cars, but you might have similar habits, just with crystals and dozens of identical yoga pants! (Or is that just me?)

Rich people are just like anyone else – the numbers might be different, but the behavior is the same. Rich people are just average human beings: some are nice, and some are assholes. But that doesn't mean that the richer you get, the assholier you'll get. Money just makes you richer – in money. It's not a cure-all for every problem in your life. Sure, you'll have to worry less about bills, but your fundamental personality won't change much. The truth is: if you're an asshole now, nothing will change! If you have bad habits now, money won't magically cure them. If you're a nice person, you'll just be a richer nice person.

What this block comes down to is scarcity – the worry that you can't possibly have money *and* other things you value, or that you have to give something up to be wealthier. Everyone has this belief, in slightly different ways. For example, you might think you have to give up good health, being a good parent, or having a happy marriage to be wealthier. Either way, it's not going to lead to something positive, so why would you do it to yourself? That's why you're repelling money – because you're not 100 percent convinced it would lead to anything good.

How Do You Know If You Have the 'More Problems' Block?

Answer Never, Sometimes, or Always to the following:

- You feel that having more money would come with too much responsibility, like extra taxes or paperwork. You worry you'll screw it up and get into trouble.

- You say you'd 'rather be happy than rich' (as if you can't be both).

- You worry that your ambition is selfish or makes you a bad person/parent/partner/friend.

- You're afraid you'll outshine, embarrass, emasculate, or have to rescue people in your life if you earn more money than they do.

Overcoming the 'More Problems' Block

Actually, the best thing you can do is to acknowledge all your fears, no matter how silly or small. The problems people think money could cause are endless. I've heard things like:

- 'If money came easily, my family would become lazy and entitled.'

- 'If I had lots of money, I'd lose it somehow.'

- 'Everyone will judge me as a rich, greedy bitch.'

Think about the 'worst-case' scenarios you might encounter if you had more money. For example: 'Life would be too complicated.' How could more money solve that problem? It might be: 'I could hire people (such as accountants) to deal with those complications.' Or: 'Making more money would take me away from my kids, and then I'd be a bad parent and they'd grow up hating me.' Chillpreneurship is all about giving you *more* time and freedom, not less.

The Truth: Money Solves Problems

'Money is power, money is freedom, money is confidence,
money is "Creepy boss, take your hand off of my leg."
Money is "I'm starting my dream business."'

SALLIE KRAWCHECK

When I was starting out, I asked my mentor Sandy Forster, author of *How to Be Wildly Wealthy Fast*, when she realized she was rich. The answer: she was buying a new blender and realized she could choose *anything* she wanted. She literally burst into tears in the department store. A blender – not a diamond-encrusted car. Every time I'm food shopping, I have that moment and realize, 'I can choose the expensive tomatoes.' That's what I want for you, too. For you to be, do, and have everything on your dream board, the big and small things, and have the peace of mind that comes with deliberately choosing what you want daily, regardless of the cost.

Life isn't going to be perfect; car tires will pop, dogs will destroy your favorite shoes, wisdom teeth will break through and cost money, toddlers will pee on your new couch. But money solves a lot of those annoying problems. If you've always lived feast-to-famine without a safety net, then it's going to take some acclimatization to the fact that you can just have spare money lying around to fix problems. It might actually feel weird – and that's why some people resist it.

I'm gonna say it, too: I love being rich. Beyond being able to build my dream homes, buy new cars, and travel First Class with my family, I love that I've completely paid off my student loans and years of government support through the millions of dollars in taxes I've put back into the system.

I love hiring people, buying from other creative entrepreneurs and small businesses, financially supporting my family, and donating to charities. There's nothing better than not having to rely on others for support. It's true freedom.

Yes, more money and success come with some complications and logistics. But you can solve a lot of problems with cash. It's the ultimate cheat/chill hack. You can hire people to solve virtually every situation. You're not going to be fixed, but you can pay for great therapy!

As comedienne Fannie Brice quipped, 'I've been rich, and I've been poor. And, believe me, rich is better.'

— *Lesson* —

Money solves more problems than it creates.

EXERCISE: IDENTIFY YOUR MONEY BLOCKS

Grab your journal and go deep into your money blocks. What do you think you'd have to give up to be wealthier? Which of the following money blocks resonates with you the most?

- You have to work really hard to make money.
- You can help people *or* make money, but not both.
- More money, more problems.

If you want to go even deeper into the conversation around money blocks, I suggest you read my last book, *Get Rich, Lucky Bitch!* after you finish this one, and consider joining my Money Bootcamp.

And don't feel bad – everyone has money blocks, even me! I'm just chill about it, and I'm very prosperous now that I've accepted it, and developed tools so they don't derail me. This is possible for you, too, no matter how much mental 'gunk' is in your way right now.

Now, would you like to learn my millionaire secrets?

— CHAPTER 3 —

Millionaire Mindset Lessons

*F*irst up, not everyone wants to be a millionaire, and that's fine! It's a somewhat arbitrary measure of success. Earning millions doesn't make you unique or clever, and you might get caught up in the definition like: which currency? Are we talking revenue or profit? But you're asking the wrong questions.

Author and entrepreneur Tim Ferriss taught us in *The 4-Hour Work Week* that you don't need to be a millionaire to live like one, and many entrepreneurs don't want a big, complicated company or to sell their business to an investor. Success looks different to everyone, but it's hard to feel successful if you don't know what that means to you or you're comparing yourself with others.

So, in the previous chapter, we talked about three money blocks that will derail your business success: working too hard, confusing your business with your charity, and focusing on the downsides of success. Let's come up with some counter-beliefs. These are the ones I live by as a legit chillionaire:

1. There's always more money.

2. There are easier ways to make money.

3. I'm allowed to be rich, too.

Mindset Lesson #1: There's Always More Money

*'If you approach the ocean with a cup, you can
only take away a cupful; if you approach it with
a bucket, you can take away a bucketful.'*

RAMANA MAHARSHI

One of the cornerstones of the Chillpreneur philosophy is that there's always more. There's enough for everyone, and we live in a world of abundance. This is the first mindset lesson I want you to master: *There's always more money.*

Of course, it doesn't always feel like that. I'm not saying income inequality isn't real, and that there's no poverty in the world. But chances are that *you* have every opportunity to change your circumstances and create a ripple effect with all the people you can help, but you're still holding yourself back. One way we keep ourselves small is by thinking that the world is a zero-sum game: if I win, someone else is going to lose; if I'm successful, it will be at someone else's expense.

But that's not true. You can do some amazing things with your wealth; there's no limit to what you can dream; and there's no cap on your earning potential if you're willing to do the work necessary in your business. There's always more money.

Never had this been so apparent to me, and in such a hilariously literal way, than when I was freaking out about buying our dream house. It had taken years to manifest and finally the day came. Instead of feeling great, I was experiencing what psychologist and author Gay Hendricks calls an 'upper limit problem,' which is the feeling that we've hit our capacity for success. It can feel like resistance, guilt, or even the sense that we're about to get into trouble.

It was as if I'd only just realized what a massive manifestation we'd pulled off. Just six weeks earlier, we didn't have all the money we needed to buy the house, and part of me still didn't believe we'd done it, even though we'd just completed the most successful launch we'd ever had. I felt sick: had we bitten off more than we could chew? Who did I think I was? Could we really afford this house in this swanky neighborhood?

During the car ride to our new property, I said to my husband, Mark, 'Babe, we're going to have to be so careful about money this year. With the new house, another baby, and two mortgages, we'll really have to tighten our belts.'

Mark looked at me in surprise and said, 'That doesn't sound like you!'

I let out the breath I was holding and said, 'You're right: there's always more money.' At that very moment, a shower of money hit the windshield of our car: at least $1,000 in $50 notes flew at us like confetti. Yes, really. This story isn't metaphorical. Actual money hit our car! The windshield wipers came on, and the notes bounced and scattered all over the road, blowing into the trees lining the highway. We both screamed involuntarily and said simultaneously, 'Did you see that?'

'Should we pull over?' Mark asked. I still couldn't quite believe what had happened, especially at the very moment I'd affirmed out loud that 'There's always more money.' But I knew that it was a big message from the universe.

'The actual money isn't the point,' I replied, 'and I definitely don't want to scrabble around on this busy highway to collect money that doesn't belong to us. The lesson is that there's always more money, and we're going to be fine.' We both started laughing because it was just too weird.

Was it a shared hallucination? All I know is that it was divine timing. Just at that moment of doubt and scarcity, the universe decided to remind me that there's *always* more money. There's always enough. And just like that, I felt better about the new property purchase. I decided to live in a world of abundance, not scarcity. To this day, I've no idea how it happened. Maybe someone was about to buy something in cash, and it accidentally blew out the window. Who knows? I've never heard another person from my town mention it. I still laugh about the divine timing, and I hope you remember it too.

There's always enough.

There Are Always Enough Clients, Ideas, and Opportunities

When I feel discouraged or worry that everyone's already seen my Money Bootcamp, I think of mentors who have 10 times the number of students. I tell myself I can quit when I eclipse their numbers because there's proof of concept right in front of me.

How many clients do you need to have a successful, thriving business? With so many billions of people in the world, there are a lot of potential customers looking for exactly what you can deliver. And you need only a tiny percentage of them to buy! So, there are always enough clients.

— *Lesson* —

Chill out. There's always more money.

Mindset Lesson #2:
There Are *Easier Ways* to Make Money

'I intentionally abandoned the hard stuff early on because
not only do I think it's useless, I think it's a distraction.'

SETH GODIN

When I was a teenager, there was a nationwide competition to win a new car. The catch was that you had to live in it with four other people. Whoever stayed in the car the longest, got to keep it. You were given a bathroom break every two hours and could order any fast food you wanted, but all the rubbish had to stay in the car, and you had to sleep there too. No showers, either. You stayed in it until you couldn't handle it any longer.

The car visited my local shopping mall as part of the promotion. It was before reality shows became a big thing on TV, so I was excited to check it out. By then, the contest had been going on for two weeks, and they were down to a few determined (and very smelly) contestants. Onlookers took turns to gawk in the window at these poor people, who were sitting in filth, wanting to win the car.

I think about that competition often because, first of all, who wants a car after it's been lived in like that? And second, there are easier ways to get a new car. Make money in your business and just buy one! Because I teach manifestation, often people ask me how they can win a competition to go on vacation or win a house through a raffle, and I think, *Just work on your business and buy what you want.* That counts too! You don't always have to win things.

Entrepreneur and author Seth Godin famously said, 'When in doubt, raise money from your customers by selling them something they truly need – your product.' Go get more clients and buy what you want.

That car story relates to the second of my mindset lessons: 'There are *easier ways* to make money.' I say this all the time when I find myself doing the opposite: overcomplicating things, pursuing an idea that's not exactly in my zone of genius, or otherwise making things harder for myself. Maybe you do the same.

In the pursuit of the entrepreneurial dream, we often take the hardest route. A lot of my early businesses failed – not because the ideas weren't good, but because they felt hard for me, and I just wanted the outcome (the money). I didn't care about the business at all. And sometimes, I pursued a good idea that wasn't really a natural fit for me.

Are You Solving the Right Problem?

Years ago, when I was still desperately looking for my 'thing' (otherwise known as a calling or purpose), I read a book that said, 'Solve a problem that you're passionate about.' I was passionate about a lot of things, but want to know what was really pissing me off at the time? The lack of hooks in public bathroom stalls.

Every time I went into a public restroom, I'd get frazzled about where to put my stuff, and I'd recently read a study that revealed how dirty people's handbags are. *Wow*, I thought, *this is my cause!* It seemed perfect for my pedantic and fastidious Virgo ways.

So, to market my new 'toilet hook' business, I thought I'd start with a name-and-shame letter campaign to businesses, and then create an app featuring a map of all the 'Denise-approved' restrooms. Fellow germophobes would thank me; fewer employees would call in sick; productivity would improve. It was life-changing stuff! I was *outraged* about this issue. I had no idea how to monetize it (that didn't seem to matter), but it was obviously something that was needed in the world, and I was the girl to do it.

So, I told a friend about the idea. He listened to my entire rant, and when I finished, he said, 'Why don't you carry around a bag of stick-on hooks, and when you're in a bathroom without one, just stick one on.' Mind blown. It was just so... zen.

In an instant, this guy had wiped my 'brilliant business idea' off the map. I looked at him, dumbfounded. 'But what am I supposed to do with my life?' I asked. I seriously thought that my entrepreneurial dreams were dead.

'Denise, you're a storyteller,' he said. 'Tell stories.' So that's what I do. I write a blog. I speak on stages. I author books. I basically make a living by telling random stories and inspiring entrepreneurial people to create the life they want. It's so much easier than being the 'Toilet Hook Queen.'

I'm so grateful to my friend because, instead of rolling his eyes at my dumb business idea, he could see that underneath my 'hook idea' was a real desire to change the world. It was a massive weight off my shoulders to hear that I didn't have to solve everything, and that my real gift was inspiring others to find their passion.

Deciding not to pursue an idea doesn't mean it isn't important to you. You can:

- Care about something deeply, sign a petition, write a letter, or make a donation – but not make it your business

- Contribute to someone else's crowdfunding campaign without making it your business

- Have a really fantastic business idea without making it your business (I promise you don't have to buy the domain name!)

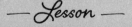

— *Lesson* —

There are easier ways to make money (for you).

Mindset Lesson #3: I'm Allowed to Be Rich, Too

*'Women get mixed messages in childhood: you can
do anything you want... but it wouldn't hurt to
find someone who will take good care of you.'*

Lois P. Frankel

One of the most powerful speakers I've ever heard was Suze Orman at the Hay House 'I Can Do It!' conference. Suze introduced her speech by saying, slowly and deliberately: 'I stand before you a very, very, *very* wealthy woman.' It gave me goose bumps.

Her words stuck with me because I'd never heard a woman claim her wealth and success like that before. Bragging isn't generally seen as a positive trait in women, but what was so compelling about Suze's declaration was that it was so matter-of-fact and made without apology. It changed my life.

The final chillionaire mindset lesson is giving yourself permission to be wealthy and successful, exactly as you are now. Most of us have a perception of what 'wealthy' means, and it's probably really outdated. Part of working through your money blocks is identifying your money stories and limiting beliefs. In this section, we're going one layer deeper, into claiming ourselves as wealthy.

When you Google 'define wealth,' some of the definitions[1] include: an abundance of valuable possessions or money; a plentiful supply of a particular desirable thing; wellbeing. Well, what if you're a minimalist and don't want an abundance of possessions – can you still be wealthy? What if you care deeply about the environment – doesn't being wealthy come with a big carbon footprint? What if you hate fancy clothes and have no desire to buy a big house or an expensive car – does that mean you won't have a big enough 'why' to generate more money?

Not at all, but it's going to take some deprogramming because, in our society, we often get incredibly mixed messages about wealth. Money becomes a personal attribute or failing, and wealthy people are often perceived as more clever, ambitious, and hardworking than the average person. You might have very fixed (but misguided) views about what a wealthy person looks like.

I talk openly about being wealthy because I want to showcase a young(ish) self-made millionaire who is a reasonably nice person (most of the time) and dresses, looks, and acts like an average person. I'm just not that fancy, and honestly, I think it disappoints some people that I'm not living a more glamorous life. I drive a mid-range minivan full of sand and McDonald's crumbs; I'm not impressed by super-fancy restaurants; I own very few expensive shoes, handbags, or clothes; and I'm just boringly normal.

Nobody who meets me would automatically think I'm rich, and most of the advisors Mark and I meet automatically assume he's the breadwinner in our family (I put them straight pretty quickly). Most people have a fixed idea in their mind about what 'rich' looks like. I know I still do: an older white lady at the country club wearing white or beige linen clothes, gold leather sandals, lots of gold jewelry and with blonde, perfectly coiffed hair.

In reality, there's no dress requirement for wealth! Steve Jobs wore jeans and a black turtleneck practically every day, and Mark Zuckerberg wears jeans and a grey T-shirt. My style? Chillpreneur. My summer uniform is shorts and a caftan, and my winter uniform is jeans and a caftan. But you can do it your way! You can pick and choose the kind of wealthy person you want to be. You can mix high-end and low-end. Who cares? There aren't any rules about how to be rich anymore, and together, we're changing the conversation so other nice, chilled-out people can join us.

If you want to open your eyes to 'real wealth' rather than 'TV wealth,' read *The Millionaire Next Door: The Surprising Secrets of America's Wealthy* by Thomas J. Stanley and William D. Danko. It offers an extensive study of wealthy people and identifies seven common traits. They're not what you think! 'Many people who live in expensive homes and drive luxury cars do not actually have much wealth,' the authors say. 'Many people who have a great deal of wealth do not even live in upscale neighborhoods.'[2]

This book changed my view about who I had to be in order to make more money because the more-is-better lifestyle just didn't sit well with me. I thought I had to 'fake it until I made it,' but I discovered that designer stuff just wasn't my bag (literally). I'm not judging people who love fancy things (a lot of my friends do) – I just realized that it wasn't for me, and that's okay. I could redefine wealth *my way* and so can you.

By the way, Stanley wrote two follow-ups that are just as good: *Millionaire Women Next Door*, and *Stop Acting Rich … And Start Living Like A Real Millionaire* – both highly recommended for helping redefine what wealth means to you.

> *'Money should never change one's values…*
> *Making money is only a report card. It's*
> *a way to tell how you're doing.'*
> THOMAS J. STANLEY

If you ignore all the other money blocks and try to get to the core of the issue, you'll find many people think that being wealthy just isn't their destiny – that they somehow lack a magical ingredient. What do *you* think that magical ingredient is? Intelligence? Ambition? Hard work? Great grooming?

It could be all of those things, but I've met some dumb people who are wealthy. I've met humble millionaires who don't consider themselves overly ambitious or competitive, and I've also met a lot of Chillpreneurs who don't work that hard, love what they do, and have a healthy work/life balance.

Maybe you think you have to look or act a certain way? Get honest and dig deep to find out what you think you have to change about yourself to be wealthy – your hair/face/skin/clothes/house/car/weight?

Choose Yourself

> *'The big break is the moment you decide*
> *to take your dream seriously.'*
> ALEXANDRA FRANZEN

This book is a perfect example of choosing myself. I self-published my first two books because I had zero appeal to a mainstream publisher. My first book wasn't that great. Nobody liked the title, *Lucky Bitch*, but I'd asked the universe for a 'bestselling book idea' and got that one in the shower. The first few versions had lots of typos and amateur covers. But I chose myself. I had a message and luckily, thanks to self-publishing, I had a platform through which I could share it. I didn't ask for permission to become an author. I just asked, 'Why not me?'

Publishing with Hay House was a long-held dream, but I didn't sit and wait for them to call. I chose myself. I built my subscriber list (starting with plenty of no-show webinars and small local events), pitched myself on podcasts, and showed up, even when I felt like an unworthy fraud. I didn't ask anyone to choose me as a speaker because I created my own events, even when only four people were in the room. I applied for industry awards and didn't wait to be 'chosen' as a winner.

Success doesn't have a weight or height limit. Success looks like you. Don't wait for someone to choose you if you have a dream, because you might be waiting a long time. Show up, show up, show up, and choose yourself.

EXERCISE: WHY NOT ME?

It's helpful to listen to your own responses when you ask, 'Why not me?' Because if you're honest with yourself, you'll have a few excuses. Here are some examples.

Why not me? Because...

- I'm not experienced/credible/educated enough.
- I'm too fat/not pretty enough.
- I'm too young/old/tired.
- I have kids.
- Nobody will listen to me.
- I'm not ready.

You're not just expressing negativity for the sake of it when you identify these excuses. Instead, they will reveal valuable information that will help you uncover your business mindset issues. In fact, you can even go one layer deeper for each excuse. Take 'I'm not ready,' for example.

Why am I not ready? Because...

- I need a perfect website to get started.
- I should get another qualification to prove myself.
- I need to lose 10 pounds.

What do you do with that information? Grab your journal again and ask yourself:

- Is this true? Or is it just a story I'm making up?
- Has anyone else done this, or would I be the first? (Most of the time, you can find a role model to emulate.)
- Am I putting off just getting on with it? (Most likely, yes.)
- Am I willing to choose myself anyway?

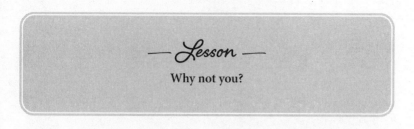

— *Lesson* —

Why not you?

EXERCISE: WHAT DOES WEALTH LOOK LIKE TO YOU?

VISUALIZING THE RICH

Close your eyes for a minute and conjure up what you think a 'rich person' looks like. What are they wearing? (Do you actually know anyone who dresses like that, or is it a cliché from TV?) What are their defining physical characteristics? How old are they?

Write it all down in your journal, and then do the same exercise for how you perceive a 'successful entrepreneur' looks. Is it the same? Or different?

VISUALIZING YOURSELF AS RICH

Stand in front of a mirror and say to yourself, 'This is what a wealthy woman/man/person looks like' (whatever feels good to you). In your journal, write down what comes up for you. Does it feel weird? Braggy, arrogant, untrue, impossible?

You can personalize it exactly for yourself. For example:

- 'This is what a wealthy Black woman looks like.'
- 'This is what a wealthy Queer millionaire looks like.'
- 'This is what a wealthy single parent looks like.'

Don't be afraid of the little voice that answers, because it's just giving you an insight into your beliefs. Ask it, 'Why *else* can't I be rich?'

Write it on your mirror so it's the first thing you see in the morning. Say it when you're looking great, and say it when you're sweaty and gross from working out. Say it when you're feeling confident and scared. It will be jarring at first, but that's the point.

The more you do this exercise, and the more you decide to claim for yourself the mantle of a wealthy person who looks like you, the more you'll start to believe that it's possible. Because, guess what? There are no height, weight, or skin color requirements for wealth. You don't have to look or sound a certain way. There's no dress code, purity test, or other conformity required. There's only what we tell ourselves from years of conditioning.

Now, I'm not saying that you won't face some challenges, or that it's easy for everyone. There are real discriminatory problems in the world that make it harder for some people than others, but it's not *impossible*. It's probably already been done, so why not you, too? You are what a wealthy entrepreneur *can* look like, especially now. There's nothing about you that precludes you from being rich. You can be wealthy and wear sweats every day, if you want. You can be rich and kind. You can be rich and normal. You can be as rich and as fabulous as you want.

Go and look for wealthy role models who have a similar life story to your own, or who look like you. They'll help you believe it's possible. And if you can't find any, guess what? It's *your* job to fill that gap! It's your destiny to be a money role model for others. Has nobody done it from your town, country, industry, or with your accent? Then it's *your* opportunity to be a role model and inspire others.

CASE STUDY: SMASHING CULTURAL BLOCKS

Name: *Sharn, UK*
Business: *Business mentor*

One of the most powerful transformations I've experienced is seeing myself as a role model for other women like me. Indian money blocks and cultural blocks are a big thing.

Through my business, I'm helping Asian female entrepreneurs with tangible and practical education, smashing cultural blocks with mindset and marketing tools. I'm also conscious that we don't see enough people 'like us' who are successful.

The more I clear my blocks and embrace my dream life, the more I encourage and give permission to others like me to do the same.

I joined Money Bootcamp in 2016 as an under-earner with so many cultural money blocks. I couldn't hold onto money. Doing the inner work hasn't always been pretty.

I remember when I held my first workshop. I didn't want to pay for a makeup artist or overnight accommodation, so I got the train into the city at 4:30 a.m. Recently, I held an event in London and had a little cry because I could easily afford to stay at the venue, hire a team, and book a makeup artist.

I had to overcome so many beliefs and blocks to get here: people like me don't get this much help. People like me can't be successful. I feel I have broken a generation of poor money mindset beliefs and habits. Why not me? Why not us? I'm what a wealthy Indian woman looks like.

— *Lesson* —

You're allowed to be rich, too.

No Man's Land

'We are the ones we've been waiting for.'

JUNE JORDAN

Did you watch Patty Jenkins' movie *Wonder Woman*? It kinda blew my mind, especially the scenes where Diana (Wonder Woman) goes off to fight 'The War.' Her love interest, Steve Trevor, says to her: 'This war is a great big mess, and there's not a whole lot you and I can do about that. I mean, we can get back to London and try to get to the men who can.' Diana shakes her head at this and says: *'I am the man who can.'*

Then, as all the soldiers are waiting in the trenches, Diana urges them to rise up and fight. Steve says, 'This is no man's land, Diana! It means no man can cross it.' Of course, she ignores him and climbs the ladder out of the trench, ready and determined to go into battle to save the world.

The words 'no man's land' hit me as a massive call to action. I felt all my excuses about my business fall away. The people who created the problems of the world won't fix them, and there's a new generation of leaders who have to step into that void. We can reject the 'old rules' of engagement. If we want a better world, we have to make it happen ourselves. My business can be part of the solution and so can yours. *I am the (wo)man who can.*

What's Your No Man's Land?

'Success doesn't come to you, you go to it.'

MARVA COLLINS

How can you work up the courage to fit in where there are no voices, faces, or perspectives like yours? What combination of skills and talents do you have that allows you into previously forbidden spaces?

We think some rules bar us from entry, but the rules have changed so much that no one really knows what they are anymore. Nobody can tell you 'no,' but waiting for permission means you'll wait forever. Maybe your no man's land is just having the audacity to show up exactly as you are. Why not you?

— *Lesson* —

**We are the ones who can. We are the
ones we have been waiting for.**

CASE STUDY: ROCKING THE BOAT

Name: *Tash Corbin, wherever my dog takes me (currently New Zealand)*
Business: *Consent-driven marketing and sales consultant*

When I listened to Denise speak about No Man's Land, I had tingles through my entire body. I was on a walk and I had to sit down, rewind it, and listen again. At the time, my business was already making multiple six-figures per year, but I was itching to cross the million-dollar mark.

I had hit a plateau, and now I knew why. As a marketing consultant, I'd wanted to speak up for a long time about the toxic and manipulative marketing practices that are prolific in the online space.

I really wanted to revolutionize the industry and bring in empowering consent-based marketing practices, but I was focusing on surface-level advice. I was hiding because I had some things to say that could rock the boat and potentially criticize leaders in my industry.

To hear Denise say that if we want a better world, we have to make it happen ourselves... I felt like she spoke directly to my heart. I recognized that my vision for change just needed to be a teensy bit bigger than my fear; it was a kick in the pants to have the courage to speak up and stop hiding.

I was invited to speak on several podcasts and event stages, my content was shared, and my social media reach skyrocketed. Instead of being shunned, I was invited into masterminds and networking groups with people I had previously only admired from afar. And that all translated into major business growth.

My income plateau was broken, and I had two record months in a row. I'm proud of myself for speaking up, and I'm now on track for that million-dollar year.

 — *Lesson* —

It's okay to speak up.

💡 THE BIG IDEA

If you remember nothing else from Part I, remember this: *Mindset is the only thing that matters. Believe that there's always enough, there's always more, and most importantly, that you are enough. You are what a wealthy person looks like. If not you, then who?*

— PART II —

Business Models

CHAPTER 4

Designing a Chillpreneur Business

'You can't stop the waves, but you can learn to surf.'
JON KABAT-ZINN

My daughter Willow loves to relax. One day after swimming class, she told me, 'Mum, floating is my kind of swimming.' I'm not being cute: her nickname is 'Chillow.' She joins her brother Chilliam and sister Chillie. Okay, now I'm joking!

Let's face it – nobody's business is a non-stop pool party. Yes, I know entrepreneurs who've made a million dollars from a single $37 e-book, but I know that thousands of other entrepreneurs overcomplicate, sabotage, and procrastinate themselves out of a semi-decent living. You can do what you want, but even simple businesses need *some* attention. Each product and service you offer has consequences and implications. That million-dollar e-book still needs marketing, technical logistics, and customer service.

A Chillpreneur creates a business that works for them. Sometimes that's about making deliberate tweaks – other times, you need the courage to ditch the things that stress you out. You can simplify or overcomplicate any business (ask me how I know). You can't create a *completely* hands-off business, but the good news is you can float more and reduce the effort of paddling upstream.

People are always surprised to hear I'm an introvert – but I am! A multimillion-dollar introvert with ADHD, three kids, and two dogs. I've set up every part of my business to work for my energy needs. I've outsourced and delegated my weaknesses and embraced the Chillpreneur philosophy: 'There are easier ways to make money.'

It's not about being lazy – it's just going with the flow for maximum results. You might resist obvious decisions, or believe your business guru told you it had to be a certain way, but being a Chillpreneur can be very profitable if you have the courage to give yourself permission to be exactly the way you are.

Who Wants to Be a Chillionaire?

'If I'd observed all the rules, I'd never have got anywhere.'
MARILYN MONROE

Honestly, six- and seven-figure goals are fun but fairly meaningless. Everyone has different lifestyle goals; we all have vastly different purchasing power depending on where we live – so you have to define your money goal for yourself.

Hence your chillionaire goal! What amount of money would make you feel successful? How much money would help you sleep well at night? Not just to survive, but to thrive and have fun. Everyone is different!

Take a piece of paper right now and write down a number, even if it's just on a dirty napkin using a blunt glitter eyeliner pencil. You might feel resistance, fear, or shame. Don't procrastinate – you're not naming a baby, it's not a tattoo – you're just picking a number and you can change it at any time.

If you don't define it, you don't know what you're playing for. A money goal can help you make important decisions, like what kind of products and services to sell or how many eyeballs need to see your website (check out The 1 Percent Conversion Rule on page 235).

Some people hesitate to name it for fear of being disappointed or jinxing the goal – remember when you were told to make a wish at your birthday party but not say it out loud? But now you're a grown-up, what are the real-life consequences? Literally, nothing terrible will happen to you! But trust me, money LOVES clarity.

Are you setting your goals for you, or for other people?

It's Allowed to Be Easy

*'If God wanted us to bend over
he'd put diamonds on the floor.'*

JOAN RIVERS

I haaaaatttte negotiating anything and find it stressful. Just tell me the price and I'll pay it. So, when we bought our first car, Mark did the haggling and asked for free car mats while I cringed in the background.

My uncle used to be a car salesman, so I was curious and asked him what profit the dealership made on our $30,000 car purchase. What would you guess? The answer: less than $500. I was shocked. Why go through the hassle of negotiating with askholes like my husband for $500? I would have assumed a 50 percent profit margin – more like $10,000–15,000.

My uncle explained the business model of his dealership; the majority of the revenue came from monthly loan commissions and kickbacks. Plus, some upsells – like fancy wheel rims, paint protectors, window tinting, extended warranties, and insurance – had a 50–90 percent profit margin.

Then he asked me the interest rate I got with the car loan. Um. No idea. I just remember the utter relief I felt when Mark and the sales guy finally shook hands. Yep, we signed up for window tinting and paint protector. Yes, we ticked the extended warranty; it only added a few dollars to our monthly repayments – but for the dealership? Ka-CHING!

Here's the lesson: car salesmen are NOT in the business of selling cars. They sell bank loans and paint protectors! The car just gets you in the door. I completely missed the details because I thought the hard work was negotiating the sticker price. Big lesson. The next time I bought a car, we paid cash and it took less than 30 minutes.

What about cinemas? They make money from movie ticket sales, right? Sorta. If a movie runs for a long time, they'll maybe recoup the licensing fee, but their biggest profit-makers are popcorn and soda. Basically, they're in the snack business, and they rent you a room to sit in and entertain you while you eat it! Obviously, this is a huge simplification. But I see it all the time; people go into business with an unprofitable product or the wrong target audience. If you're going to set up a business, at least know how you're going to make money!

— *Lesson* —

Know where the money comes from.

CASE STUDY: UNCOMPLICATE ANY BUSINESS

Name: *Hannah Gilly, UK*

Business: *Knitting courses and patterns*

Chill and Prosper *has taken me on a journey of unravelling my beliefs about myself. I stopped doing things the way other people did and instead built my business to my strengths, knowing that my brain works differently.*

I don't need to write out long to-do lists or over-prepare for workshops and live events; all I need is a few bullet points and to trust my expertise. Previously, I only made sales through fancy workshops, but I felt braver and sold mastermind spaces on live, unscripted videos.

I set up a knitting kit shop – yes, actual physical products, not passive income – because I finally trusted myself to just get the yarn out and create a few patterns without an overcomplicated design process first.

The knitting kits have more than doubled my business income in the last year, and I absolutely love this arm of the business.

Becoming a Chillpreneur has made a big difference in my life. I often look at my processes and consider how I can make it easier and what I can leave out. It's empowering to let go of an idea or leave a project for another time or another entrepreneur. My focus is on keeping the chill.

— *Lesson* —

Trust yourself. You know what feels good.

Know Thyself and Prosper

'If you don't know yourself, you can't
live the life of your dreams.'

Iyanla Vanzant

I won a business award recently, and the runner-up apparently said, 'I can't believe I lost to a blogger!' Ha, ha, yeah, you did, a *multimillionaire blogger!* Of course, I'm not really just a blogger. I'm a writer, speaker, and business mentor, and part-time accidental rose farmer (more on that later).

By the way, if your family doesn't understand how you make money, self-publish a book (any book), so during the holidays you can tell Uncle Bob and Grandma you're a writer, and they can print one out to show her bingo friends.

I help people in all different types of industries and business models, like:

- **Makers**, who make actual, tangible products

- **Creatives**: artists and designers

- **Service providers**, who provide done-for-you services

- **Consultants/mentors**, who help others with their expertise

- **Teachers**, who provide training and education through courses

And yes, different business models have unique challenges. Most entrepreneurs I know have overlap, like my friend Karly Nimmo, who has a service-based voice-over agency but also does one-on-one consulting for wannabe podcasters (like me) and hosts business retreats. My friend Nicola Newman is a fine artist who does large-scale commissions for commercial buildings, sells permaculture and art e-courses, and hosts a business mastermind for introverted entrepreneurs.

And of course, many entrepreneurs use their business as a catalyst for social change. Brandon Love's candle company started with an anti-suicide mission and has grown into a large, loyal community with multiple consumer products – all focused on spreading love and joy (like candles called Sexy Lumberjack and Corgi Butt).

There are no rules, and your business doesn't have to focus on one thing. You can try your hand at anything. But there are nuances within each business model that totally depend on your personality.

For example, if you love:

- **Constantly creating**: Consider offering a membership site. Many creators resist making money out of their talents and end up giving away too much for free, for little return. If you're prolific, charge your community for it! Create small batches so you have variety.

- **Forming deep relationships**: Create a mastermind so you can work intensely with a small group of clients. Have minimum retainers so you work with clients long-term.

- **Connection and fun**: Create VIP days or experience-rich conferences.

- **Low commitment**: Sell hands-off e-courses, host stand-alone retreats, or offer one-off consultations rather than done-for-you services.

- **Coming up with new ideas**: Instead of feeling guilty for not following through, be an ideas consultant for other people. Be the midwife and let others raise the business baby.

- **Playing matchmaker**: Get paid through affiliate marketing or referral fees.

You can do it all your way! Just make sure:

- It suits your personality.

- You're charging well.

- It feels good.

CASE STUDY: THE 'BEST' BUSINESS MODEL IS PERSONAL

Name: *Emily Osmond, Australia*
Business: *Business coach and speaker*

I believed that there was one 'best' type of business model and invested a lot of time and energy trying to find and emulate it. But that meant doing things I didn't love and ignoring my intuition. I thought it was normal for a business to feel hard.

While infuriating at first, it was liberating to hear Denise explain that the 'best' business model is personal. As a result, I simplified my business to play to my strengths and restructured my core offer, removing other offers from my business, and let go of the feeling that I should be doing more – what a relief.

Allowing money to feel easy has been huge for me. I'm much more discerning about what I take on in my business and often hear Denise's words in my head – 'There are easier ways to make money' – when considering new projects. I no longer compare my business model to other people's and think they must be doing it 'right,' because I know that I have designed my business model to work for me.

My business is now extremely simple, and I love it. I have created my low-stress, higher-revenue and -profit, Chill and Prosper business!

— *Lesson* —

Discernment creates simplicity.

You can change your mind at any time. Literally any time. But remember, each product and service you offer is like adding another kid or pet to your family. It needs to be nurtured and fed, so you should set it up for maximum ease and flow. You can be a starving cartoonist or you can be a chillustrator – you choose.

Don't take any more courses to overcome your weaknesses. Instead, focus on your strengths and eliminate, outsource, or delegate your weak points to other people (we also use Kolbe for recruitment – *see page 75*). You might think, *Wait, Denise, shouldn't I research my target customer and design my business for the market?* Nope, do what you want.

I once had someone ask me to buy her business, which, on the surface, was a fantastic fit because she taught people how to create passive income. I couldn't figure out why I was hesitating to make an offer until it hit me: I don't teach how-to; I teach *mindset*. So, even though the topic was perfect, the method wasn't. It was a small distinction that had a huge impact on me: I tightened up the content on my blog to focus more clearly on mindset lessons rather than how-to stuff that could date.

CASE STUDY: A CHANCE TO REMODEL WITH BUSINESS 2.0

Name*: Kathryn Hocking, Adelaide, Australia*
Business*: Business astrology and branding*

In business, I've experienced the highest of highs (including $500,000 years) and the lowest of lows. I've made bad decisions, accumulated personal debt with a failing business, and have experienced significant financial stress. But nothing is forever, and I'm thankful to have learned from it and built back better.

I was often sick and burned out. I had severe adrenal fatigue two years in a row, and I was in a place of desperation, working harder and harder. I took a corporate job to go back to basics, and decided only to do work and create products that lit me up.

I focused on what lit me up and how I wanted my life and business to look. In the meantime, I asked myself what I would do even if I didn't get paid. Well, I was giving people complimentary astrology readings all the time – the answer was staring me in the face!

These days I live and work cyclically in alignment with moon cycles and astrology, and I allow myself to rest and restore as often as I need. When I recreated my business, I was also aware that there were a lot of cheap astrology services – and I was determined not to price my services based on a starving healer mindset. So instead, I price in a way that compensates for my time investment, which also feels really good.

I now embrace the easier ways to make money with multiple streams of income, effective boundaries, and the right foundations and structure for success. I still offer non-leveraged services like astrology readings and brand design. However, these are not the bread and butter of my business. I get to choose how many clients I service because I have leveraged income flowing in all the time through e-products, e-courses, and my year-long astrology certification.

My business earns on average $20,000 per month and is growing all the time. I've paid off significant personal debt, and I'm back to being full-time in my business.

I'm grateful I can choose to do only work I love and have designed my business 2.0 as one that works for me.

— *Lesson* —
It's okay to take a break and build back better.

Shortcut Your Success with Personality Tests

It can take years to learn business lessons from trial and error, or you can shortcut it with personality tests like Myers-Briggs, Kolbe, the Enneagram, StrengthsFinder, The Fascination Advantage, Human Design, etc., and build your business around your results.

I'm a '9 Quick Start' in Kolbe, which means I can be impulsive, love spontaneity, and don't need a lot of preparation. I just thought I was impatient and lazy! I can run a three-day conference with virtually no notes, and I write 80 percent of my books in the two weeks before the deadline (shh, don't tell anyone).

Getting an official ADHD diagnosis was validating for both my life and business. My team keeps me out of the minutiae and asks me simple yes/no questions. Every part of the business is set up for my preferences – I'm the Queen Bee, and there's no business without me. I've stopped criticizing myself for it, because it's way more profitable and fun just embracing who I am.

I think you can learn something from almost any personality test, even if it's not designed specifically for business. The goal is self-knowledge for more pleasure and profit, and less stress or friction. For example, I loved the book *The Five Love Languages* by Gary Chapman. It's about love relationships, but I could also apply it to my business.

Chapman says there are five ways that you express and prefer to receive love.[1] They are: receiving gifts, quality time, words of affirmation, acts of service, and physical touch. My love language is quality time (such as sitting on the couch watching a movie with Mark, but not *talking* to each other) and acts of service (I love that Mark cooks most of our meals). Knowing that about myself means I need to make sure I don't have to work evenings or weekends. Otherwise, I'll feel resentful toward my clients and business for cutting into my couch-not-talking-time with Mark!

You can learn just as much from your preferred way of being as you can from your least favorite way. For example, words of affirmation are not important to me. I just don't need to hear praise – in fact, it often makes me feel uncomfortable. I ask my team not to forward fan mail but to capture them for testimonials, and I ask people not to send me thank-you presents. You might love receiving gifts; I don't, and I've put boundaries around this preference.

You can use any personality test to create more flow in your business, but sometimes you have to dig deep to find the money lessons. That's why I love the Sacred Money Archetypes® (SMA®) assessment and even became certified in teaching the method. It's been life-changing for me, my business, and everyone who takes the quiz.

Your SMA® result tells you how your personality can make or repel money. I'm a Ruler, Maverick, and Romantic; my sabotages tend to overwork, taking impulsive risks and ignoring details! You might be an Alchemist, Accumulator, Celebrity, Connector, Romantic, or Nurturer – each with its own financial strengths and weaknesses. This is seriously one of the best tools I've ever seen, and it's spookily accurate.

You can get a free Sacred Money Archetypes® personality report at denisedt.com/chill. Do the quiz now because it will give you crucial information about how to prosper from your personality. Why make it harder than it needs to be?

'Wherever you go, there you are.'

Confucius

— *Lesson* —

It's okay to build your business around your strengths.

CASE STUDY:
LEVERAGE BUT DON'T LOSE THE JOY

Name: *Angela Henderson, Queensland, Australia*
Business: *Coach and consultant*

Most business experts teach leveraged hands-off marketing, but I've always felt resistance to that model. I'm a big connector and thrive in small, intimate groups, developing deep, long-term friendships with my clients.

I've focused my business on one-on-one VIP offers and hosting intimate, high-connection retreats in beautiful locations. Looking after people and creating fun experiences feels magic to me – I never get burned out by people, and the more I connect, the more money I make.

Chill and Prosper gave me permission to recognize that my business needs to be built to my strengths. But the question remained: how could I scale my offerings and create leverage when I thrive working in such a high-touch way?

I experimented with a low-ticket product – but instead of an automated, pre-recorded e-course, I decided to run an online two-hour group workshop. We could still connect live (which I love) but in a more leveraged way. The result: 200 people registered and we made $53,700 in sales, with a conversion rate three times the industry average. I give myself permission to run business my way – fun and profitable!

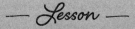

— *Lesson* —

Do it your way. It's the only way to prosper.

EXERCISE: IS YOUR BUSINESS FLOWING?

In your journal, write down the first answer to the following questions that comes to mind:

- What are my top three strengths?
- What are my top three weaknesses?

Now, get honest with yourself:

- Where is my business working for my strengths?
- Where am I working against my weaknesses?

You're allowed to shift, quit, tweak, or pivot every part of your business to suit yourself.

My Three Biggest Business Mistakes

I mean, I've made so many mistakes that it could be a whole book, but luckily, with my inattentive-type ADHD, I often forget about them instantly! I always take things a little too far; I always underestimate how long things take (like writing books), agree to commitments I immediately regret (like speaking gigs), and get excited about random off-topic projects all the time. I almost always come to my senses and remind myself that 'all roads lead to Money Bootcamp,' but not before taking a few detours.

Here are three times when I've gone against my strengths, got distracted, or forgot to make it easy:

1. Making bee-branded merchandise.
2. Making a mobile app.
3. Selling the world's most expensive roses.

Mistake #1: Making Bee-Branded Merchandise

My path to physical products started innocently: I got fake money made with my face on it instead of business cards. It was fun and cute. Then, during my live events, I gave out branded notebooks, pens, and a Lucky Bitch calculator. I almost made giant $50-note beach towels but stopped myself just in time when the budget blew out.

Then, during a spectacular procrastination session, I started making Lucky Bitch swag for no reason (I didn't even sell it). But, of course, I didn't get out my sewing machine or buy my own kiln – there are tons of companies who'll support your procrasti-branding by making things on demand; all you have to do is upload your logo, and they'll ship it. So, for example, I made Lucky Bitch cushions, a towel, wrapping paper, Christmas ornaments, stickers, etc.

And then, I found a site that does print-on-demand clothing. So, naturally, I made my own branded kimonos. Now, to be fair, my staff can wear them to my events, but still... branded kimonos. The clothing company had many options, so I also made a bee-branded jumpsuit, mesh tank top, one-piece swimsuit, and zippered clutch bag – all matching my website brand colors. I almost went for the yoga pants, but my accountant started asking questions and I cut myself off.

To paraphrase Jeff Goldblum in *Jurassic Park*: 'Your scientists were so preoccupied with whether or not they could, they didn't stop to think if they should.'

Just because the technology exists to make cheap branded merchandise, it doesn't mean you should do it – unless it's a strategic business decision (and you can afford it). My business is helping entrepreneurs release money blocks, not making branded bikinis and Christmas ornaments. I'm a big advocate of fun marketing, and people regularly ask me where they can buy the branded Lucky Bitch/Chillpreneur merch. But the answer is: you can't. It's not my business, and I don't care if I might make a few bucks from it.

Beware shiny object syndrome.

It's okay to say no, even to good ideas. Your community wants live events, but you don't want to travel? Say no. Clients want you to get up at 5 a.m. for a coaching session in their time zone? Say no. People ask me to create a men's version of my book *Get Rich, Lucky Bitch!* What would I call it – *Get Rich, Lucky Dick*? *Lucky Dude, Lucky Bastard*? Sorry, no.

If you ask them, your audience will give you tons of random ideas, but you don't have to act on them if you don't want to! Not all money feels good to earn. For example, people often ask me to create a business mastermind, which is not my zone of genius and not something I can hold space for while our kids are young. No amount of money would actually tempt me to do it.

Before you start something new, ask yourself: *Is this useful, or am I bored?* Now that my business has been successful for a few years, I do sometimes get itchy fingers. I recently discovered a company that makes branded clocks. Could I make one with my popular affirmation: 'It's your time, and you're ready for the next step'? Should I make 'Chillionaire Juice' KeepCups? Yessss – I mean, NO!

For most entrepreneurs, the 'rush' of being in business comes at the beginning. This is why you'll feel compelled to create a new website even when your current one is fine. Resist the urge. Seriously, get a hobby instead. Get a new haircut. Don't blow up your business just before things start working.

Beware of how your procrastination manifests itself. Whether it's collecting another certification (procrasti-learning) or starting a new business offering because your mentor (or business nemesis) does, get real about how it's impacting your income.

— *Lesson* —

There are easier ways to make money.

I should put that on a T-shirt and sell it! Wait... no!

Mistake #2: Making a Mobile App

On the surface, launching a money-tracking app was a business win that felt cool and cutting-edge. This is embarrassing, but I only made it because the author Danielle LaPorte had one, and I got FOMO (fear of missing out).

I invested $12,000 in design and development, and when I had to choose the app price, I realized my big mistake. Apps usually charge just a few bucks; my philosophy is 'free or expensive.' I don't want to be in the app business, even if it can market my Money Bootcamp. I could have created a cheaper, more effective lead magnet than an app.

I made the app free because I didn't want to deal with technical support. If it's free, I can apologize but we don't have to spend time and energy fixing every tech problem (which is guaranteed to happen with anything). I'd rather help my Money Bootcamp customers than deal with angry app refund requests. *(Check out The 3 Percent Customer Service Rule in the Money section on page 243.)*

Almost every day, someone pleads for or demands an Android version, but the answer is no because eventually I'll discontinue the whole thing. Yes, it's hard to disappoint people, but I'm not going to invest more money now I've realized my mistake. I'm just not in the app business. Not everything has to be my business. What I offer is free or expensive.

— *Lesson* —

Don't create something because of FOMO.

Mistake #3: Selling the World's Most Expensive Roses

One day I'll write a whole Lorn Rose Farm book because the business lessons come thick and fast (just like the thorns). During my pregnancy with baby #3, I started reading *Country Style* magazine. It's full of stories of people who fell in love with some derelict property on a weekend mini-break and found themselves a few months later shoveling pig poop in the middle of nowhere. I'd think, *Who are these idiots?*

But… a country house would be a fun goal one day, right? So, like an idiot, I convinced Mark to start visiting country properties on weekends 'just for fun.' Not to brag, but I'm an excellent manifester, and sometimes I have to control this superpower.

You know where this is going. As soon as my foot hit the soil, holding my newborn in my arms (middle name: Rose), I looked at Mark with literal tears in my eyes, and he said one word in return: '… Fuck.' We called our financial advisors, and they said one word too: 'No.'

Sometimes that's all I need to hear… to do the exact opposite. I said, 'Tell me how much money I need to buy this, and I'll go away and make it.' So, if you bought Money Bootcamp in October 2018, you helped me buy a 10-acre hobby rose farm.

First lesson: selling my Money Bootcamp is a way more chill business than selling roses. On our first Valentine's Day, we spent all night learning how to de-thorn and arrange roses from YouTube, and we made… $1,300. The following year we made $20,000 from roses – WHOOHOO… and it cost us at least $100,000 in staff, fertilizer, and other expenses. It would have been cheaper to give away origami roses made from dollar bills. The next obvious business was hosting weddings, but after maintenance costs, customer service, and dealing with brides, I could make the same from a few Money Bootcamps.

Don't worry; there's a happy ending. We found a young couple to live in our caretaker's cottage in exchange for yard work. They started their own organic vegetable business from the farm, and harvest and sell our roses too. It's a win-win situation. So, I'm keeping the farm for personal joy and a few retreats each year for my most special clients – come visit one day and smell the world's most expensive roses!

— *Lesson* —

Just because you can, doesn't mean you should.

CASE STUDY: A HOBBY GREW OUR BUSINESS

Name*: Nathalie Lussier, Canada*
Business*: Software solutions for entrepreneurs and farmer*

I read Chill and Prosper *during my second maternity leave, with a business already at the seven-figure level. I felt restless, asking, 'What's next?' and trying to envision the next steps for my business and family life, and all of the issues we're all facing at the global level.*

Wanting to start fresh is a huge tendency for me because I'm an action taker. So it was an important time to read about not blowing up your business because you want to try something new or different, particularly Denise's advice: get a hobby.

So, we moved my family from Texas back to our home province in Canada and bought a hobby farm! We've since gotten chickens, geese, ducks, and sheep. Our business success helped us buy the farm with cash, grow food, and raise animals, without the pressure of turning the farm into a profitable business.

Our software business keeps growing; we're able to pay ourselves a great salary and reinvest profits into hiring more female engineers (putting more wealth and power into the hands of women), planting trees, doing rotational grazing to help with carbon sequestration, and growing fresh food for our family and neighbors.

Plus, I get to take photos and videos of our farm and pour my creativity into both places. We're aligned with our values and feel like we're doing something bigger than just earning for earning's sake.

— *Lesson* —

A hobby can refresh your love for your business.

EXERCISE: FINDING YOUR CHILLPRENEUR BUSINESS

In your journal, answer the following questions:

- Are you in the right business, really?
- What parts of your business do you (secretly) want to quit?
- Is there an easier way to make money?
- What could you tweak? Could you find an alternative win-win solution?

— CHAPTER 5 —

Protecting the Golden Goose

*'We need to do a better job of putting ourselves
higher on our own "to-do" list.'*

MICHELLE OBAMA

*D*o you know the story of the Golden Goose? There are many
variations, but it goes like this:

A man has a goose that lays a golden egg every day. It makes
him very rich, but he's impatient to become even richer as fast as
possible, so he kills the goose to get all the golden eggs he thinks are
inside. But of course, all he discovers is goose guts, and he realizes
that, in his greed, he's killed the source of his wealth.

Aspiring Chillpreneurs can learn a lot from this story; namely *you*
are the Golden Goose. You can profit for a long time if you take care
of yourself, but not if you kill the goose.

There's nothing wrong with ambition. Entrepreneurs like us are
wired to create, and I'm the kind of person who goes on holiday
and gets business downloads during a 'relaxing' massage. I love my
business. Let's accept that we're lifelong entrepreneurs, and we'll
never run out of ideas.

I used to be ashamed to acknowledge burnout because it felt like admitting weakness, but I don't know too many people who haven't experienced it at least once. Unfortunately, in my quest to churn out more golden eggs, I overcommit and overschedule, and forget that I'm a human being, not a money-making machine.

As my friend Amber McCue says, 'Don't try and boil the ocean.' I know you have a lot of ideas gestating, and they all want to be birthed *now*, but you don't have to write all the books of your life right now. You don't need all the domain names. Be discerning and respect your season of life.

If your business requires every drop of blood, sweat, and tears, it's only a matter of time before it catches up with you – either in the form of a health wake-up call or another type of 'forced intervention' from the universe.

Instead of having a long and profitable career, do you really want to burn out in a few years? Me neither! We can avoid that intervention by consciously protecting the Golden Goose, and it's never too late to start.

CASE STUDY: A CANCER DIAGNOSIS WAS MY WAKE-UP CALL

Name: *Michelle Swan, Australia*
Business: *Personal branding photography*

When reading Chill and Prosper, *it was glaringly apparent that I wasn't honoring my energy at all. I was the photographer, editor, admin assistant, social media manager, content creator, marketer, and accountant in my business. I was wearing all of the hats, utterly resistant to handing the reins over to someone else.*

Unfortunately, it took a cancer diagnosis and surgery for me to take a step back and realize it was no longer sustainable. I was killing the Golden Goose, and working harder was not going to fix the problem.

I realized that my capacity is three photoshoots per week, with a day off in-between to rest and recharge. So, I raised my prices and began charging clients for their gallery upgrades. Those two upgrades alone resulted in the first $20,000 month in my business.

I hired a private editor who is brilliant. The onboarding process was easier than I anticipated; we had a few lessons over Zoom, and I recorded some training videos so she could easily emulate my editing style. It feels so nourishing and expansive to have this task taken off my plate.

My online system can now take bookings, send contracts, and accept payments via credit card; it links with my calendar and online accounting program. My accountant also has access, which makes tax time feel so straightforward.

My next step is to hire a virtual assistant to help refine my workflow and support content creation. I'm excited because this will free up even more energy for rest and give me the time and space to create my first passive income products.

— *Lesson* —

Honor your capacity.

CASE STUDY: NOT ALLOWED TO HAVE BOUNDARIES

Name: *Sarra Cannon, USA*
Business: *Young Adult author and author coach*

When I read about the Golden Goose, it struck a chord and suddenly my vision of my life cleared. Growing up with a narcissistic mother, I've always struggled with setting boundaries. I spent my early years thinking I was responsible for everyone else's happiness, and my own was an afterthought or a luxury.

I had an epiphany: 'My entire business depends on me and my energy, and yet I'm consistently taking myself to the edge of burnout and exhaustion.'

While I'm pretty good at getting things done, I struggled with relaxing and having fun. During group assignments in high school, I decided that I'd have to do it all myself if I want it done right – so I've resisted hiring help and taking time off when there's always so much to do.

I love my work, but the creative side of my fiction-writing was getting pushed to the sidelines, along with gaming, reading, exercise, and a ton of other things I genuinely enjoy (especially with a new baby in the house as I was reading the book).

I hired an assistant and online marketing manager, outsourced some bookkeeping, cut things off my to-do list, and created new boundaries at home with my husband. As a result, we started having a daily huddle in the mornings to share duties when I needed to sleep in or step away from the house for some brainstorming or creative daydreaming.

Things immediately began to shift in my life and business. I focused on the tasks that only I could do and outsourced some of the others. After implementing what I learned in Chill and Prosper, I had my best year in business ever. I'm still working harder than I want to, but I'm making changes all the time to free myself up for more fun, joy, and creativity.

I need and deserve fun and downtime to preserve my energy. I'm the Golden Goose, and I have to take care of myself.

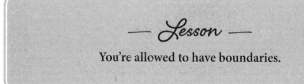

— *Lesson* —

You're allowed to have boundaries.

Three Ways to Protect the Golden Goose

Nobody is going to give you permission to change what's not working. You have to decide for yourself. I have three suggestions:

1. Take imperfect action.

2. Know when to quit or pivot.

3. Stop doing it all yourself.

Way #1: Take Imperfect Action

> *'There are people less qualified than you doing*
> *the things you want to do simply because*
> *they decided to believe in themselves.'*
>
> UNKNOWN

Marilyn Monroe was not a perfect actress; she often forgot her lines, medicated with drugs and alcohol to overcome her anxiety, and regularly turned up late to set. Yet her legacy has endured for decades. Billy Wilder, her director for *The Seven Year Itch* and *Some Like It Hot*, was asked why he put up with it. He said something like, 'My Aunt Minnie would be punctual and professional, but nobody will pay to see my Aunt Minnie.'[1] Marilyn had priceless magic that couldn't be replicated.

When my husband, Mark, joined the business, I was already generating a million-dollar revenue working part-time and half-assing all my systems. He had a lot of fresh ideas – what if we perfected everything and did more launches? Then we'd make even more money!

I made my branding and sales pages slicker. It made no difference to conversion statistics (in some cases, it made it *worse*). I hired a 'sell from stage' coach and bombed. Instead of one or two launches a year, we did four long, complicated ones. So, add all the pre-launch promotional work plus the actual delivery of my course: it was like being in all trimesters of pregnancy at once – while trying to give birth AND breastfeed the (thousands of) babies simultaneously.

I was not a happy goose. Yes, we made more money, but our expenses went up too. Most importantly, my fruitless quest for perfection killed my enthusiasm for the business. Worse, I felt like a failure. So, we needed a Golden Goose intervention, known as the 'two-card ultimatum' – I asked him which business card he wanted: a divorce lawyer or a marriage counselor. We had a lot of counseling that year and, don't worry, we eventually found our groove.

Mark's a former Boy Scout who loves following rules, but he had to learn that I was the one that brought the magic in my business, not my systems. Obviously, working with your spouse is a strange dynamic. I'm the Queen Bee, but I'm also his wife and business partner. He wanted me to be the show pony who made us money *and* the plow horse doing everything behind the scenes.

If I'm not happy and thriving, there is no business. Maybe I could squeeze out a few more eggs under pressure, but I want to lay big juicy golden eggs for a long time.

— *Lesson* —

People want your magic, not perfection.

The Truth: Perfectionism Costs You Money

If I were having brain surgery, I'd want my surgeon to be a perfectionist. I want our bridges and planes to be built by perfectionist engineers. But, and I say this with love, your business doesn't require that level of perfection.

Let's see what your perfectionism is costing you. Years ago, I created a free audio called 'Seven Money Blocks and How to Release Them.' Unfortunately, the slides were crap, the audio was a bit echoey, and there was no follow-up funnel. It killed me to publish it because it wasn't perfect.

Here was my 'sales pitch' at the end of that audio: 'Okay, guys, so if you want my help with your money blocks, I have an um... Money Bootcamp and um... I'll just put the link under this video if you're interested. Okay, thanks, bye.'

Two years later, I was about to delete it out of shame and create something super-perfect, but out of curiosity, I had my SEO guy run the numbers: 21,737 people had visited the page, and around 1 percent of them bought my Money Bootcamp that day. At $2,000 each.

In two years, that placeholder made at least $200,000 and helped over twenty thousand people, even though I didn't think it was good enough. The first version of Money Bootcamp was filmed at home on an iPad because I had something to say and wanted to share it. I've upgraded it every few years since then, and honestly, it's *still* not perfect.

While some of my biz friends waited for the stars to align, I've made more than 20 million dollars showing up with half-assed systems and a sincere intention to help people. If I'd waited, I'd still be living in a tiny apartment and driving a car with a roof that sagged around my ears.

Yes, I know you still want things to be perfect, but can you publish an imperfect placeholder today? There is no ideal time to start. You're the right weight, age, and height to get started right now.

My imperfect magic has created millions of dollars for our family and a ripple effect for my Money Bootcamp students worldwide. I've helped thousands of people make money (and birthed a few millionaires, too) because I dared to show up imperfectly. You can, too.

— *Lesson* —

Half-ass, full heart, can't lose.

CASE STUDY: I STOPPED TWEAKING AND STARTING SELLING

Name: *Christine Collins, Mississippi, USA*
Business: *Content coach and certified master hypnotherapist*

My first hypnosis recordings were made on my cell phone and edited with a free music app (and I would cringe if I heard them now), but those were some of my first sales.

I eventually bought better equipment and improved the audio quality. But after I re-recorded my entire hypnosis audio collection more than twice, I needed to shift my focus from constantly tweaking to actually marketing and selling.

Denise helped me realize that 'pretty good' to me might be 'amazing' to someone else and can offer them a lot of value. In addition, Denise's message that 'done' and 'perfect' are much less distinguishable to others helped me to let go of some of my natural perfectionism.

I stopped upgrading and started exclusively marketing my hypnosis audios. And I started selling them! REALLY selling them. Each year since I internalized that piece of advice, I've increased my hypnosis audio sales by two or three times. Every year it goes up. It's easier to make those sales than when I was in perfectionist mode.

Chill and Prosper *helped me to be able to get my work out there and allow upgrades to happen later (or not!).*

— *Lesson* —

Imperfect placeholders can be profitable!

EXERCISE: BUST THE PERFECTIONISM

In your journal, answer these questions:

- What product or service could be launched right now?
- Could it help at least one person right now?
- What's my next action?

Way #2: Know When to Quit or Pivot

> *'Know the difference between a bad day, and a bad business.'*
> YVETTE LUCIANO

I had a perfect early introduction to hard work. As a child, the dance school I attended performed every weekend at shopping centers and old folks' homes, and then I was a professional children's performer from ages 16–22, including being an Olympic Games mascot.

The lesson drummed into us was 'the show must go on.' No matter what. If your leotard went up your butt during the performance, you were never to touch it. If your top hat fell off during the tap number, you ignored it and mimed your hat. Sprained ankle? Tape it, plaster on your smile, and don't forget to point those toes!

This lesson steered us well because we had our share of costume malfunctions, and we could roll with unexpected mishaps, like subtly adjusting our spacing if someone got injured mid-performance (or the time we tap-danced on concrete).

You never missed a rehearsal or show; you pushed through any pain because you never wanted to let the team down. I loved it and credit my dance teacher, Simone Mann, for keeping me out of a lot of teen-related trouble. 'Sorry, I can't come to that party; I have a rehearsal in the morning!'

> *'I hate canceling anything, I'm "the show must go on" mentality. If you can crawl, you can take the stage.'*
>
> SUZI QUATRO

When I started my business, I went into it with the same 'show must go on' mentality. Work ethic is a fantastic quality, to a point. But then, after a while, you have to learn an important lesson. It's okay to say no.

When I was super-pregnant with baby #3, I was invited on a morning TV show to talk about my newest book, a three-hour drive from my house. I said no, but agreed to appear about six weeks after my due date. *Why, Denise, why?* Because they asked me. Because it was 'show time.' Strap up those leaking boobs and smile!

I worried about the logistics for weeks – three hours (each way) of driving with a newborn, and an hour of hair and makeup. I'm not a fan of live TV, to be honest, and at best it was a three-minute segment that didn't even necessarily reach my target audience.

Then, finally, I had a great idea! I'll tell them I got into a car accident! Or I'll wait till the day before and say I have explosive diarrhea! It never occurred to me to tell the truth. I had just had a freaking baby and had two other young kids.

Finally, I emailed the producer two weeks before: 'I sincerely apologize. I shouldn't have committed with a newborn; I just can't make this work.' And I felt like the biggest loser. I *could* have made it work, but I didn't want to. So I canceled a show for the first time in my life.

The actual consequences were minor – the producer never responded and probably put me on a 'never-book-again list' (I hope so) – but the impact of that moment was huge for me. Finally, permission to *choose*. It was liberating, and I felt inspired to quit even more stressful things in my life and business.

> *'Yes, the show must go on, but it's also important*
> *to survive until the curtain calls.'*
>
> MARSHALL THORNTON

CASE STUDY: SLOW DOWN TO BUILD IT BETTER

Name*: Mason Aid (they/them), USA*
Business*: Diversity and inclusion coach for small businesses*

I was caught up in hustle culture to the degree that it was dramatically affecting my mental health. I decided to do 75 coffee chats in a month and was literally losing my sanity. Chill and Prosper was the initiator of a long process of chilling the EFF out.

I realized I was putting too much pressure on my business as my only income source. I needed a reset. I shut down my business almost entirely and got a full-time job. I knew I needed to make ends meet without putting more pressure on the business than it was ready for.

I'm now diving back into business, building it chill from the start because I want a sustainable business that works for me instead of against me. While I still have progress to make, I'm so much further on the road to recovery – both from my mental health crisis and in building that sustainable business.

— *Lesson* —

Nothing is forever.

The Truth: You're Allowed to Quit Anything

In Stephen King's book *On Writing: A Memoir of the Craft*, he writes, 'Kill your darlings, kill your darlings, even when it breaks your egocentric little scribbler's heart, kill your darlings.'

What does he mean? Author Ruthanne Reid says, 'Darlings, in writing, are those words, phrases, sentences, paragraphs, and even chapters that we're often most proud of. We love them, to the point that we *almost* don't care if those bits are clear to readers or not. We love them, and we want to keep them.'[2]

In business, we have to 'kill' our darlings, too. When I started my first blog, I tried to solve every problem. My website had a tab for every conceivable issue. I created a 'Manifest Your Soul Mate' course and wrote a book called *Get Hitched, Lucky Bitch*. It hurt to delete it, but it was the right decision.

My business motto, 'All roads lead to Money Bootcamp,' helps me stay on track. I even bought Mark a sign for his office that spells out 'Sell More Bootcamps' to keep us from complicating our business.

You might resist killing your darlings because:

- It's a good idea, even though it's not The One.

- You spent money on a domain name or website.

- You don't want to turn down or give up money.

- The 'perfect' idea hasn't turned up yet.

- It's part of your identity.

- You've developed a reputation for fixing any problem.

- You're worried people will think you're a flake if you change or pivot (again).

- You don't want to disappoint people (clients, suppliers, staff).

It doesn't matter if it's your first or 30th attempt, a bad business doesn't get better over time, and it can totally kill your Golden Goose.

Keeping a business out of stubbornness or the 'sunk cost fallacy' is a waste of your potential. It's okay to quit. Even if you've invested time and money, nothing is ever wasted. My first business, Raw Brides, only sold one course, but I learned how to write a sales page, set up payment systems, run a webinar, and do a million other things.

I actually love seeing people quit their businesses – I find it just as inspiring as business successes. Have you ever been to a Cher or Elton John concert? They both sing songs that are decades old and have probably made them millions of dollars. Do you think they get sick of them? Maybe they do, but they remind me that if you're going to put a song out into the world, you'd better make sure it's one you really like!

What could you sing about for decades? Choose wisely. Money is a subject I've been passionate about for a long time, and I'm beyond grateful that I gave up my early business ideas and I'm not still talking about weddings or toilet hooks. Nothing is wasted; you retain every skill you learn, and even your screw-ups can be invaluable lessons. Every 'practice' business is one step closer to your Chillpreneur one!

— *Lesson* —

Nothing is wasted.

But what if you actually do make money out of a business you no longer love? Now, killing your darlings takes courage when you rely on them for financial support. Sometimes you have to transition slowly; other times, you need to rip off the bandage quickly and create a vacuum for new income streams. Giving up the old enables you to move forward and welcome the new. It's so empowering to let go. Not only does it free up a lot of time and energy, but it also creates space for new things to be birthed. You're allowed to walk away from a business, even if it's a hugely successful one.

Many entrepreneurs have a defining moment, such as burnout or the birth of a child, that necessitates change, while others realize that their business doesn't bring them joy or enable them to work to their strengths.

Sarah Walked Away from Millions of Dollars

Sarah Wilson, a former journalist and magazine editor, created a multimillion-dollar business out of a thyroid disease diagnosis. She quit sugar for her health and wrote about it on her blog. One recipe book turned into numerous bestsellers and then she created an online 'I Quit Sugar' course. She had 1.5 million students go through the course. 1.5 million!

Then, in 2018, she closed it down. She was done. I debated about it with my friends for weeks because we couldn't believe she quit such a lucrative business. We mapped out her funnel – why not make it an evergreen course? Why not sell it?

I wasn't the only one questioning her decision. So, she wrote on her blog: 'Seven years into a movement, five years into a business, I feel my work in the realm is done. Success is a funny thing. It requires feeding. It requires growth. Which sees you become caught up in the cycle eventually, sometimes without realizing.'[3]

Remember, even a Chillpreneur business requires attention. Everything you create has its own energy. Even if you send your kid to boarding school, they're still your child. Putting Sarah's course on autopilot would have demanded energy. Even if she outsourced most of the work, it's still her name attached to the business.

I actually respect the decision so much now.

How do you know if you should quit?

- You're completely bored.

- You've run out of steam.

- You start dreading opening up your inbox.

- You're resenting your clients.

- You're making mistakes or unconsciously sabotaging the old business.

- You're exhausted and something's got to give.

You could sell your business, wind it down, or rip off the Band-Aid and quit. There are no rules!

CASE STUDY: GIVING UP PROFITABLE BUSINESSES

Name: *Jodie Minto, New South Wales, Australia*
Business: *Resort-wear designer and e-commerce coach*

I couldn't have picked up Chill and Prosper *at a more pivotal time. I was burned out and overstretched because, as I realized, I was running FOUR different business models at the same time:*

- *Designing, manufacturing, and retailing resort wear in my own online store.*

- *Offering Facebook ads management for other online fashion stores.*

- *Business coaching for up to 12 e-commerce clients at a time.*

- *Teaching an online e-commerce course with dozens of students.*

I wasn't just killing the Golden Goose; I'd totally cooked it!

After that OMG realization, I closed the ad management and one-on-one coaching businesses, both profitable revenue streams but totally unscalable. I had to refund thousands of dollars to clients, which really hurt, but it was the right decision. I used Denise's scripts to have those difficult client conversations, and I've bookmarked them all for future use – they are absolute gold! (See Awkward Money Conversations on page 187).

I reminded myself of the Chill and Prosper affirmation, 'There's always more money,' and I had more time to think strategically on the growth of my other two businesses.

Within two months of refocusing my attention to my e-commerce fashion business, we did our first-ever $100,000 month, ending with $1.4 million annual sales! It was like a sign from above saying, 'Yes – you are on the right track!' I'm also *working a lot less, with more time to focus on growing the business and enjoying life, without feeling like the hamster on a wheel anymore.*

I've also had the time to refresh and update my online course, and I've just had 22 students finish a live round. I enjoyed every minute of working with those students and didn't feel overwhelmed or overstretched at all.

— *Lesson* —

You don't have to implement ALL your good ideas at the same time!

The Truth: You're Allowed to Renegotiate Anything

When my eldest kid started school, she started saying to her younger siblings: 'You get what you get, and don't get upset.' It's drummed into all of us at school. Mark and I teach our kids to make deals with us. If they disagree with us, they have to use their negotiating skills and convince us otherwise. We want to teach them that their reality is totally up to them.

If you grew up hearing 'You made your bed, now lie in it,' you might feel like any decision you make in business is forever. But you're allowed to renegotiate anything, even if it worked for a while, even if people get upset with you.

Before you throw out your whole business, ask yourself: 'Is it a bad business, or do I need to renegotiate?' You have permission to shape your business to suit you.

Renegotiate Your Prices

A florist told me she hated doing weddings, but it was by far the most profitable part of her business. I asked her if she hated the work itself. She said, 'No, but I find it overwhelming.' I asked if she could make it more enjoyable and worthwhile if she made more money. She decided to become a more premium business, raising her prices and taking on fewer clients.

Renegotiate Your Schedule

Ignore other people's preferences. Some people love the '5 a.m. club' life, and others get their best ideas between 11 p.m. and 3 a.m. When I first started out, I coached people six days a week depending on their preferences, not realizing I could choose. So, I gradually eliminated Mondays and Fridays from my coaching calendar and freed up so much space. What works for you?

CASE STUDY: I HAD TO BE AVAILABLE 24/7

Name: *Joy Bufalini, Florida, USA*
Business: *Business coaching*

> I used to have a hard time turning off from work, and I felt obligated to stay connected and available 24/7.
>
> As an introvert, I needed a lot more 'no people' time during the week to be at my best. Chill and Prosper prompted me to reduce my client schedule to three days a week. It was fantastic for my energy and the enjoyment of my business.
>
> I kept Mondays for planning and Fridays for flexibility and fun. The next step was to create a firm work boundary and end those days by 4 p.m. at the latest.
>
> My next-level upgrade was to remove all calls in the last week of the month. Wow! What a gift! It didn't matter if

someone wanted to interview me on a podcast or get on a call. I politely gave them my schedule for the following week.

The best part is the result. My business continued to grow at the same upward rate, and my clients kept getting excellent outcomes, but without needing as much of me as I thought. As a result, I hired more team members to serve my clients, and I grew from $40,000 months to my first $100,000 month a year later.

— *Lesson* —

You're the boss – you can choose everything in your business!

Renegotiate Your Work Environment

Do you need to invest in a co-working space or upgrade your workspace at home? Maybe you need a better computer or more comfortable chair. Don't destroy your health because you don't want to spend the money. You're allowed to thrive. Maybe you need a business partner.

CASE STUDY: EXPERIMENT AND FIND YOUR SWEET SPOT

Name: *Natasha Johnson, Black British living in Spain*
Business: *Celebrant business training and mentoring*

> *Before Chill and Prosper, I'd never read a business book where nearly every chapter resonated with me and what I was going through with my own business. It felt like it was written for me. The biggest problem in my business was that I was working too hard and doing too much unnecessary work.*

I was a solopreneur, and I took that to mean that I had to do every damn thing by myself – literally, every damn thing: sort tech issues, send login details, record and edit podcasts, chase people for missed payments, reply to comments in the Facebook group – all before I even did anything that drove my business forward. It was ridiculous.

Denise showed me that I'm a precious asset to my business and need to protect myself to continue delivering the goods. The affirmation 'I attract abundance with ease and grace' struck a chord because my business didn't feel abundant. Instead, it felt like hard, unrewarding work, and the revenue didn't reflect my effort. I started resenting my work, which was heartbreaking because I created the business with so much passion.

The changes didn't happen overnight, but I started taking baby steps and instantly felt so much lightness and relief knowing the situation was not permanent. My first step was to automate as much as possible. The elimination aspect was so revelatory, too. Do you mean I can stop doing all the crap that doesn't serve me? Yes, you can! Do you mean I can get rid of unaligned products or services? Yes, you can! Do you mean I can take stuff off my website forever? Absolutely!

After three years of being a solopreneur, I joined forces with my friend Claire and we became co-directors of our company. I don't have to do this alone, and a partnership was the next and best step. Claire and I are a fantastic team, and we have taken our business to the next level.

— *Lesson* —

**Don't throw out an almost-good business
if you can tweak it into a great one!**

Renegotiate Your Offerings

You can ask yourself this for anything in your business – the type of clients that feel good to you, the kind of work that feels best – and then make changes.

For example, as a favor to a friend, I gave a keynote speech at her conference – to an entirely different audience than usual, one that wasn't even close to my target market. Although the speech was well-received, I came off-stage feeling horrible and used up, as if I'd pimped myself out for someone else's gratification.

Renegotiate Your Time Off

Maybe you just need a break! You're allowed to take holidays. You're allowed to have fun. You're allowed to have hobbies! Sometimes it refreshes your love for your business. Give yourself space for pleasure in your life – including time for creativity, rest, relaxation, and all the things that fulfill you.

CASE STUDY: BREAKING THE PATTERN

Name: *Tina Tower, New South Wales, Australia*
Business: *Business coaching and consulting*

I sold my previous business because I burned out and couldn't figure out how to handle the growth. I vowed never to get myself into that situation again. But of course, that was my pattern, so I ended up right back in overwork mode in my next business too!

Chill and Prosper opened my eyes to why I was doing this and how I could change it. Honestly, when I read about 'Protecting the Golden Goose,' I got mad about it, but I knew I had to pay attention.

I acknowledged I was getting my self-worth from my business, and I felt guilty for 'slacking off.' One of the simple yet powerful changes I made was around my work routine. I take Thursday to Sunday off each week, and one week off per month.

I'm so much happier; I can serve my customers better, create higher-quality products, and be there for my family. I'm feeling so much healthier. I still struggle with the feelings of guilt and laziness and will be working on this for a while, but my number-one priority is to protect the Golden Goose (me!) so that I can continue to make an impact in the world, provide for my family, and employ my team.

I'm grateful for Denise opening my eyes to the different possibilities and helping me to live better.

— *Lesson* —

Taking time off is good for business.

Renegotiate Your Boundaries

Many people I know have quit a perfectly good business because they had horrible clients. And rather than have an awkward conversation or set new boundaries, they let the whole thing go. So, don't let your fear of being called a bitch destroy your love of your business. It's always okay to renegotiate or fire a bad client. There's always more money.

CASE STUDY: WRONG BUSINESS OR BAD CLIENT?

Name: *Bianca Aiono, Australia*
Business: *Sales confidence coaching*

When my triplets were six months old, I wanted to return to work but no longer felt called to my body-confidence coaching business. So, I took Denise's advice about 'living like a 1950s man,' hired help, and outsourced as much of my home duties as possible. This gave me the bandwidth to take on engagements with friends to sell their online programs.

After I sold over $1.2 million between breastfeeding the triplets, it gave me the confidence to work with a very successful, multimillion-dollar business owner. I negotiated a 10-hour work week and set boundaries around my work hours.

It was quickly apparent that the boundaries weren't going to be respected. Instead, the CEO pressured me to work extra hours, constantly presented my ideas without acknowledgment, and even took over sales conversations when they were on holiday.

I rationalized it because I was supposedly 'learning from the best.' Maybe this was the only way to succeed? But more and more, I felt anxious about the work, affecting my mental health and my time with my children. I started to question whether it was even possible to chill and prosper Denise's way. Maybe she was just an exception to the rule – just a Lucky B.

Eventually, I had enough and resigned. I'm now collaborating with two friends, earning six-figure months working part-time. We prove that you can have a successful business without stress and burnout or abandoning family time. I love being part of the movement of women who embody and role-model the Chill and Prosper way.

— *Lesson* —

**Set boundaries before
you ditch your business.**

Give Yourself Permission to Upgrade

You don't have to change everything. Maybe you tweak your model, discontinue products or services, or change up how you offer things. You have permission to make things easier or more pleasurable for yourself!

- **Cailen Ascher**, creator of the 3-Day Workweek Schedule, moved from coaching and teaching one-off courses to a membership model. She says, 'I'm a content creator and community leader at heart, so this shift feels much more aligned with my natural energy and talents.'

- **Ashley Stahl**, founder of Cake Publishing, says, 'I moved from private coaching to e-courses, and back to private coaching after burning out on funnels and tweaking. I've gone high-end, and I've had a lot more joy in my work!'

- **Tammy Guest** started as a naturopath who also offered massage. She didn't love massage, but people kept booking, so she did it. I kept telling her people would keep booking as long as she offered it. Finally, she took massage off her website and her naturopathy business exploded. After a few years of building a practice and then coaching other Naturopreneurs, she's pivoting again to host retreats for fellow mavericks and adventurers.

Way #3: Stop Doing It All Yourself

For years, I've been smug about having one program (all roads lead to Bootcamp), but it was still the Denise Show. I answered every question myself in the online forum of up to 5,000-plus students. Why, Denise, why? I don't know. I can't give you a good answer. Do you see an over-delivering pattern?

It was my fault; I was being taken for granted in the business I had created. People would tag me day, night, weekends, Christmas Day, and I would answer! I found myself answering messages during 3 a.m. feeds or before serving dessert on Christmas Day.

One day it hit me: *I'm trying to be their mum! The unappreciated, martyred mother who is always there without complaint.* The combination of my desire to serve, my performer's stamina, and my inability to say no was the perfect storm.

Here's the change I made. I summoned my inner performer and decided to become… Mickey Mouse.

At Disneyland and shows like *Disney on Ice*, they always treat Mickey Mouse like the star! He opens and closes the parades and shows. Then, when he enters the stage, the lights dim, the music fanfares, and the other performers turn and look at him expectantly. Everything is about the Golden Goose of the Disney empire – Mickkkkkkkey Mouse!

Mickey Mouse doesn't moonlight on Main Street, picking up trash between shows. He doesn't play second fiddle to anyone. You wouldn't dare put Mickey in the corner. He gets the respect he deserves with Mickey ears hidden all over Disneyland and billions of dollars of merch.

To channel Mickey, I needed to hire some more cast members. So, I very timidly hired a community manager. I worried, *What if everyone likes them better than me?* See? Total martyr. But I knew I couldn't grow my capacity without help. It was utterly transformational once I got over myself.

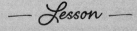

— *Lesson* —

Mickey Mouse doesn't moonlight.

CASE STUDY: I BOUGHT BACK TIME AND ENERGY

Name: *Victoria Gibson, Melbourne, Australia*
Business: *Marketing for life coaches*

Despite being in business for some time, I had never quite figured out how to stop over-delivering for my clients. I would respond to questions day and night, coach for hours until they ran out of questions, and helped them whenever needed, even if this was outside my program's scope. I often felt like nobody could do things like me, so I just did it all.

In Chill and Prosper, I read, 'You resist delegating or outsourcing, preferring to do everything yourself because it's quicker or because nobody else can do it the way you do,' and that really sunk in for me. I was keeping my business small due to my resistance to systems and growing a team!

In my new program, I wanted to expand my team to give my clients and me more support and, in the process, allow me to let go of doing ALL the things.

Mindset is a big block for many of my clients, and I knew a fantastic life coach who wanted to coach for other entrepreneurs rather than build her own business. So, I brought her into the program as a mindset coach and added a bonus coaching call that I didn't have to attend personally.

I couldn't believe this was all I needed to do to buy back 90 minutes of my time. It was the first time I got to experience *not showing up live for a group call and it was amazing. Even better than that, my clients got extra support from a skilled mindset coach that helped them through so many of their big marketing blocks. Embracing this made my offer juicier, and I'm sure it had an impact on its success, creating an additional $50,000 in one quarter (and the cost of hiring support was significantly less).*

Sometimes we're so attached to our blocks it can be hard to let go, but simple action can help us move through them and create an amazing upside, and freedom too.

— *Lesson* —

Buy back your time to focus on income-producing activities.

Find Your Chill-Team

'On the six-figure path, seeking support is not an option, but a requirement.'

BARBARA STANNY

You've heard of the A-Team? To protect your Golden Goose, you need the C-Team (the Chill-Team). This is about finding the right people for the right thing, not hiring for the sake of it or because other people tell you to. Remember how I told my friend James that I could get to six figures on my own? What's so great about doing everything yourself? CEO doesn't stand for Chief Everything Officer. That's a Golden Goose killer.

Amber McCue, founder of the course 'How to Clone Yourself,' gave me a wake-up call too: 'Self-made millionaires and billionaires outsource nine out of 10 times when there's someone else out there who can do it better. Other people tend to try to DIY everything – that's just not an efficient use of time.'[4]

In the next chapter, we'll talk about how to get started and build your 'Chill-Team.'

CASE STUDY: I FELT LIKE A DIVA ASKING FOR HELP

Name: *Erika Tebbens, USA*
Business: *Sales strategy*

I've always valued simplicity in my business, but I was doing too much and not valuing myself enough. I was only working 20–25-hour work weeks, but my ADHD brain was still juggling too much, and I was chronically undercharging, making it harder to hire support.

The business was working, but something needed to change. So, I promoted my assistant, who'd been with me over a year, to my business manager, and outsourced content repurposing and sales emails. I also hired a life coach to support me during this mental up-level.

I then raised my rates to accommodate this new level of support. Additionally, I didn't just get further help; I learned to embrace communicating with my team better about my needs, asking for help and doing it unapologetically, without feeling like a diva. This was huge!

Being able to fully embrace my role as the Golden Goose in my business, and coming to terms with the fact that the more I lean into that role, the greater impact my work will have in the world, has been life-changing.

It feels so good to pay great rates for team support; I feel cared for and rested, and that allows me to be so much more present for both my paying clients and in my free content, which I take a lot of pride in. By mid-2021, I had already surpassed what I made in all of 2020, and I had exceeded my sales goal in 2020 too!

In a world that increasingly asks more and more of us, the easier we can make our businesses on ourselves, the bigger and more sustainable success we'll have.

— *Lesson* —

Hiring a team helps you be more present.

EXERCISE: PROTECTING THE GOLDEN GOOSE

In your journal, write down some reflections about how you could be killing your Golden Goose:

- Where are you feeling resentment in your business?
- What products, services or offerings no longer feel worth it?
- What tasks feel really hard for you?
- What does your Golden Goose need in order to thrive?

— CHAPTER 6 —

The Keyless Life

'It is always the simple that
produces the marvelous.'

AMELIA BARR

When I first had kids, the simplest things suddenly felt really hard. Like getting in and out of the car with the bags and an actual baby (or two). Life suddenly seemed overwhelming, and I felt I'd lost my easy-breezy, chilled personality. Instead, I became a frazzled 'busy mom!'

I got a new car with keyless entry, so as long as the car key was somewhere on my person (usually covered in crumbs at the bottom of my bag), I could get into the car without needing to fish it out. It was just one tiny thing off my mind, but it made a massive difference in my life.

I got addicted to finding even more shortcuts (or chillcuts) in my life. For example, I added all my credit and debit cards to my phone, put everything on autopay, started using a meal-delivery service, and replaced my house locks with electronic keypads so I never had to deal with losing my keys again (handy for ADHD). Between the keyless entry on the house and car, I haven't had to use a set of keys in years! Thus, a *keyless life*.

I asked myself, 'How could I make life as easy and stress-free as possible?' and found every bit of friction to eliminate. Multiple phone chargers for every room and car; extra headsets so nobody fought over them; a water filter for my office. I turned off my voicemail and redirected emails to my assistant.

Nothing is too small! I didn't realize it would be life-changing to have electronic keypads on my door, but it is! When you systematically eliminate the things that cause you inconvenience, you'll have more energy to create your chillionaire life.

You might not even realize how much energy these irritations take up in your life until you release them. It's like an old computer full of viruses that runs too many programs at once – you don't realize how slow it's become until you get a new one.

Creating a 'keyless life' is so much fun, and I'm constantly looking for new ways to create simplicity. So please, if you're inspired by this chapter, tag me on social media @denisedt using the hashtag #keylesslife and let me know how you're implementing it in your own life.

> *'Be a curator of your life. Slowly cut things out until you're left only with what you love, with what's necessary, with what makes you happy.'*
>
> LEO BABAUTA

The Keyless Business

The truth is that we make business way more complicated than it needs to be. Myself included. Yep, I don't always have it together; I often create unnecessary work for myself, resist making things easy, reinvent the wheel, and frequently change my mind midway through a project (driving my team, including Mark, crazy).

A keyless life is about simplicity and ease – whatever that looks like for you. It could be:

- Finding the path of least resistance
- Hiring a team to help you
- Setting up a home team
- Creating passive income

I'm not perfect, but I've created a pretty chilled million-dollar business without a big team or large overheads, and I want to share all the details with you, including how I set up my home life to support my business and vice versa. Most business books ignore the home stuff because, frankly, they are written by men who don't have to think about it too much. However, the reality for many entrepreneurs is that our business and home lives are intertwined and impact each other, especially if we work from home or have a family.

Here's one of my most recent lessons on making things easier.

The $100,000 Book Tour

A few years ago, I spent $100,000 on a self-funded book tour, including event hire, A.V., video production, staffing, and travel costs. I traveled with the whole family (including my kids and my mum), which was honestly a stupid decision. It was only four events, but it cost me $100,000, and it was incredibly stressful. On the plus side, I got to meet hundreds of Lucky Bees and, best of all, it was the inspiration for the Golden Goose chapter.

Recently, faced with the prospect of another self-funded promotional tour, I asked myself, 'How can this be the most chilled, easy, and fun event ever?'

If you've ever organized events, you know the most challenging part is booking all the venues, so I had a brilliant (if I say so myself) idea. What if I held each event at a cinema? Every city has one. They seat a lot of people and have parking and accessible facilities. They have inbuilt A.V. equipment. They sell snacks and have cup-holders. And best of all, they are always available!

I contacted the Event Cinema chain, and it only took a few hours to book a 12-city tour! Then, I found a nationwide book chain that agreed to set up a book table at each event to sell my books. I created guidelines for my team to book all my travel, pick-ups, hotels, and hair and makeup artists, so all I had to do was rock up and speak. Could it get any easier?

I may not be a perfect Chillpreneur all the time, but I was so proud that I pulled off such a potentially challenging tour with a minimum of stress.

CASE STUDY: THE PATH OF LEAST RESISTANCE

Name: *Lien De Pau, Belgium*
Business: *Business coaching*

My business was thriving, yet it was complicated and felt like a lot of hard work. During my first years in business, I was still fine-tuning who I wanted to serve. But rather than changing what I offered, I kept adding to my product suite.

At one point, I was selling, launching, and managing nine different products and services for different niches. I automated a lot, but I still felt spread thin. I was always running from one launch to another, which was not my goal for my business or life. So, I urgently needed some simplification. And some extra chill!

I loved Denise's quote: 'Follow the path of least resistance' – I repeat it all the time, not only to myself but also to clients and friends. This quote was the driver for me to simplify my offerings down to three products, which had an amazing flow-on impact on my procedures and back-office systems.

Overall, my revenue tripled, and I quickly broke through some income glass ceilings. As a result, not only is my business more chill, but my life is far more aligned to the one I had imagined for myself.

— *Lesson* —

Simplifying can have a huge positive impact.

Getting Started with Outsourcing

'*The smartest thing I ever did was to hire my weakness.*'

SARA BLAKELY

Chris Ducker, author of *Virtual Freedom: How to Work with Virtual Staff to Buy More Time, Become More Productive, and Build Your Dream Business*, is an incredible resource for figuring-out tasks to outsource. Google his '101 Tasks to Outsource to a Virtual Assistant' for some ideas. He suggests that you start with a simple exercise writing what he calls 'Three Lists to Freedom':

1. Things you hate doing.

2. Things you struggle to do.

3. Things you shouldn't be doing at all.

It's your business, and you're allowed to get help. You're allowed to focus on the things you're really good at, and you're allowed to create more chill in your business.

- **You might hate** bookkeeping, customer service, scheduling clients, or sending out your newsletter. When you hate something, it takes forever. Customer service stressed me out so much I'd lose sleep over it.

- **You might struggle** with technical things or graphic design. If it's costing you money (because nobody can pay you), it's worth outsourcing. My newsletter came out sporadically and sometimes not at all when I was responsible for it, but when I finally outsourced it to my assistant, it went out like clockwork every single week.

- What about things **you shouldn't do at all** – this might be doing your own graphic design or website. Maybe you regularly break stuff or get caught up in the weeds and forget to focus on income-producing activities.

It's okay to:

- **Start small**: It's not all or nothing. A few hours of help could be life-changing.

- **Pay experts**: Just find someone who can do it quicker, better, or with less stress.

- **Do short-term**: I love hiring people to batch projects for me.

My biggest tip: Don't hire people like you – hire for your skill gaps and weaknesses instead. I screwed this up initially because I wrote job descriptions that sounded exciting, and I ended up hiring Mini-Me types who were fun to interview. Guess what? When I worked for other people, I'd get bored, get a new business idea, and quit. That's precisely what happened with my employees, except they all quit after our first onboarding session because they got so excited by the possibilities of my business – it was like a free coaching session.

I use personality tests like Kolbe to write the job description. If you read the job description yourself and think 'Yuck,' then you're probably on the right track to finding someone to complement your skillset perfectly!

— *Lesson* —

CEO doesn't mean Chief Everything Officer.

I've always had a lean team because I don't want to manage lots of people; I want to keep my costs manageable and keep the business as simple as possible. I reached the million-dollar revenue with just me, one part-time assistant, and a few key contractors.

Before you hire, try asking yourself whether you can take these steps first:

- **Eliminate**: Nobody should be doing this, not even me.

- **Simplify**: How can this be done more easily?

- **Automate**: Can software or a system take care of this?

- **Batch**: Can I or (or someone else) batch this?

- **Outsource**: Can another person or business do this?

Then you can decide if it's worth hiring an actual employee. For example, do you need an assistant or do you need an online scheduling system? Just systematically look for areas in your business that stress you out, and make a plan. Less friction, more joy!

There are no rules. You're allowed to keep things lean or you're allowed to get as much help as you like. Some people get scared about adding payroll costs, other people can't wait to build a team. A keyless business might mean having a lean team because you want less complication. It's up to you!

> — *Lesson* —
>
> **You can tweak until you find what works.**

CASE STUDY: DON'T HIRE OUT OF FOMO

Name: Tyler McCall, Chicago, USA
Business: Online business and marketing strategy

The constant push to hire and build a team in the online business space is causing more harm than good. Messages like 'Hire before you're ready,' and 'Outsource as fast as you can' are prevalent. That leads to entrepreneurs (myself included) building teams without the right financial footing, HR structures, training processes, and leadership skills in place.

Not taking hiring seriously can lead to stress, and harm you, your reputation, your business, and the people you hire. And don't forget about the time and resources you waste when you hire the wrong person or don't have a plan, and end up broke within months of building a team.

There was a solid year in my business (back in 2018) where I tried to hire multiple times because I was stretched so thin. Guess what? I wasn't able to hire someone for months (because I didn't have the time to do it), and when I finally hired help, each person was a terrible fit and lasted only a few weeks (because I didn't have time to do it right). Hiring out of desperation creates drama for you and a shitty experience for your new team member. Spend some time getting your act together, THEN reevaluate if you need to hire someone or if you just need some boundaries and systems.

Don't just hire because everyone else is. What if the best decision for you right now is to focus on embedding what you know, systemizing, and stabilizing your foundations before embarking on the next growth phase?

— *Lesson* —

Hiring is always a personal decision.

EXERCISE: WRITE YOUR HIRING 'WISH LIST'

In your journal, answer these questions:

- What's causing me the most amount of stress in my business right now?
- What's stopping me from making money? Technology? Marketing? Systems?
- What can I outsource right now?
- What do I need to thrive as the Golden Goose of my business?
- What would my dream C-Team look like?

The Keyless Home

I've really nailed my keyless home life, and I'd rather spend more money outsourcing things at home than in my business. I don't have to think about changing the toilet paper or picking up mail.

My laundry fairies always deliver nice clean clothes into my drawers, and my bedsheets and towels are changed weekly without any effort on my part. My housekeeper makes me snacks, goes to the post office, or calls the handyman if something breaks. I rarely cook, yet somehow breakfast, lunch, and dinner appear on the table each day.

Basically, I live like a 1950s dad, and I love it! My life is set up for two things: maximum quality time with my family and maximum freedom for my work. I'm not 'too fancy' to clean my own toilet, but nobody will pay me to do it and I don't want to spend my limited time or energy when I can outsource it. Women are often taught that it's noble to do housework for their own family but shameful, lazy, and exploitative to pay others to do it. Have you noticed that nobody judges men who live this way?

My keyless home life gives me the freedom and mental space to do my work; I outsource every boring, mundane, or unpaid task that I can think of, and I don't feel guilty at all.

CASE STUDY: MY HOME IS MY CASTLE, NOT MY JOB

Name: *Sami Wunder, Germany*
Business: *Dating and relationship coach*

> *I felt quite tired and annoyed by the number of times my family expected me to do household chores while still running my very successful seven-figure business. We had a house cleaner to support us twice a week, so it wasn't about not having help. It was more about the mindset. There was a silent, subconscious expectation that I should manage the responsibilities of the house.*
>
> *I would get requests 'on the fly,' such as asking me to do laundry or go grocery shopping when I had just finished a launch webinar with thousands of participants or I was working on my newsletter.*

I wanted to say no because I wanted to stay focused on my zone of genius (and I was making millions per year), but at the same time, I felt guilty for saying no. I felt like people would judge me for not being a caring enough mother and wife. And yet I felt annoyed and resentful, all at the same time. I would question, Can a girl have a chore-free life? Then, Chill and Prosper showed me – of course, we can.

I sat down with my husband, looked him in the eye, and said, 'I'm the Golden Goose in my business and this family! You guys need to love me, support me, and nurture me; please help me operate in my zone of genius by making space for me to do things that I love doing with my full energy and attention. We can easily find people to help us with the laundry and dishes and ironing clothes, but not everybody can do what I do in the world.' The point was well received. It really landed.

We increased how often our cleaner came to help us from two to four days per week. We also hired a gardener to help us with taking care of our outside space. We decided to order healthy, fresh meals to not feel the pressure to cook unless I wanted to. Suddenly, there was so much more freedom to be me, to be Queen Sami, to be the Golden Goose. So much more guilt-free energy was available for things that actually mattered to me. I could spend more quality time with my kids rather than do the dreaded laundry.

There is so much more connection with my husband too, because now he gets it. He gets me. It's like he 'gets the math' around why protecting and preserving my energy is so important.

Now the Golden Goose is a running metaphor in our house and we all giggle at it. But I'm so grateful for how this tool shifted everyone's psychology around how they saw me, my place in the world, and, importantly, my place in the family.

> — *Lesson* —
>
> **Reduce your home stress**
> **so you can make more money.**

CASE STUDY:
THE KEYLESS CARAVAN

Name: *Karen Gunton, South Australia, Australia*
Business: *Books and workshops to help people get unstuck*

My business was pretty chill already. I've kept things simple, and I stick to what feels easy and fun. But I realized that the rest of my life stressed me out and sapped the mojo I had for my business.

We recently bought a caravan, and packing to go away for a quick weekend escape was so complicated! So, my goal became to make it a 'keyless caravan,' so we could hook it up and take a bucket-filling vacation whenever we wanted.

It has become a fun challenge to time how long it takes to get ready to go (30 minutes) and find ways to make it even easier. For example, I forgot my headphones one time and was so excited to buy an extra pair to live in the van so I'd never had to remember them again.

Recently we invited friends to come away for a weekend. They said no because it takes them a whole day on either side to pack and unpack their caravan. I love our 'keyless' camping life. We can take a mini-vacation without stress, ready to get back to work refreshed. Self-care and having fun shouldn't require sacrifice, long lists, and hard work!

— *Lesson* —

Your whole life is allowed to be easier.

The 'When I Earn More' Myth

'I've seen women insist on cleaning everything in the house before they could sit down to write... and you know it's a funny thing about housecleaning... it never comes to an end.'

CLARISSA PINKOLA ESTÉS

Every hour you spend on growing your business will positively impact the lives of your family members for years to come. So, stop the procrasti-cleaning; let your house get a little dirty and focus on income-producing activities instead.

Many parents cite lack of childcare as the most significant stressor holding them back from being successful in their business. Single parents, especially, find this so incredibly hard.

I often hear, 'My partner said that when my business earns more, we can pay for childcare.' This is the ultimate chicken-and-egg situation, but let me be clear: it's going to be hard for you to gain traction in your business if you never invest any time in it. The day will never come unless you're willing to get up at 4 a.m., and that's not sustainable or advisable. Sleep is really, really important.

On the few occasions I've tried working while caring for the kids, it's made me want to tear my hair out, and one of them will ultimately tell Mark, 'Mama said the F-word a lot today!'

Before you spend money on your business, could this be better spent investing in childcare (even for just a few hours a week)?

What do you need to thrive at home?

- More childcare at your productive work times? That could be someone to pick the kids up from school, entertain them, or help you during school holidays?

- A cleaner to do the bathrooms and floors?

- A meal-prep delivery service?

- A garden and maintenance service?

- A daily housekeeper?

- A laundry service?

- A private chef?

It's all doable when you're earning more money.

Set boundaries with people who think 'work from home' means 'always available.' Mark used to ask me to pick up his dry cleaning and friends would drop over unannounced. I had to learn to say, 'Sorry, I'm working.'

You need dedicated time and space to grow your business. Outsourcing home tasks is highly symbolic because it means your time is worth something, even before you have a lot of clients. The opportunity cost is too high to spend your time doing small, inexpensive (and frankly energy-sucking) jobs. Instead of cleaning your bathroom, you need to be out there getting your next client.

You have permission to create an easy life for yourself, so you can focus on growing your business.

EXERCISE: WRITE YOUR HOME 'WISH LIST'

In your journal, answer these questions:

- What's causing me the most amount of stress at home right now?

- What's stopping me making money? Childcare? Messy house?
- What do I need to thrive?
- What can I outsource right now?
- What would my 'dream home team' look like?

~~~~~~~~~~

Keyless Income (AKA Passive Income)

When I was starting out in business, I was seduced by the concept of passive income – because I loved the idea of sitting on a beach and making millions doing 'nothing.' HA!

Are you ready for some truth bombs? Creating passive income still requires work; both to set it up and keep it going. Doesn't that defeat the purpose? No! It can be very leveraged and automated, but it doesn't happen by itself.

My passive income comes from book royalties (published and self-published), e-courses, and affiliate income. I also have investment properties and shares in the stock market.

But it doesn't all run by itself. I still have to write (and update) the books, market and launch my courses, and invest money in customer service. But I'm not going to lie – it's an awesome way to make money.

A keyless business should include some form of passive income. Why?

- **Money.** Duh. Making money while you sleep is fantastic.

- **Choice.** You don't have to say yes to every client when you have other sources of income.

- **Energy.** Passive income conserves your energy – which you can then spend on things you prefer doing.

- **Impact.** You can help a lot more people when you're not burning yourself out.

Your passive income product could be so many different things: e-books, courses, drop-shipping revenue, affiliate money, advertising or sponsorship revenue, book royalties, music royalties, templates, licensing fees, software subscriptions, or membership fees.

You might be lost for ideas on what to create, but the truth is that it's best to look at why you might be sabotaging it. Why haven't you done it yet?

Because you have an underlying belief that you have to work hard to earn money. It doesn't feel like an equal exchange if someone gives you money for something you no longer have to sweat over. Making passive income goes directly against the concept of 'fair pay for fair work,' and that's why you resist it.

The reason why it took me so long was guilt. If I didn't need to pull all-nighters, stopped waking up at 5 a.m. to coach clients, or stopped hustling to make money, did I really earn it with integrity? Was I disrespecting the women in my family who had to work to make money – like my mother, who cleaned houses or worked long shifts in a nursing home? Who was I to have this easy life?

What Are Your Excuses?

- 'Everyone knows this already; why would anyone pay me for that?' Something easy for you might be incredible for someone else, especially if you create a system or tools for someone to follow step by step.

- 'It's not personal enough.' If you're someone who likes high-touch connections, you might feel like it doesn't count if it's an automated product. But it does! It can still help people, and they'll want to connect with you even more!

- 'It doesn't feel like real work.' When I wrote my first e-book, I felt incredibly guilty, like I hadn't earned it properly or I was ripping people off by charging for something I'd already created. I wanted to call each purchaser and read the book to them over the phone to 'earn' that $10.

- **'Anyone can figure this out themselves.'** People (like me) are busy and/or lazy. So, package and curate your knowledge, create extra value (like shopping lists to save them time), and make it easy to buy, even if people can find the same information online for free.

- **'What makes mine different?'** Sometimes customers have a desperate need for specific information for their particular problem – like how to get their six-month-old formula-fed baby to sleep – rather than generic information that applies to everyone.

- **'It's not perfect.'** You'll be waiting a long time! My first attempt at a video course was basic: a $50 manifesting course that I filmed using my iPad. It wasn't sexy or professional, but my audience loved the information. For me, creating that course was life-changing. Waking up having made $50 while I slept was a huge mental breakthrough.

I've bought so many things to help me shortcut to success or deal with a pain point, like:

- **E-books** on how to get my baby and toddler to sleep, how to pluck my own eyebrows, how to create a month's worth of freezer meals (with done-for-you shopping lists).

- **E-courses** on how to write a memoir, how to start a wedding venue, how to renovate antique furniture, how to run a five-day challenge.

- **Shortcuts:** I've bought templates, software, and systems galore. I always look to see if someone has created something before our team starts from scratch.

Start Small, But Start

Even if your topic has been covered a million times, think about how you can create something especially for an underserved market niche. Think about how you can add YOUR voice. Be a contributor, not a guru.

If you do it once, you'll get addicted. A Chillpreneur doesn't have to hustle for every dollar. It's okay to solve problems for people while you sleep!

Lesson

**Don't let your money blocks derail
your passive income dreams.**

CASE STUDY: FREEDOM IS MY HIGHEST GOAL

Name: *Marissa Roberts, Australia*
Business: *Home organization for busy parents and actor*

Freedom and ease are my biggest motivations in business. I follow my own path and go at my own pace. I love the Chill and Prosper *principles: that there are easier ways to make money, and that there's always more money (and time, and ideas).*

When I set goals, I don't base them on the goals of my mentors or peers. I want to feel calm, confident, relaxed, and free from pressure so I can go to the movies in the middle of the day whenever I want. FOMO was easy to let go of once it clicked that I was working in alignment with my own long-term goal.

It wasn't always like that. I was worried that people would judge me for being too lazy or having too many different money-making ideas. I worried I was too old for YouTube and not focused, polished, or professional enough. But not a single person has ever commented negatively – most people get inspired by the possibilities.

I previously did a lot of one-on-one work with clients, but it made me resentful and burned-out. So now my business is 80 percent passive income. My first product was the unedited 'Busy Mum's Guide to Making Life Easy,' recorded on my iPad in my kid's bedroom. Now and then, someone still buys it! You don't need to be perfect to help people.

I don't follow the 'rules' of being on YouTube – I don't even edit my videos anymore. My favorite thing is to cook dinner live or have a cup of tea and talk about decluttering. Think about it – people make money from videos of them eating lunch!

Strategies that worked in 2011 still work for me now. I suck at updating things, but the conversion rate is still 1 percent on everything I've created. I'm lazy, and it's still working. If it stops working, then I'll change it!

My business created so much free time that I got into TV and film acting – a fun dream since high school drama classes. The passive income from my business gives me the freedom and confidence to be super-relaxed in auditions. So, when my acting money comes in, it's a nice surprise!

Ultimately, you get to decide what you want and what goals are important to you. I choose freedom, ease, and fun. And that's the life I get to live. Why not you, too?

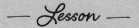

— *Lesson* —

Passive income gives you choice.

EXERCISE: MY KEYLESS PASSIVE INCOME PRODUCT

In your journal, answer these questions:

- Is there something I've mastered that my friends always ask me for advice about?
- Do I have a unique method or system that I use in my business or life? What's really obvious to me but hard for others?
- What resources have I already created for myself that others could buy (templates, plans, spreadsheets, e-books, blog posts)?
- Why am I resisting creating passive income?

Your Simple Business Plan

This was a big section, and now we're going to put it all together and create a simple business plan to keep you on track. You can download a template at denisedt.com/chill

THE BIG IDEA

If you remember nothing else from Part II, remember this: *You are the goose that lays the golden eggs. Set up your business and home life in a way that ensures you'll keep laying them for a long, long time.*

— PART III —

Money

INTRODUCTION

Money

*'Making money and doing good in the
world are not mutually exclusive.'*

Arianna Huffington

I see memes floating around on social media asking, *Would you
stay in a haunted house for $100,000?* Hundreds of people
comment on them, saying 'Sign me up!'

Why, though? You don't have to *suffer* to make money. You
don't have to do things that are scary, against your values, or cause
problems in your life. It's totally okay for you to make money doing
things you love!

Why are we in business? To help others and to make money. It's
straightforward. If you don't help enough people, you won't have a
sustainable business. And without the money part, all you have is a
hobby – sometimes a very expensive one! Helping people probably
comes very naturally to you. In fact, you've probably done it all your
life. Creative entrepreneurs tend to be great at the helping part and
not so great at the money-making part. That's where I can help.

Here's some Denise real-talk: if you can support yourself, you should. Many people don't have the opportunity, ability, energy, or capacity to do it, so if you can create a ripple of abundance for yourself and others through your success, why not? We live in a time of great opportunity – use your privilege and create financial independence for yourself and your family. Don't let money fears hold you back from starting or growing your business. Claim your worth, support yourself, and use your money to do good in the world.

In this part of the book, I'm going to take you through the trickiest thing creative, heart-centered entrepreneurs face in business: *money!* We're going to talk about setting and increasing your prices, where and when you should *never* work for free, and how to deal with awkward conversations about money (you're going to have *plenty* of those).

Let's get started!

— CHAPTER 7 —

Big Pricing Mistakes

*'If you undervalue what you do, the
world undervalues who you are.'*

Suze Orman

A simple question that's often difficult for business owners to answer is: 'So, how much does it cost?' When asked that yourself, do you stammer, or deflect the question? I have, many times! Now that I'm on the other side of it, I get impatient when a business owner clearly doesn't want to tell me how much something costs. Please, just tell me the price so I can pay it! It's annoying! Money is just money!

When I was a fledgling life coach, I was just as clueless about pricing as everyone else. I'd never had to think about it before – all of my previous jobs either had fixed day rates set by my boss or were an internal cost to the company. I didn't like having salary conversations and *never* asked for a raise or bonus. I took what I was offered (like a good girl) and never thought I was worth more.

When I decided to go into self-employment as a full-time life coach, it was suddenly *my* responsibility to assign a monetary value to my skills, and that was scary. Too expensive would make it look as if I was too big for my britches, too cheap and I'd look inexperienced. I wished someone would just *tell* me what to charge.

In working with thousands of business owners over the years, I've seen pricing patterns emerge among the mistakes they make and, believe me, I've made them all too! Knowledge is power, though, and if you can recognize these mistakes when they arise, they'll be less likely to derail you. In this chapter, we'll look at the *big* pricing mistakes I've seen, namely:

1. Pricing by committee

2. Undercharging and over-delivering

3. Working for free for too long

4. Taking 'you're too expensive' personally

Mistake #1: Pricing by Committee

The worst thing you can do is ask other people what they think you should charge. It's an innocent mistake: we think we're being inclusive, collaborative, and harnessing the wisdom of others by asking them for their opinion. But it's a dangerous practice.

Here's why: every time you set your prices by committee, you're taking on other people's beliefs around money, regardless of their qualifications, experience, or money mindset. Imagine that your money blocks are physical things – like rocks – and you have to carry them around in a backpack. Obviously, the more money blocks you have, the harder you have to work just to go about your daily life. When you crowdsource your pricing, you're not just carrying *your* backpack of money blocks, you're taking on everyone else's too!

Not all feedback is useful. If you don't believe me, try it yourself. Go to your favorite business forum and ask a pricing question. You'll be astounded by the variety of responses. Everyone has a different perspective on 'worth' and 'value'. Before you pay any attention to what others say, ask yourself the following questions.

Are They My Target Market?

Taking advice from people who are nowhere near your target market – for example, your non-business family and friends or a random stranger – is a big mistake. I remember talking to a 50-something guy about my business at a networking event and on hearing what I did, he said, 'Wow. It sounds like you're charging *too much.*' I felt chastised and embarrassed because he was reflecting my own worst fears about my business. 'Yeah,' I said, 'I think you're right.'

This dude was the complete *opposite* of my target market, but I let his opinion sway one of my most important business decisions. His view of my pricing could have been based on what his own target market could afford, or on something more sinister, like an ingrained misogynistic view of what women are worth.

Either way, it was totally useless, but the interaction played on my mind for days. He wasn't my coach, and he wasn't a pricing or marketing expert. He knew nothing about my business or target market. He just made a snap decision based on what he 'felt' was too expensive, and I believed him!

His opinion was none of my business, so why was I soliciting it? Why even have this money conversation with some random stranger? Honestly? Because I didn't want to think about it: I wanted someone else to *tell me* what to charge so I didn't have to confront my fears about money. I thought someone else would know better than me.

> *'… if you're just looking to your friend, co-worker, husband or wife for validation, be careful. It can stop a lot of multimillion-dollar ideas in their tracks in the beginning.'*
>
> SARA BLAKELY, FOUNDER OF SPANX

If you have a specific niche (and you definitely should), then how tightly do the people offering their opinions fit that profile? For example: age, gender, geographical location, income level, stage of life, or business. If your ideal target market is parents with a healthy income, why would you take the opinion of a childless senior citizen, or vice versa? It doesn't make sense!

If you market to other business people, what stage of business are they in? What's appropriate for a beginner to pay is entirely different from someone who's financially successful in business. Nobody knows more about your business than you do. Nobody knows your target market's hopes and dreams as well as you do. And nobody is more deeply and emotionally connected to your business goals than you are.

Another question to ask yourself is:

Are They in the Market for What I Do?

Until people actually need something, they don't really know what they'd pay for it. When I think of what I've paid for things, either because I needed them ASAP or because I got excited about the results I was promised, it must be hundreds of thousands of dollars by now! If you'd asked me what that product or service was worth beforehand, I probably would have vastly underestimated what I would've paid.

My budget is way more flexible than someone starting out in business and, to be honest, my time is worth more now, so I'm willing to pay to outsource to an expert. I've always appreciated paying for professionals in my business – for example, copywriters to help me with sales emails. But I never considered paying a ton of money for copywriting until I needed to create 35 scripts in two weeks for a new course I was filming. I procrastinated over it until I had no choice, and ended up paying four times my budget because I was suddenly in the market and needed it done ASAP! It was totally worth it, even though I had unrealistic expectations about what I should pay beforehand.

So, unless the people giving you advice represent your target market *and* need you now, they won't give you accurate or useful advice. If you need a ballpark figure, a better question to ask your business buddies would be *What do you do, and how much have you paid for X?* For example, 'If you've been in business for at least two years, what did you pay for your website?' or 'Hey, health coaches, what did you pay for your website photography?' That way, you're getting advice from people who have put some money in the game, and it's useful market research rather than confusing random opinions.

Asking Competitors or Peers

What about other people in your industry? Should you ask them or sneak a look at their prices and place yourself accordingly? Again, this isn't even remotely helpful. You might believe that the seniority (or popularity) of your peers means you can't charge as much as, or more than, they do. Maybe you're judging yourself against the 'kool kidz' in your industry and think that social media followers mean superior experience?

At the start of my business I decided that I didn't deserve to charge as much or more than established coaches who were decades older than me, regardless of their skill level. Now, that sounds reasonable on the surface, but I was discounting my years of adjacent coaching and mentoring experience, of which I had plenty – both in jobs and as a volunteer. In my own mind, that didn't 'count,' and I told myself I needed to start at the bottom of the ladder.

However, longevity doesn't always mean you're great at your job. I know lots of 'experienced' coaches whose skills have been stagnant for years and, frankly, aren't that great. Maybe you know those types too? Plus, look at professions like social media management – a long career in that field isn't even possible since technology changes so quickly. In a case like that, results and knowledge are just as valuable as experience.

Lastly, your industry might have massive money blocks (the alternative healing professions come to mind). So, remember, when you're averaging out the competition, you're basing your income potential on collective insecurities and industry myths. Money coach Kendall Summerhawk says it best: 'Don't base your net-worth on someone else's self-worth.'

If you can't survey your audience (or a rando guy on the street), and you can't sneak a look at what your competitors are charging, *what's a Chillpreneur to do?* The simple answer is: you have to trust in your own wisdom and set your own prices. Nobody is going to do that for you. Just pick a price and try it out. The truth is that what you charge is entirely personal and not as black and white as you'd think. You're looking for the 'Goldilocks sweet spot,' which is the 'just right' price for you, regardless of what other people charge.

Author Danielle LaPorte calls this being 'comfortable in your money shoes.' It has to be the right fit. Too big price-wise and you'll feel like a fraud, like you're a little kid playing dress-up in your mama's high heels. But wearing too-tight money shoes that you've outgrown (prices that are too small) is incredibly uncomfortable too. You have to feel as if you're in alignment and in integrity with your rates, and only you can decide what that is for your business. Sorry!

— *Lesson* —

Stop comparing your prices with other people's, or soliciting unqualified feedback from unqualified people.

Mistake #2: Undercharging and Over-Delivering

'All underearners, without question, share one
common trait: a high tolerance for low pay.'

BARBARA STANNY

Ah, what a classic combination! Often, if an entrepreneur finds charging difficult, when they finally do accept money, they'll feel compelled to over-give to the point where they might not make much money at all. And even then, they'll feel guilty!

I've done this often. Picture this: I was on stage leading a free workshop, and it was time for the 'upsell.' This is my least preferred way of selling, and I hate it, so I always overcompensate with the bonuses. My offer was a one-day live workshop, teaching all my secrets of manifesting success, for $97. I'd undercharged in the first place, but then, in my desperation to offer value, I also threw in two 60-minute, face-to-face coaching sessions. A crazy, awesome bargain, right? But I wasn't done: 'If you decide today, you also get these bonus earrings.' Yes, *earrings*.

In my defense, they were cool earrings with 'Love' written on them, and one of my manifesting tips is to wear affirmation jewelry, but it was a completely unnecessary bonus. The $97 offer was good enough as it was! People came up and threw cash at me for the workshop, and why wouldn't they? I was practically giving away the naming rights to my firstborn child! Hey, why don't I come over to your house and clean your toilet while I'm at it? Cook you dinner? It was like a bad infomercial. But wait, there's *more*!

Of course, once I added up all the expenses for the event, the cost of all those in-person bonus coaching sessions (parking, coffee, and the hassle of putting on a bra), *plus* those stupid earrings, I wasn't making much money at all, certainly not for all that effort.

And that, my friend, is a *huge* mistake around pricing: being over-generous to the point of self-sabotage. Maybe we do it because we don't believe we're worth it without all the bribes, bells, and whistles. We want people to like us, and we desperately want to help people make changes in their lives. Here's the thing: *What you offer is already amazing and life-changing.* Read that again. Let it sink in. Your work can stand alone without making you broke, or making you resent your clients. Plus, you're allowed to make lots of juicy profit!

Almost every time I create a new product or event, I fight the urge to over-deliver. We usually think it's a good thing to give our clients more, but it's not. A course stuffed to the gills with extra information becomes incredibly overwhelming and failure-inducing. I know this because I looked into why refund requests were creeping in for my Money Bootcamp. It turned out we had too many modules and too much bonus material. People thought they had to complete it all and felt like failures before they'd even started. When we reduced the amount of content, the refund requests went down. Less really is more!

Over-giving can disempower your clients. For that reason, I don't recommend *ever* offering bonuses like unlimited email coaching if you're a service professional (it's a pain in the butt that really doesn't teach your clients self-reliance or boundaries). And I don't recommend adding premium services like face-to-face coaching unless you're charging appropriately for it (your personal attention should always be your most expensive offering). Over-giving can also be terrible for the environment. Branded stress balls and endless USB flash drives end up in landfill or clutter up your office. Don't add to the problem!

The same goes for over-delivering in terms of time. Humans need time to integrate and apply information, so if you're a coach and you're having monster three-hour sessions with your clients, you're probably overwhelming them with information, most of which they'll forget almost instantly. When we try to jam our years of experience and knowledge into one session, it's often incredibly tiring and uncomfortable for our clients. Then they don't rebook because they want to implement everything from the last session (which is impossible). So, over-delivering can ultimately derail your client. Again, less is more.

CASE STUDY: OVER-DELIVERING ISN'T THE ONLY WAY TO CARE

Name*: J. Nichole Smith, UK (American living in London)*
Business*: Brand design and color psychology consultant*

After increasing my prices, one of the most significant shifts I made was paying myself first – what a symbolic and important shift. I also made money choices based on how I wanted to feel, which meant choosing not to commit to big expenses that would give me anxiety all year, such as retreat deposits. I'm charging way more, my profit margin is higher, and, more importantly, the way that I feel about money and finances has changed.

Previously, I felt I had to 'give it all away' to feel that I was serving, so that people would genuinely know I care. The amazing thing is that now that I have overcome this, I can give more in more aligned ways, such as donating to causes I'm passionate about, and giving time and money to the change I want to make in the world. I also invested more into myself, including joining a powerful mastermind full of high-achieving women.

I found the 'this is what a millionaire looks like' idea transformative, accepting that 'millionaire me' is still me, just with more money. This helped me more fully embody my wealth, goals, and imperfections.

I feel so much more on-fire AND at peace simultaneously. Obviously, the work is ongoing, and there are lots more changes I'd like to make, do, be, give, and earn – but I'm not in a hurry now. I don't call myself 'busy' anymore, and as I move into this next stage of life, I've never been more excited or relaxed about my lifestyle, my role in my business, my family, and the potential I will watch unfold over the coming years.

— *Lesson* —

You can care deeply about your clients, but still charge well.

Are You Making Enough Profit?

> *'Profit is not an event. It's a habit.'*
>
> MIKE MICHALOWICZ

Guess what? Not only are you allowed to charge what you're worth, you're also allowed to make a healthy profit. *Say what?!*

I once bought a beautiful handmade soapstone jewelry box from a local bookshop for $14. *Fourteen dollars.* I said to the owner, 'I think these are underpriced. It's clear that a lot of love goes into them.' He replied: 'I know – my wife does an amazing job, but we'd rather be affordable for people.'

First up, 'affordable' is different for everyone, right? Those soapstone boxes would still be a bargain at $25. Plus, handmade items *should* be more expensive than mass-produced ones, and many people are happy to pay a premium for something that's made by an actual human being. I hate to think how little profit they are making on those boxes, especially when factoring in the woman's time (which I suspect they aren't doing). It's a shame, because I bet she'll give up, get discouraged, and lose her enthusiasm for the craft pretty quickly.

My first-ever business was selling handmade bracelets made of wetsuit remnants. I bought the raw materials for two dollars and sold each bracelet for... two dollars. Okay, I was nine, but still. The thing is: I loved having a business. I loved creating, and I even loved selling. It didn't occur to me that I could make money too!

Entrepreneurs often feel guilty about making a good profit, especially on something that feels good, is easy for them, or is something that helps transform people's lives. But that's the whole point of being a Chillpreneur: it's *supposed* to be easy and feel good. So, make sure you're adding up all the true costs of doing business – including your time and expertise – and make sure you're *actually* making a profit! If you're not, you have to increase your prices.

You're even allowed to pay yourself a salary! I know, *crazy*, right?! Paying yourself is incredibly symbolic. Why? Because most of us will move heaven and earth to pay our suppliers and make sure they are taken care of. In fact, I've been so stressed about not being able to pay an invoice on time that I went after more sales or chased down clients who defaulted on invoices I sent to *them*. I hate letting other people down.

But guess who comes last? Who works their ass off? Who does the buck stop with? You. You deserve to get paid, and not with the leftover scraps. There will never be any 'spare' money left over for you until you stop undercharging in the first place. Charging appropriately is an act of self-care and self-love. It's not greedy or unethical to charge well for what you do. Money is a tool that helps you take care of your own needs and use your extra energy and resources to help others.

You might think you're doing people a favor by undercharging, but it rarely works out. It can lead to burnout and resentment, and you won't have the energy and vitality you need to make a difference in the world. So, stop being cheap with yourself – it serves very few people, least of all you. *You are enough.* You might not believe that, yet, because it's so deeply ingrained. But you are.

> — *Lesson* —
> You don't need to bribe people to work with you.
> And you're allowed to make a healthy profit.

Mistake #3: Working for Free for Too Long

'Time is money.'

BENJAMIN FRANKLIN

Many entrepreneurs confuse their business with a charity, which leads to burnout and resentment. You're a chillpreneur first, then a chillanthropist; give from your abundance, don't sacrifice your life force.

One of the most symbolic milestones of your business journey is graduating from free to paid work. For many, it feels like a leap too far, which is why otherwise talented entrepreneurs get stuck in their day jobs for way too long.

I very deliberately use the word 'graduating' when it comes to charging for your work, because it should be a natural progression, like moving on from an unpaid internship into an actual paid job. Real-talk: graduating from being a moonlighter (or hobbyist) to a full-time entrepreneur requires you to actually charge people money!

At some point, you just have to decide that you're ready and that, even if you never believe you're good enough, you're going to move forward. The Chillpreneur way is realizing that your imperfection is perfect – because you'll never feel ready, have enough testimonials, feel validated enough, or be free of doubts about whether you're good enough. That's the inner work you need to do, not the actual hard work and hustle.

Now, there's a difference between working for free and intentional volunteer work. It's healthy and generous to build some philanthropy into your business, whether you're giving time or money. But know the difference. Philanthropy usually feels good and has no other motive than giving back. If you're being exploited, you'll feel out of alignment.

> *'To be in business you must generate a profit;*
> *otherwise, it's called volunteering.'*
> Susan W. Antal

Reasons to Work for Free

Beyond philanthropy, you might decide to work for free strategically, and there's nothing wrong with that. Valid reasons include the following:

- **To gain valuable experience**. Maybe you're working toward a certification and need to log client hours. Or you need testimonials for your website, test cases for your portfolio, or case studies for your blog. In that case, working for free is the quickest way to achieve your goal. It's totally fine: get 'em booked ASAP! Just decide in advance how many clients you'll take on for experience purposes and cap it at that. You don't need to live in apprentice mode forever. You're allowed to earn while you learn.

- **To promote your work**. Most businesses can find a way to let customers 'try before they buy.' For example, if you've got a course, you can give away some lessons for free and finish with, 'If you liked this, here's where you can buy the full version.' Don't forget to make the payment link really obvious: you don't want to make people work to give you money.

- **As a sales strategy**. People understandably want to see if there's an energy fit before they commit to working with you, so doing a small (emphasis on *small*) amount of work for free can be an awesome sales strategy. A lot of different service-based businesses can do this. You could offer 'mini makeovers' for a web page (not the whole website), a free critique of a sales page, or copywriting feedback. This isn't working for free, and you have to be clear that it's a taster or trial to see if working together is a win-win.

- **To gain exposure to your target market.** I do several interviews on podcasts each week, just to get in front of my target market. It's totally a win-win situation. However, nowadays I'm more selective about what I say yes to. It has to be a good fit, and it has to be a sizable audience. I've done my apprenticeship and have been interviewed for a blog with five followers, but I've since graduated to blogs with a bigger reach. When you're starting out, say yes to almost every opportunity for the experience, and then become more discerning as you go on. You'll figure out what to say no to over time.

It's also OK to charge for all of these things, even if you're starting out.

What About Speaking for Free?

I get asked to speak for free all the time – not just at events in my hometown, but in different states and countries – by organizers with zero budget. Some think that 'there's no harm in asking,' just in case I happen to be in their neighborhood on the other side of the world at the exact time and date of their event. Um, no thank you. There's a 100 percent chance I'm going to decline that 'opportunity.'

Back in the blissful, carefree days before I had kids, I traveled the world attending conferences all the time, so it was no big deal if I spoke at an event I would have paid to attend anyway. Why not? After I had kids, I started adding up the true cost of speaking for free. Most conference organizers booked the cheapest flight available, so

I had to pay extra to check in a bag or have more legroom, and they didn't always pay for a taxi to the venue. You'd be surprised how many organizers don't provide food for speakers, so there are meals, snacks, and beverages to pay for. There are also internet costs at the hotel, plus tipping everyone from waiters to bellboys to taxi drivers.

To feel confident enough to perform well, I need to look my best, so I usually have my hair and nails done. And, now that I have kids, there's the additional cost of childcare and the indirect cost of being away from my family. Like many mothers, I feel obligated to make up that time with Mark and the kids when I return. Then there's prep time. All the 'brain power' invested in speaking for free comes at the cost of developing my own income-producing assets. As an introvert, I also have to factor in recovery time. Putting on a bra and Spanx to leave my house and be in a room full of hundreds of people can wipe me out for hours and sometimes days at a time!

> *'If you don't value your time, neither will others.*
> *Stop giving away your time and talents. Value*
> *what you know and start charging for it.'*
>
> KIM GARST

Let's face it, though: it's wonderful to occasionally sleep through the night without my kids waking me up, or use a hotel room to write or take a quiet bath. But get honest with yourself and calculate your costs: *all of them.* Then you can decide if it's worth doing. Sometimes it is! Sometimes speaking for free is worth it if the audience is your target market and if enough potential clients are there to make it worthwhile.

Don't get guilted into speaking for free just because it's a good cause or you feel like you should. Appearance activist Carly Findlay often gets asked to speak for charities, to provide disability awareness to organizations, and, ironically, to participate on panels to promote equality and women's empowerment. All for free.

After being asked to speak fro free at a career day for disabled students at a for-profit educational institute (another irony), she wrote on her blog: 'No doubt they'd pay a consultant specializing in an area outside of disability. No doubt the person running the event gets paid. For me, it'd mean an afternoon away from my day job, plus several hours preparing the presentation.'[1]

When Carly said no, the organizer said she was disappointed (ouch, the D-word always stings), and that she should have been 'happy to donate her time' because it was a worthy cause. Carly says, 'I believe the work that people like me and [other disability activists] do in educating people is important in facilitating change and improving access and inclusion, and it deserves compensation. Our work is not to be given away for free.'[2]

— *Lesson* —

**Be intentional about your free work and
calculate what it actually costs you.**

Melanie Ramiro, one of my Money Bootcampers (and someone I hired to coach me on speaking), advises having a personal quota for free events – say, one per quarter. When you've fulfilled that, it's okay to say, 'Sorry, I've reached my quota for pro-bono work this year.'

Before You Work for Free

Many people have a seemingly unlimited capacity for giving, and they feel greedy if they expect something in return. If this sounds like you, here are some tips that will help you 'check yourself before you wreck yourself.'

- **Put clear boundaries around your giving.** If you're giving away a certain amount of coaching or consulting hours, or designing a small website for someone, put it in writing, and when it's done, it's done. If you're speaking for free, don't feel obligated to stay for the whole event. One keynote and you're off the clock. Don't feel like you should market the event for free, either – that can be part of your paid speaking package.

- **Be clear about the expected reciprocity.** If you're doing free work in exchange for something, e.g. a testimonial, professional pictures, or video footage, make sure you follow up and actually get it. You'd be surprised how often people overlook this because they don't want to nag or bother others, even when they agreed to it up front.

- **Make it worthwhile.** If you do pro-bono work, let the recipient know what your rate is going forward, and make an offer for further work. If you're a speaker, can you sell books or products at the back of the room? Can you use the time to meet up with some paying clients around the event?

- **It's always okay to say 'No, thank you.'** Working for free isn't bad in itself: just make sure you're doing it intentionally and for strategic reasons – not because you feel bad about charging.

CASE STUDY: JUST TELL THEM THE FEE

Name: *Adele Bates, UK*
Business: *Behavior and education specialist*

I didn't think that I could charge in the education industry at all. Organizations contact me assuming I'll work for free, and yet sometimes it's as simple as writing back with, 'Great, here's my fee.'

I'm not worried about rejection anymore because even if they can't match my fee exactly, I'll still get paid a lot more than the initial offer of £0. Then, I'll negotiate other benefits if they're still below my fee with their budget.

I also write articles for many education publications. Editors always set the fee, so I never thought about it further. After a while, I realized that these fees weren't matching my other price increases, so, with all the Chill and Prosper lessons behind me, I dared to at least ask. I couldn't believe it when they upped the fees for me.

I recently raised the prices of my online and in-person training. I decided not to shy away and wrote a letter to my email list explaining what I do, my values in education, and how that crosses over into my values with money. I shared with them where the money went and which organizations I support with my money, and it was so well received! I would never have done this before working with Denise.

I loved Denise's affirmation, 'I serve, I deserve,' and all the mindset teachings around it. I also found the price-increase scripts and advice so valuable in helping me communicate my changes in a gracious way that matches my work's integrity and value system. Sometimes it's as simple as asking!

— *Lesson* —
Any negotiation is better than free!

Mistake #4:
Taking 'You're Too Expensive' Personally

*'If you think it's expensive to hire a professional to
do the job, wait until you hire an amateur.'*

Paul Neal 'Red' Adair

A tenet of the Chillpreneur philosophy is to 'take nothing personally.' You have to give up the illusion that there's a perfect price for everyone and that you can avoid criticism when you find it. *You can't please everyone.*

It feels horrible when you have the perfect solution for a client but they tell you flat-out that they can't afford it. That's when people feel shame around their pricing, decide they're being too greedy, and give discounts or concessions to fit into the client's budget. But 'expensive' is a relative term: something that one person sees as obscenely expensive can seem dirt-cheap to someone else.

Nowadays, I'm much more chill about hearing someone say I'm too expensive because I know I'm just out of their budget at that *particular moment.* It also might mean they *can* afford it but just don't want to spend the money. Or that I need to do some work on my sales page to better showcase my value. It's not personal.

You'll have people say no to your very reasonable quote because they 'can't afford it' and then see them spend money on something totally ridiculous the next week. It's not your business what people value or spend money on, and you don't have to change your pricing to meet their financial expectations. It's just a mismatch of budget, money mindset, or values – not a moral failing on your part. Your pricing is not a literal translation of your value as a human being. Money is just money. A price is just a price.

Having said that, yes, you can price too high. That might sound weird coming from a money mindset mentor, but I don't want to

BS you. For example: you can price too high for your ideal client. If you've consciously chosen a target market that's on a low or fixed income, your prospective clients probably won't have the money to pay premium rates. So, it's a trade-off. Remember, don't confuse business with your charitable giving because you want so much to help a particular type of person. There's nothing wrong with that. But you have to be the right match price-wise with your target client, and you must have the right business model to support it.

You can also set your price too high for your client's business level. I don't often recommend that brand-new entrepreneurs work with super-high-end coaches, because they're rarely in a place to get immediate value for their money. For example, I've seen newbies get flustered when they receive advice about how to up-level their business or create high-end branding when they don't even have the basics in place. It's okay to work with someone in line with where you're at.

I once invested $7,000 for an intimate group business day with a high-end coach. Half the room thought it was worth the money, and the other half felt like it was a big rip-off. What was the difference? Half were six-figure business owners and the rest had million-dollar businesses. We all heard the same advice, but it was mostly applicable to the million-dollar half of the room. Not because we were smarter (far from it), but because at that point in our business journey, the advice we received was more useful to us and had a quicker return on investment. We got the same information, we paid the same price, but we experienced completely different value.

> *'How you perceive yourself is*
> *how others will perceive you, too.'*
> LORIE GREINER

Understanding Pricing Psychology

What do you think when someone is 'cheap'? Remember, cheap is relative: what you consider cheap might feel expensive to someone else, and vice versa. When people's prices seem too low, we often think they're just starting out or are inexperienced in business: I know I do. Are you giving that perception with your current prices? Do they make you look like a beginner? Or someone who is insecure about their worth?

When people charge too little, it doesn't automatically mean they're inexperienced or bad at what they do, but it makes me second-guess working with them because I'm suspicious of their price and the value I'll get in return, especially when I know that it often indicates unresolved money blocks.

In my experience, that causes problems for me; like the supplier who is slow to invoice (even when asked repeatedly), they will often over-deliver in a way that's not always useful (which can take longer to complete the original work) or be timid in taking charge because they aren't in their true power. I can feel their money 'stuff' leaking into every interaction and it makes me feel uncomfortable, or even as if I should coach them, when what I want is for them to take care of *me*.

As someone with money to spend, I want to work with people who have clean and clear money boundaries, and who don't buy into a power dynamic just because I earn more money than they do. I'm coming to them because of their expertise and how they can help *me*, not so I can help *them*. Quite simply: I like working with people who have worked on their money blocks! That doesn't mean they are perfect, but I can tell the difference.

Whether you're just starting out or an established professional, you don't want to offer the cheapest services in your industry. If clients say 'You're so cheap!' or refer others to you by emphasizing your low prices, take it as a sign that people have a different perception than you do around your worth. It's not necessarily a compliment!

As I said, I get suspicious when something is too cheap. It's like, what's the catch? With low-cost flights it often means a horrible seat on an old plane or a big layover. It's usually cheap for a reason. Now, let's look at the flip side. What do you think when you see someone with 'expensive' pricing? *She must be really good and worth the money!* I'm not saying this is true or fair, but that it's the reality of pricing psychology. A higher price often gives the perception of experience, mastery, skill, confidence, and higher self-worth.

Here's another reaction to high pricing: *That's not for me.* Does it feel unfair, exploitative, or exclusionary? Pricing yourself out of someone's budget or comfort zone doesn't make you greedy. It's okay for those people to be served by someone else. And it's okay that some people have to save up to work with you.

Do you remember wanting something that was financially out of your reach? You felt a sense of accomplishment when you could finally afford it. Why rob potential clients of the sense of triumph they might feel when they can work with you? I'm definitely not advocating price gouging. Most people know the difference between knowing their worth and being flat-out evil.

It's not evil or manipulative to make a significant living from your business – not only to put food on the table for your kids, but also to have enough money to live an extraordinary life. Because, unlike greedy scammers and unethical tax-dodgers, I know you'll do great things with your wealth.

Remember, there's no magical critic-proof price, which is why the Goldilocks sweet-spot pricing method is so personal. Even if you undercharge, someone will ask why you're not serving clients for free – guaranteed! Don't be offended; it's just a business rite of passage. People will ask you to lower your prices, no matter how low they are already, and it's okay to say no. I've heard this so many times. An entrepreneur agonizes over the price and finally quotes what they think is a low but reasonable proposal and the response is 'too expensive.' Those people aren't your customers. There's always more money.

One of my Money Bootcampers, Ingrid Tuffin, got an email from a prospective client saying, 'We have received your proposal. Your price seems high for this job. Would you like to amend your quote?' She wrote back simply saying, 'No.' We cheered her on! Make sure you're surrounding yourself with people who believe in charging what they're worth, otherwise you'll constantly second-guess yourself.

Every time I've set my prices, I've had completely opposite reactions to the same amount. On the same day I've heard 'That's too expensive,' and 'Wow, that's great value!' Who would you rather serve? I'm not saying you can just sell a bag of horse poo for $10,000. But, if you're giving good results for $10,000, and it's appropriate for someone to pay that because they'll get a great return on that investment, charge the ten grand. *With pride.* Then wait for somebody to say, 'Oh, is that all? What a bargain!'

That's the truth about pricing. There will always be someone who thinks it's too expensive, and there will always be someone who thinks it's a great deal. You're not required to serve everyone, and many aren't going to be a match for your services or pricing. You don't have to convince them. You won't get your pricing exactly right the first or the 100th time. So, try not to worry about what other people say or think. Chill out and just pick a price.

— *Lesson* —

It's okay to be expensive for some people.

CHAPTER 8

How to Increase Your Prices Without Losing Clients

'Price is what you pay. Value is what you get.'

WARREN BUFFET

*I*f you want to earn more in your business (and you're not ready to add passive income sources), you have two main ways to accomplish it: work with more people or charge more. You may have already done the math and realized that you can't work harder without going into burnout and overwhelm. If that's the case, raising your prices is probably the easiest way to earn more money.

But you're going to resist it like crazy. One of the mistakes entrepreneurs make – even after they get over the initial hurdle of setting their prices in the first place – is to rarely review or change those prices. If that's true for you, you're either going to love this chapter or want to run away from it screaming.

I once mock-chastised my *very talented* photographer friend Claire Thomasina because I felt her prices were too low. She said: 'Denise, last year I was doing this practically for *free* – you've inspired me to increase my prices, but I need to sit here for a while before I jump again.' That's fine. Claire knew she was probably still undercharging, but she needed to acclimatize to her new rates before she raised them again.

Four Signs You Need to Increase Your Prices

You don't need any particular excuse to increase your prices, you can do it simply because you want to – but if the thought of doing it makes you feel a little sick, there are some undeniable signs that will help you determine whether it's time. Ask yourself:

1. Are you booked out, over capacity, or carrying a long waiting list?

2. Do you have high-maintenance clients who are no longer worth working with at your current prices?

3. Are your results incredible, and do clients often say you've changed their lives?

4. Do you attract 'I-need-it-now' clients who ask for fast turnarounds but find you're not charging enough to make that worthwhile?

If you answered 'yes' to three or more of these questions, it's time to increase your prices! Nobody is going to give you permission – you have to claim it for yourself, and decide that you're worth it and that *now* is the perfect time. Let's dig into these signs a little deeper.

Sign #1: You're Booked Out

Are you in such demand that you're booked out for weeks, if not months, in advance? Time for a price increase. Are you seeing clients back to back with no time in between to grab a cup of tea or take a quick pee? I've been there! Remember, I used to get up at 5 a.m. for my first international client of the day and had all-day sessions without a break.

Sound familiar? One biz friend told me that she once peed in a towel during a call because she had no time for a toilet break! This is not good, but highly relatable. I didn't do the towel thing, but I'd mute myself on the phone so I could sneak to the bathroom and relieve myself without my client overhearing.

It's nice to be popular, but if your client schedule is starting to impact your life (or your bladder), it's a sign you're ready to increase your prices. In fact, you can increase your rates and the demand probably won't drop off that much. *Trust me on this.* A long waiting list is a big sign that you're too inexpensive for your reputation or for the results that you give people. Before you try and justify this, let me first say that everyone's version of 'booked out' is different. Your capacity is entirely personal.

Pricing is all about supply and demand. If you have a lot of people clamoring for your services, chances are that you can afford to increase your prices, at least a little bit – if not a lot. Working an over-demanding schedule because you can't say no is unsustainable, and one of the ways you can recalibrate demand is to charge in greater alignment with your actual value in the marketplace. No more metaphorical (or literal) peeing in towels!

The bonus is that you'll work less and either earn the same amount or *more* money than before. And you'll have more energy to serve your clients or to reclaim some creative space to focus on other projects, like writing a book or creating a course, that could help you serve even more people.

Now, you might resist this because it feels like cheating if you're earning more for doing less. If that's the case, it's time to reread Part I: Mindset to work on your blocks and Part II: Business Models to find a model that causes less stress.

> — *Lesson* —
> Being booked out is often a sign
> that you're charging too little.

Sign #2:
You're Attracting High-Maintenance Clients

One of my Money Bootcampers, creative coach Bonnie Gillespie, told me that her motto used to be 'drama costs more,' but after working on her money blocks, she now says, 'drama is someone else's client.' Ah, that feels so much better!

Most entrepreneurs have a low point in their business when they think, *This isn't worth it. I should just get a job.* You've been there, right? If you're attracting clients who always complain, try to negotiate on price, criticize your work, and generally make your life hell, it's a *huge* sign that you're an energetic mismatch to your current pricing.

It's the universe's way of forcing your hand to increase your prices, not a sign that you should quit your business, that you're in the wrong line of work, or you're not 'cut out' for being in business. Please listen, otherwise those nightmare clients will keep coming! You deserve to have clients who gladly pay you for what you do without stress or drama.

When you charge too little, you think, *I'm delivering so much, and I'm trying to make it so affordable. Why aren't they happy and grateful?* It's not the price. You're an energetic match to people who don't appreciate you because you're not appreciating *yourself.* You're just attracting clients who mirror the energy you're projecting.

Many well-meaning entrepreneurs ignore the signs and work with someone because they feel obligated to (or they need the money), not because they feel like a fit. Listen to your gut. Pay attention to the red flags that tell you someone has the potential to be a painful client. You can recognize these people by their demands for a discount when you know you're already affordable, requests for accommodations above and beyond what you're comfortable with, and the constant overstepping of boundaries.

Do you feel good or resentful when you work with a client? When you charge appropriately for what you do, you'll attract those who mirror your self-worth back to you. Plus, when you're not desperate for every single client, you'll feel empowered to say no to the ones you know aren't going to work out!

My friend Natalie MacNeil, an author and coach, calls this a 'fuck off price.' She says, 'This is your internal, pre-determined number of what you're willing to work for. If the client isn't willing to pay at least this as a minimum, then you can absolutely say no to the project, no questions asked.'

Natalie says her fuck off price came from the 80/20 rule: the lowest-paying 20 percent of her clients were the ones who caused the greatest amount of stress. Increasing her prices helped her focus on clients who actually appreciated her. You don't have to work with painful people. Increase your prices and often, they go away!

— *Lesson* —
**High-maintenance clients
are never worth the money!**

CASE STUDY: LEARN FROM THE RED FLAGS!

Name: *Jody Jelas, New Zealand*
Business: *Online marketing*

When I was broke and desperate in my business, I'd take money from anyone, even if there were giant red flags. It never ended well! They were always an energy suck compared to our quality clients.

We complete projects super-fast because my team are masters and I'm a 22-year 'overnight' success, but one client questioned the quality of our work because we're so fast. He was rude to my team and made them feel undervalued, so we fired him without a second thought. I ended up refunding him 100 percent, and I didn't even explain why. Not worth it.

Within 10 minutes of refunding the client, we made two more sales worth far more than the refund. Keeping our firm boundaries means the energy in my business is clean and opens up space for more money to flow in without stress.

With our new boundaries embedded in our terms and conditions, we've fired three other clients and turned down many others. If we see red flags, we won't even get on a sales call anymore, even with someone begging to pay us 'whatever it costs.'

It wasn't until I stopped desperately seeking money and trusted the Chill and Prosper way that more money flowed in. And, best of all, we don't seem to attract red-flag clients anymore!

— *Lesson* —

You're allowed to choose your clients.

Sign #3: Your Results Are Incredible

Someone recently told me that she wanted to lower the price of her coaching packages because she was so good at getting results that her clients ran out of things to talk about in multiple sessions. She basically 'cured' them in one session, so she wanted to reduce her prices drastically because she felt guilty. Hell, no!

I don't know about you, but I'd pay a premium to work with someone who was so good that they could get me better results in less time. I highly value speed and efficiency, and I'm willing to pay for it!

There's a price point for every market and budget, and that's true of any business. Lots of industries have tiered pricing, like consulting firms and even hair salons (senior stylists are more expensive than apprentices). Experience often means better results for your clients, and the better you get, the more you can justify higher prices. After all, you can help save or make your clients a *lot* of money when you're fantastic at what you do. If you get amazing results for your clients, you deserve to charge accordingly! Business isn't necessarily a meritocracy; you have to decide for yourself you're worth more. (Does that make it a chillocracy?)

Here's the problem: most people in business vastly underestimate their value to clients. Sometimes you need to do research and quantify it for yourself. For example, advertising specialists might look at the return on investment their clients are getting for the ad money they spend. Coaches can quantify whether they've helped people to lose weight, find love, or hit other personal goals. What value would your clients put on something that's *priceless*?

Don't forget that your knowledge didn't come to you for free. Your clients are borrowing your years of education and experience so they don't have to learn on their own through trial and error. They're paying you to shortcut their success and give them the best results possible. Your investment in mastering your craft saves them time and money.

Remember to factor that in to your pricing. Experience gives you the right to charge more for what you offer, especially when you create results that have an impact on your clients' time, income, happiness, love life, health, security, or desire for a better life. I'll teach you how to (ethically) tap into these desires in the Marketing section.

Sign #4: You're Attracting 'I-Need-It-Now' Clients

'Fast, Cheap, and Good... you can only pick two.'

ANON

You can't be extremely good at what you do, deliver results faster than everyone else, *and* be the cheapest in the market. That's a recipe for disaster, and not even remotely chill. You might have a reputation for being the 'emergency go-to' who does things quickly, or maybe you're just a sucker for sob stories. It's flattering to be in demand, but it's more fun to make money and not live in stress all the time, especially if you've developed a reputation for being someone who can fix disasters.

I've heard lots of horror stories. For example, the résumé writer who worked all weekend to finish a client's 'emergency' request (without asking for payment up front), and the client then ghosted after receiving the CV. Unfortunately, this is way too common. Some clients urgently need a logo by the end of the week, even though they've failed for months to provide the necessary design information. Some coaching clients 'desperately' need to talk *today* due to their own bad time management. (I'll admit I've been *that* client, but I'm always prepared to pay for it!)

Do you need lots of time and space to do your work, or do you love the adrenaline rush of finishing jobs quickly and meeting intense deadlines? Your capacity is a huge consideration when setting and increasing prices, as is your lifestyle. Do you really want to work evenings and weekends for little money and ungrateful clients? Hell, no!

The problem is that many well-intentioned entrepreneurs unwittingly create this scenario by saying yes to last-minute requests and not charging enough in the first place. If you keep attracting clients who are disorganized and expect you to fix their problems, you either need to change your marketing, put some new boundaries in place, or create a whole new offering with a price that works for you. Recognizing the fact that you're attracting high-maintenance clients is actually an opportunity to create a lucrative premium service for your business.

You could set two-tiered pricing: a standard one and a premium to 'jump the queue,' for impatient people like me. For example, if your wait time is now several weeks or months, you could easily increase your prices. But if you added a premium service, you could cut the wait time down to a week. Here's how that works: you could allocate three days a week to regular clients who have to wait in a queue, but you could reserve one or two days a week for people who don't mind paying a premium to see you sooner.

Does that feel unfair? Why? Lots of businesses offer this kind of service, like printing companies, and people don't balk at paying more for speed and convenience. Online retailers charge extra to deliver your package faster, right? Why shouldn't you do it too?

Some businesses use the higher premiums paid by 'express service' customers to keep prices low in other areas. So, if you feel bad about charging for fast-track service, you could use a portion of the proceeds to create scholarships for people who couldn't otherwise afford you. And by the way, just because what you do is easy and fun for you, doesn't mean it should be cheap for clients. Fast turnarounds are a premium service no matter how long it takes you to complete a project.

*'Poor planning on your part does not
necessitate an emergency on mine.'*

Bob Carter

Tips for Offering Premium/Fast-Track Services

- **Plan ahead.** If you work in an industry in which rush jobs are the norm, *create space in your schedule in advance* to accommodate inevitable last-minute requests.

- **Get organized now with crystal-clear contracts, terms, and conditions.** Rushed verbal agreements can go haywire, and you're more likely to make (and regret) them when you're under pressure.

- **Know and communicate the process.** Specify precisely what is and isn't included in each of your services, exactly what you need from the client, and *when* you need it. That way, you set clear expectations up front and minimize the chance of scope creep.

- **Automate the process.** If you need clients to fill in a form before you start work, make this an automated email with automated follow-ups. Use an online scheduler so you're not wasting time with endless emails. Consider outsourcing or batching some of the work too.

- **Get paid up front** (or at least take a hefty deposit). Don't release or ship the final product until you receive payment in full. Urgency gives you more power in this situation, so now's your time to be clear about your boundaries.

What to Charge for Fast-Track Work

Some service-based entrepreneurs add a certain percentage (anything from 10 to 50 percent) to their standard rate for rush work. Others have one price for their usual timeframe and another for a faster turnaround. Charging a premium rate can feel scary, but as I said, it's standard in almost every industry. The key is to identify a cost that gives clients what they need *and* feels good for you.

Lastly, reframe a 'rush job' into premium service. It's all about marketing. *Don't make your clients wrong for wanting quick results!* Instead of berating them for being disorganized or framing your premium price as a penalty fee, make it something positive. Call it a 'VIP rate' or a chance for them to 'skip the queue,' so they'll feel special instead of penalized.

Whatever you decide, attracting these clients is a tremendous opportunity to serve people who want instant gratification – or who have more money than time (like me). Just make sure you charge accordingly!

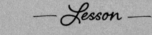

— *Lesson* —

Instant gratification should cost more.

CASE STUDY: IT'S YOUR CHOICE WHEN YOU RAISE PRICES

Name: *Yael Bendahan, Israel*
Business: *Business coaching for moms*

I was due to have my fifth baby, and my service-based business wasn't going to work for life with a newborn. I was offering too many things, working late into the night, and definitely wasn't charging enough.

I decided to raise my prices and create new offers that were a better fit for my needs and life with this new change on the horizon. I created specific packages that weren't customized, and even with the higher price point, my audience jumped on them.

I also decided to go for it and relaunched a group program I had run in the past, which ended up having a five-figure launch and attracting the best clients ever. Raising my prices and changing the way I worked were necessary with the baby on the way, and I wasn't attached to the outcome. The way I worked was going to change regardless.

I ended up having my highest income month ever and then was very close to it again the following month. This was when the Covid-19 pandemic was really expanding, and the world was imploding. At a time when others online were creating lower-ticket offerings and saying that people weren't buying, here I was increasing my prices and making more money than ever before.

— *Lesson* —

You're allowed to increase your prices, even when everyone else is discounting.

EXERCISE: KNOWING YOUR VALUE

After looking at all the clear signs that you should increase your prices, ask yourself the following questions:

- Is demand outstripping my available energy right now? How many clients would I like instead, and for what money?

- Do I need a 'fuck off price' to deter painful clients? If so, what would feel good?

- Am I undervaluing the results I give to clients?

- Do I want to offer a 'skip the queue' or fast turnaround service? If so, what would make it worthwhile?

And then take action! Add a new service to your website, set new prices, or set some new boundaries for clients.

— *Lesson* —

Amazing results can attract a higher price.

Announcing Your New Prices

The simple way to break the news about your new prices is to announce them – just tell people the new prices. The more complicated way is to second-guess them a million times, chicken out of telling anyone, backtrack a few times, vacillate between the old and the new prices, and then finally bite the bullet and feel like vomiting every time you say your prices. Ask me how I know this.

The method for picking a new price is the same as for setting the original one: *you just pick a number.* I've muscle-tested numbers, I've used random-number generator websites, and I've literally flipped a coin. You could add 10 percent (or any percentage) to your current packages or pick a number that's visually pleasing or meaningful to you.

Stop thinking there's a special pricing strategy; most people are winging it (and second-guessing it) as much as you are! You'll realize pretty quickly if there's a mismatch and you can tweak it accordingly. There are no rules about how often you can change your prices – there's no pricing police!

The most important thing to deal with is the fear. You'll convince yourself that nobody will ever pay your new rate and that taking this step will spark a downward spiral into bankruptcy and homelessness. Then (trust me), one day, someone will pay the new price, and you'll feel relieved for a while – until it's time to increase it, and the cycle starts all over! Isn't this fun?

I asked a few of my Money Bootcampers for their recent price-increase success stories to inspire you:

- **Tara Daylami**: 'I recently increased my prices by 26 percent, and I got a client at the new rate within 48 hours of making that internal decision (I had previously hesitated to price at five figures).'

- **Michele Helton O'Neil**: 'I just did a price increase on my Patreon. I was terrified everyone would unsubscribe. Nope. They all stayed, with a couple saying, "It's about time you started charging more."'

- **Brandy Quick**: 'I was over-delivering and undercharging. I raised my prices by 20 percent and felt much more energetically aligned. When a potential client confronted me on my price increase and asked for the original pricing, I declined, and he still bought at the higher price.'

- **Debra Heim**: 'I increased my prices today! I got a call for a same-day appointment, explained I was fully booked and implemented the VIP rate Denise talks about to try it out, and it worked!'

- **Carol Kozulin**: 'I just raised my prices. I'm still using an hourly rate for my side hustle, and after going through the "increasing prices" exercise, I've landed at just over double the old rate. The client didn't even question the rate but opted for fewer hours – which was fine with me!'

It's normal to feel nervous, so always remind yourself that it's *okay* to make money doing what you love. You're allowed to be successful, charge more than others in your industry, and have a wildly profitable business. You have to believe in the value you're creating for your customers and then be unattached to the outcome. Remember, some people will complain, some will think it's a steal. No big deal. To be really chill about this, you need a plan, so I've got some specific advice for:

- Increasing prices for existing clients

- Transitioning a freebie into a paid client

- Increasing prices for a course, program, or for new clients

Increasing Prices for Existing Clients

Some of your clients are getting an absolute bargain, and it's high time you increased your prices. How does that sentence make you feel? Terrified or relieved? It's natural if you're scared about losing some clients. And I'll be honest: some people won't want to continue working with you at your new price. But that's okay. Some customers happily shop at both Target and Armani, but that's not usually the case. You can't force a Target customer to pay Armani prices, and vice versa.

A lot of entrepreneurs worry that charging more excludes people, but the truth is that you *can't* serve everyone. As you charge more for your work, you won't be able to take all your customers with you – especially the ones you served during your entrepreneurial apprenticeship (your Target days).

We often think that, if we price ourselves out of someone's budget, nobody else will help them. But this 'savior' syndrome can burn you out, make you feel resentful and cynical about your business, and limit the impact you can truly make in the world because you have no extra energy to give.

If some of your customers are no longer aligned with your pricing, it creates space for someone else to serve them at rates they can afford. It creates opportunities for new people in your industry to learn their craft and become leaders in their field. You're no longer an apprentice and, since you're your own boss, *you* have to promote yourself and give yourself a higher salary.

Maybe your expertise has increased rapidly since you first started out. Or you've invested a ton in your business and personal growth, so you're adding even more value to your clients. Or, now that you've been working on your money blocks, you simply know that you're worth more. You might even realize that these clients are costing you money or other opportunities. This is especially true if you find yourself feeling resentful or that the energy exchange between you is unequal.

Guess what? You're not trapped. You're allowed to charge more, no matter how long you've been working together. You didn't sign up for a lifetime of servitude. You can revoke your vow of poverty any time and hand in your martyr badge.

Below is a 'script' for communicating a new price to an existing client. This works best for clients who are coming to the end of an agreed timeframe or project, but you can adapt it for those open-ended clients too. You can do this over the phone (which is best) or via email (which is still okay). Either way, you can read it out word-for-word so you don't get nervous. (You can download all the scripts in this section at denisedt.com/chill and customize them to suit your particular circumstances.)

Before you talk to your client, read my guidelines for successful money conversations below.

Tips for Price Increase Conversations

- Remind yourself of the immense value you add to your client's life. Take a moment to affirm to yourself: 'I'm worth every cent!'

You might reread testimonials the client has sent you or review the outcome of the work you've done together.

- **Have the conversation at the start of your session or meeting, not the end.** That way, you won't chicken out or end it with any awkward money talk.

- **Pause and breathe** in between each sentence, to let them add their thoughts or agree with you. It stops you from speaking too quickly, or sounding nervous and, if they love working with you, let them tell you and sell themselves!

- **Keep it light and don't ask permission.** This is not a negotiation process – it's a heads-up, so you don't need to apologize or justify your decision.

- **Don't feel rushed.** If they have questions, take a note and say you'll answer them after their session is over. Clients shouldn't have to pay for the time in which you're explaining your new prices, so make sure you add extra time to their session at the end.

Script for Existing Clients

Before we get started today, I just want to remind you that your current package with me ends on [date].

[Pause for a moment and let the client speak.]

I'm really proud of the work we've done together, including...

[List some of the things they've achieved as a result of your work together, particularly as it relates to increased revenue or success for them. Pause for a moment and let them respond.]

I'd love to continue working with you to take your [business/life/ health] to the next level. You're such a great client to work with!

[Pause to let them respond.]

I'm discontinuing this current package, but I'd love to transition you into my new [awesome package name], which I think is much more appropriate for where you're going in your life/business.

[Briefly explain the new benefits. It genuinely has to feel as if you're graduating them to the next level, not just charging more for the same thing.]

Because you're one of my existing clients, I'll also give you [a VIP day, free access to another program, or some other benefit] as a thank-you for renewing your contract.

The investment for the new program is $x, and I have a payment plan available. I'll send you an email that contains all the information you need to renew.

You don't have to decide today – this is just a heads-up before the current package ends. Do you have any initial questions?

[Definitely stop talking here.]

Okay, I'll send you an email about the new package soon. Now, let's get started with today's agenda. Are you okay if we go an extra [amount] minutes to make up for the time we spent on this?

Note that I recommend offering a bonus when you increase your prices, as a way of rewarding repeat customers. Remember the warning I gave earlier: don't be too generous and over-deliver in an attempt to 'bribe' your clients. The result they get by working with you *is* the reward. The bonus is just a cherry on top! The bonus you offer can be extra time with you (not too much), access to another course or program you offer, or some additional things that don't cost you too much time or energy (which just perpetuates the problem).

To come up with the most appropriate bonuses, I create a matrix with perceived value on one axis and my investment (in time, energy, and money) on the other. I brainstorm everything I'd like to offer in a package and plot it all out. Then I pick one or two bonuses that make the most sense. You'll find the template for a blank matrix among the book bonuses at denisedt.com/chill. Think win-win. Don't give away the farm, as that will defeat the purpose of a price increase!

After the session, you can follow up via email with the details of your new package (have this pre-written), and during the next few meetings, remind your client of the deadline for both your rebooking incentive and your price increase. Every single time, follow up with an email that contains the information they need to sign up. Some people want to take action right away. Make it easy for them to give you money.

In your last meeting with your client, *ask for the sale*. It's totally okay if they say no, but if you don't ask, you'll never know!

Transitioning a Freebie into a Paying Client

People you haven't charged before might be ones you've been bartering with, have been working with in exchange for a testimonial, or just feel bad about charging. Either way, get clear about the value you offer and the value of a client having invested in themselves. Receiving something for free versus paying for it results in a totally different energy and accountability. Give clients the gift of investing in themselves!

The script for this is pretty much the same as the one above, with a few variations.

Script for a Freebie Client

Before we get started, I just want to remind you that your free sessions with me end on [date].

I'm really proud of the work we've done together, including...

[List some of the things they've achieved as a result of your work together, particularly as it relates to increased revenue or success for them.]

I'd love to continue working with you to take your [business/life/health] to the next level. We seem to be a great fit.

When our free sessions end, I'd like to transition you into my [awesome package name], which I think is a great next step for where you're going in your [life/business/health].

As a special bonus for coming on board as an official client, I'll also give you [a VIP day, free access to another program, or some other benefit] to reward you for committing to your success.

The investment for the program is [amount], and I have a payment plan available. I'll send you an email containing a link to all the details you need to sign up.

You don't have to decide today, but do you have any initial questions?

[Stop talking here.]

Okay, I'll send you an email soon. Now, let's get started with today's session.

Increasing Prices for a Course or New Client

In theory, this is the easiest one. Just stick your new rates on your website and new clients or students will pay the new prices. But as we've discussed so many times in this book, easy on the outside means nothing when it comes to money. Raising your prices for people who haven't worked with you before is actually a really great sales opportunity. I've used this as a brilliant strategy, both with one-on-one coaching services and courses.

It's totally fine to increase the price as your results, quality, and value increase. My Money Bootcamp has had five different price points as I've added more value to the course! Each increase provided an opportunity for a 'Get it now!' marketing campaign, so don't increase a price without a big announcement that gives people one last chance at the old price.

If you're a service-based business, send personalized messages to anyone who has expressed interest in your services in the past year. It might be the perfect time, and they'll be bummed out if they've been quietly saving up to work with you and didn't know about your price increase. Send them a simple message like this:

Script for a New Client

I'm touching base about working together this year. I have a few spots available on my calendar and want to let you know that my prices are going up on [date].

I'd love to help you achieve your goals, and I think we'd be a great fit because [explain why].

If you decide to sign up before [date], you'll get the current price of [amount] and, as a special bonus, I'll also give you [a VIP day, free access to another program, or some other benefit] to reward you for committing to your success.

The current investment for the program is [amount], and I have a payment plan available.

You'll find all the details and booking information for my current prices here: [link]. After [date], the new price will be [amount].

Would you like to have a brief conversation about working together? You can book a time to talk on my calendar here: [link].

Honestly, you don't have to overcomplicate it. Just be really clear that your prices are going up and they have to take some action to work with you at your old rates. They can't book with you if they don't know about it.

More Tips for Increasing Prices

- **Give people notice** of exactly when your prices are going up – 15–30 days in advance is the perfect time, or at the end of the month.

- **Reach out to people** who have been 'thinking' about working with you and give them an excuse to get off the fence before your rates increase.

- **Give regular reminders**, both in your newsletter and social media, to encourage people to get in at the current rates, before they go up!

- **Create urgency!** Put a countdown timer on your sales page. This is also really useful for people in different time zones than you.

- **Show integrity** – actually change the prices on your website and marketing materials after the deadline. Don't chicken out. This small but symbolic action will make you feel like it's real!

Resisting Increasing Your Prices?

Let's talk about a mindset shift you need to make before increasing your rates. You might be saying, 'Nobody will ever pay this new price,' and if you believe that, you actually might struggle at first.

I noticed this in myself when I offered an 'early bird discount' for my Money Bootcamp. I told myself, *Nobody will pay full price for this.* And guess what – nobody did! Well, hardly anyone. Ninety-five percent of people took the early bird offer. At the next launch, I told myself: *This is amazing value, even at full price,* and that time, just 70 percent of registrations were early bird. Nothing had changed except my belief that it was still worth it at the higher price. You might need to go back and read client testimonials to remind yourself of the same thing.

You don't have to make huge price jumps. You might need to acclimatize to new price points every few months. There are no rules, it doesn't have to be annual, and you can do it whenever you like!

EXERCISE: GETTING READY FOR A PRICE INCREASE

In your journal, answer the following questions:

- Are you okay with letting some of your customers go?
- What limiting belief is behind your reluctance to charge more?
- What would you like your new prices to be?
- On what date are your prices going up?

Then take action based on your answers!

— *Lesson* —

You're the boss! Give yourself a pay increase.

You might really resist the idea of raising your prices and procrastinate about acting on this chapter. Just remember that you're in business to make money, and you're allowed to profit from your skills and talents.

Money is power. The more collective wealth we have, the more independence and control we have over our own lives. When you make more, you pay more taxes into the system to support others and reduce your own burden on public services. You can support political candidates who can enact change on a large scale, and you can put your money behind creating a better and more just world for everyone.

The world will become a much better place when more people like you prosper financially and are financially independent, so stop holding yourself back! Charging what you're worth is the first step.

CHAPTER 9

Awkward Money Conversations Made Easy

*M*y biz friends and I laugh about the fact that being in business is just a series of potentially awkward and scary money conversations. Unfortunately, these very normal situations are just too much for some entrepreneurs. But don't let any of them stop you from playing the game of business. Back to the snakes (chutes) and ladders analogy: this *is* the game!

Just like having people unsubscribe from your newsletter, having to talk to people about money is an inevitable and *unavoidable* rite of passage. Don't be surprised when weird stuff happens. The truth is that people will make unreasonable requests all the time! Clients will be demanding and ask for exceptions to your policies. They'll ask for discounts or freebies. Some will demand refunds and others will default on their commitments to you.

But it's honestly no big deal and is just part of being in business. The rewards are worth a few awkward moments, and they're why you need some business besties. Together, you can call or text each other, say 'WTF!' and laugh at the audacity of some people. Entrepreneurs often struggle with these money conversations because we believe we have 'no choice': we want to be accommodating and 'nice,' and we want people to like us. But nothing drains your energy faster than saying yes when you really want to shout *no!*

You don't have to make exceptions, you don't have to help everyone, and you don't have to feel bad about it (even though the first few times you say no you'll feel like a mean ole bitch!) It will make you feel better to know that it happens to everyone. I've experienced every single one of these scenarios multiple times, and I can tell you that it gets easier. The requests don't stop; you'll just get 'gatekeepers' who'll stop you having to deal with it yourself, or you'll just feel less bad about saying no.

Strategies for Awkward Money Talks

Remember, what scares you today, won't scare you tomorrow! I'm not a big fan of confrontation, but I have some really simple strategies for handling the difficult money conversations that *I guarantee* you'll have to deal with too.

- **Get a gatekeeper.** You don't have to be the one to hold all of these conversations. Your assistant (or fake assistant) can help you with this – everyone needs a 'Dave from accounts.' (I'll explain who he is later.)

- **Boundaries are your friend.** You don't have to put up with rude behavior or unreasonable requests just because there's money involved.

- **Assume that people want to pay you.** You'll feel a lot more empowered doing that than you will second-guessing whether you're worth paying in the first place.

- **Where possible, follow a script.** That way, you won't chicken out or say the wrong thing. It's so much easier, especially when you're on the phone.

- **Practice clarity.** Before you send anything by email, take out all the apologetic or unclear language you've used to try and be the 'nice girl' or avoid hurting feelings.

- **Create a bank of 'canned responses.'** You or your assistant can customize and send these without thinking too much about them (you'll find some examples in this chapter and in the book bonuses at denisedt.com/chill).

- **Update your policies.** People seem to respect things that are written in black and white, so if something is a recurring problem for you, make it an official policy on your website's terms and conditions and/or in your contracts.

> *'Balance is not better time management, but better boundary management. Balance means making choices and enjoying those choices.'*
>
> BETSY JACOBSON

CASE STUDY: OUR BOUNDARIES ARE ROCK SOLID!

Name: *Hibiscus Moon, USA*
Business: *Crystals and Crystal Academy*

Whenever Denise shares a script for something her team uses, I forward it to my team and ask them how we can use it to automate or otherwise increase efficiency.

One specific instance was creating new boundaries around refunds. It was so simple and easy with the right words. It also allows my team to let go of guilt. Instead, they feel empowered because they know there's a firm boundary and a response ready to go.

Another change was with the requests to meet with people for a cup of coffee so they could pick my brain. Being an introvert, this sort of request always caught me off-guard and gave me a bit of anxiety.

But Denise is so freaking proficient at setting a solid boundary and putting it into action so seamlessly, professionally, and in such a courteous way. How could I not follow her example?

I now have a file where I keep scripts handy (with my personality added to them), so I have them at my fingertips.

— *Lesson* —

Boundaries feel empowering.

'Can I Pick Your Brain?'

When you're starting out, it's flattering to have people ask you for advice. Requests can range from a subtle, 'Hey, what do you think of this?' to a blatant, 'Can you help me?' These requests will come from friends, family, peers, competitors, and even random strangers. You'll be shocked how entitled people can get when you start to make a name for yourself. This is where nurturers with 'go-to' personalities can get stuck because we want to be helpful and solve problems. Any problems.

I used to be everyone's agony aunt, travel agent, business coach, and general mini-Oprah. That started in school and continued into my working life. I just couldn't say no to requests for help, and I couldn't resist solving particularly tricky dilemmas, even if they weren't my business specialty!

If you're a go-to entrepreneur, this can quickly result in you giving away your genius for nothing. It's pretty rare that back-and-forth emails giving free advice turn into paid work. In fact, it comes at a huge cost to you. Most of the time, you actually can't solve people's problems over email – at least not in a sustainable way. People need to invest in themselves and solve the problem with an expert – you. So, you're doing them a disservice by enabling them to keep procrastinating or by putting a temporary bandage on the issue.

The tricky thing about social media now is that there are so many ways for people to contact you: it's an introvert's nightmare! These 'brain picks' might come in the comments on a social media post, a sneaky private message, or via email, and they can quickly get overwhelming. If a member of one of my paid programs wants extra information on a lesson, I generally say something like this:

Script #1 for a Brain-Picker

Great to hear from you – and great question!

I can't answer private questions about this course, but if you ask it publicly in our networking group and tag me, everyone can benefit from my answer, and you'll get input from other members, too.

If the brain-picker isn't in a paid program, I say I'll answer the question in an upcoming blog post or, if it's something that can be solved in one of my paid programs, I point them there. **You. Don't. Owe. People. Free. Information.** Your time is valuable, but others will value it only if you do first. A straightforward way to deal with brain-pickers and freebie-chasers is to:

- Acknowledge their question.

- Express sympathy.

- Tell them you have a solution.

- Tell them how to get that solution from you.

For example:

Script #2 for a Brain-Picker

Thanks so much for your message. It sounds like you're in a really challenging situation.

My program is perfectly designed for people in your circumstances and can help you in the following ways [list of benefits].

You'll find all the details here: [link].

Your reply doesn't have to be long or apologetic, because the logical next step for brain-pickers is to work with you! Assume that's what they want in the first place. If you're getting into long back-and-forths with people asking random questions, then you can create a FAQ on your website and point them to that.

What about people who want to meet for 'coffee,' but you know that actually means 'free advice?' I prefer to assume they want to be a client, so I send a similar message to the one above.

Script #3 for a Brain-Picker

Great to hear from you, and thanks for your interest in my business.

My schedule can't accommodate a meet-up, but I'd love to help you out. It sounds like my mentoring package might be the best option for you.

You'll find details and scheduling here: [link].

If they write back and say, 'Oh no, I just want to meet you for a casual coffee!' or want free advice, you can elaborate and say something like:

Script #4 for a Brain-Picker

Thanks for your interest in meeting with me. Unfortunately, I can't meet because the time I don't spend with clients is dedicated to my family.

But seriously, if you love meeting with people, *do it*. It can be a great way to make new friends. Just make sure you don't coach or mentor them during the meet-up. That's for your paying clients. Keep it light, and if they ask for specific business advice during the meet-up, you can say something like:

Script #5 for a Brain-Picker

It's difficult to give advice when I don't know the whole situation, and I'm not your official coach. How about I send you information about my rates and packages when I'm back in the office?

Setting Boundaries

It's also okay to protect your time (and your Golden Goose) by simply saying no. Have you noticed that the people who demand the most free help are also the least gracious? I've given advice to people via email or coffee dates and never received an expression of gratitude in return, and often I had to pay for my own coffee anyway!

Setting boundaries around offering free advice needs to become a *practice*. The first time you do it, you'll probably feel mean, but put yourself in their shoes and consider what's in their highest good. If you have an excellent solution for them, don't get sucked into giving them a sub-par experience via email or in-person advice without accountability. Hold them to a better standard so they get better results.

I *still* have to be disciplined about not responding to brain-pickers' requests. One came through as I was writing this chapter and I had to restrain myself from stopping work and sending them free advice. The truth is: people who want to take advantage of you will never go away. The only thing you can do to prevent yourself from dispensing free advice is to establish better boundaries and redirect brain-pickers to the paid service you offer.

Lastly, see if there's a reason you're attracting brain-pickers. Are you afraid to charge? Are you training people to get your valuable services for free by always being available and never saying no? You're worth the money you're charging!

— *Lesson* —

Giving people advice for free isn't in their best interest.

'Can I Have a Discount?'

I was shopping recently and noticed something interesting: some brands never go on sale and don't give discounts.

I found a tiny rack in fashion outlet Country Road marked 'Last of the bestsellers' with a discreet discount sticker on each item. The message was 'This isn't our crappy stuff, we're almost out of our most popular stock, and this is your last chance to buy it.' Then I noticed that on workout clothing brand lululemon's website, there isn't a 'sale' tab: instead, there's a section called 'We made too much.' They don't want to be perceived as a discount retailer – especially in their flagship stores – and they don't want to train their customers to expect regular discounts or to wait until things go on sale.

Maybe you think this is just semantics; however, there's an *energy* behind the way you frame discounts. Are you known for always offering a discount or are people happy to pay your full prices? It's totally okay to say 'I don't offer discounts or scholarships' without having to justify anything! I'm not saying you should never offer financial incentives for your customers, but the way you market them and the reason behind them are really important.

Here are some script ideas for you:

Script for an 'Early Bird' Incentive

I don't offer a discount, but if you purchase by [date], you can take advantage of my early bird offer/special bonus.

I love rewarding action-takers, so I often give a financial incentive to people who buy on the first day, either by offering an early bird discount (that's okay in this case) or by offering a limited-time bonus. Here's the thing: you have to be strict on this. If you don't stick to your date or quantity policy, you're sending the message that what you do isn't worth full price, and you're training people that deadlines don't matter.

Script for a 'Package' incentive

I don't offer a discount, but if you purchase my [awesome package name] , you can get six sessions for the price of four.

Packages are always my preferred recommendation, especially for service-based companies, because it's way less work for you and better accountability for your clients. Even though my initial private coaching rate was low, I created packages of six sessions because that gave the best results for my clients. Eventually, I took on only clients who would commit to six months or more. Packages are good for your clients. If you're realistic and honest about what clients need to achieve excellent results, one session with you just isn't going to cut it, right?

If you're a product business, offer a subscription option rather than just a one-time purchase. I've seen this work really well with supplements, beauty products, and even candles and crystals. Make the offer and give people the choice.

Script for a 'Returning Client' Incentive

I don't normally offer a discount, but because you're a returning client, I'd be happy to book you at the old rate [or offer an additional bonus]. This offer expires on [date].

When you've worked with people before (and only if you liked working with them), you might want to offer a limited-time incentive or added value if they rebook with you. If your prices have increased since they originally booked, your incentive could be that they continue at their old rate – but only if they rebook within a specific timeframe. Bonuses are good too – just follow the win-win rule.

Script for a 'Pay-In-Full' Incentive

I'd love to offer you the special rate of [amount] if you book by [date] and pay in full.

I don't mind offering payment plans, but I also love incentivizing people who want to pay in full by offering a slight discount (and some people *love* that), especially around tax time, when they're trying to maximize their business deductibles.

Script for the 'Buy Everything' Incentive

I don't offer a discount on that service, but if you buy this package, you'll save [amount] overall.

I've bundled some of my bestselling courses and offered a significant discount on the set. Some people just want all your stuff in one go, so give it to them! As before, boundaries are essential: be firm in your expectations of what people need to do to be eligible for special offers and incentives.

Introductory/Beta Pricing

What about your first-ever course or program? Many entrepreneurs think they should offer a free trial run or low introductory price if they're new or starting out. You might have heard this called a 'beta price.'

I'm firmly against this. Why? Because the energy is all wrong. When you offer a beta price, the power dynamic is off. Your participants go into 'review mode' and aren't fully experiencing the true transformation of being a paying client. They feel like they're doing *you* a favor and can often be way more critical because they're experiencing your program as a reviewer not a student. You've given them an energetic 'out' from doing the actual work.

You can, however, offer a 'special introductory price,' which is basically the same thing but energetically different. It feels celebratory, as if people are lucky to be the first participants. But be clear that future customers will have to pay the higher price and stick to it!

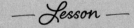

— *Lesson* —

Reframe discounts into incentives!

What about Pay-What-You-Want Promotions?

I get asked this a lot, and you might not like my answer. I don't love pay-what-you-want (PWYW) for services because, most of the time, you're just chickening out of actually setting a price. You might think you're being generous and flexible, but often your customers spend a lot of time worrying if they are under- or overpaying.

Some people use PWYW as a way to gain approval or test their value to others, and then feel rejected and unvalued by what people choose to pay. With PWYW pricing, you'll still need to get the offer out to lots of people and, if they don't take you up on it, that, too, can feel like rejection.

As a customer, I *never* buy things on PWYW because it forces me to do the pricing work that others failed to do. That stresses me out: *just tell me the price and I'll pay it!*

Tips for Offering Pay-What-You-Want

If you still feel drawn to it, here are a few guidelines:

- **Be genuinely unattached to the outcome.** Don't obsess over the individual amounts people pay. Look at the overall result, not who paid what.

- **Set boundaries.** Limit the timeframe and number of people who can take up the offer. Make this a special event and emphasize that it's a one-time thing.

- **Give a realistic price guideline.** For example, display clearly what the service would usually cost, or give a realistic scale so people don't worry about over- or underpaying. Remember, a confused mind always says no.

- **Be clear in your ask.** If there's an expectation – for example, that people have to give you a testimonial in return for their offer – say so in advance and follow up.

- **Value your time.** Don't offer PWYW for one-on-one time; it works much better with e-products or courses. Otherwise, you'll have to cap how many you can realistically deliver.

- **Set your limits.** If there's a price you wouldn't accept, be upfront about it and set that boundary (if possible, by using software that enables you to set a minimum). Otherwise, people *will* take advantage of you.

Again, be genuinely unattached – you'll get people who hardly pay anything and others who overpay. I've heard of people paying literally one cent, so go into this with your eyes wide open.

— *Lesson* —

Make sure you're not using PWYW because you're chickening out of setting prices.

'Can We Barter?'

I wrote about this in *Get Rich, Lucky Bitch!*, but want to reemphasize it: I'm firmly in the 'no bartering' camp. Why? Simply put, bartering has a detrimental impact on your ability to earn money, and it's a trap that too many people fall into.

Bartering means swapping your products and services for somebody else's without money ever changing hands. It seems like an excellent idea for entrepreneurs – especially at the start of your business, when you have little money. What could go wrong? Plenty! Have you fulfilled your end of the bargain and received something crappy in return? Or did the person you bartered with fail to fulfill the swap *at all*, leaving you feeling taken advantage of? It rarely works. Sometimes, you agree to a bartering arrangement out of obligation or guilt, even if you don't need the service the other person is exchanging.

It sets up a weird power dynamic, which is particularly true if you're both coaches and coach each other for free. Being both the expert and the client is *hard* and not particularly useful for either of you. If there's someone you'd love to collaborate with, set up an informal mastermind or accountability group, rather than swapping your services. Respect each other.

Declare Yourself Open to Paying Clients

The biggest reason I discourage bartering is the symbolism of it. I understand that bartering feels convenient, collaborative, and even 'post-money.' It feels warm, fuzzy, and generous to help each other without 'dirty money' polluting your relationship. But we live in a society in which women especially are already financially disadvantaged. Why continue to perpetuate an environment in which we don't have actual, spendable money?

If you aspire to have a thriving business (and quit your day job), then bartering can stop the flow of money into your business. You're not open for business literally or energetically. Bartering sends out a message that you're willing to work for free, and that can cause you to attract clients who don't respect your prices. It's a highly symbolic milestone to receive money for what you do and to pay others in return. Trading money is much cleaner than bartering, even if it means you have to do bookkeeping and pay taxes.

You might think it's more convenient to avoid those things by not 'complicating' transactions with payment, but that's rarely true. Plus, do you see how you're telling the universe that you're not willing to create a 'real' business because you're afraid of bookkeeping or paying taxes?

Even with the best intentions, bartering can get messy. For example, I once let one of my affiliates use her accrued commission toward coaching with me. That got complicated at tax time when she thought I owed her more money, forgetting that we had this partial payment arrangement. She should have paid me, and I should have paid her, so we had a proper record. We should have respected the transaction, even if it felt 'easier' to trade. Does that feel like an extra step? Maybe, but it can avoid practical problems later on.

If something is worth paying for, just pay for it. Respect the flow of money and each other's talents, even if it means paying taxes on the income. After all, you're in business to make money. Taxes are just an inevitable part of that and very symbolic for entrepreneurs.

Unexpected Benefits of a 'No Bartering' Policy

When you draw a line in the sand and refuse to swap your services, exciting things start to happen. But first, you have to energetically close down free work and declare yourself open for business. Make that decision now. Even if it feels silly to, say this out loud: *'I am no longer available physically and energetically for bartering arrangements. I declare myself open for business.'*

You have to be resolute on this. *No more.* Not even one more time. Guess what will happen? I'm not psychic, but I've seen it hundreds of times. As soon as you make this decision, you'll be tested on it. You'll get a request for bartering within the next 24 hours, and a really good offer might even tempt you. *This is just a test.*

Saying no is a symbolic rite of passage for you in your business and will open up many avenues for you to receive *actual* money. Think of it as the final test of your apprenticeship. Are you ready to pass the test and graduate to being paid for your skills and talents?

How do you turn down a bartering request (especially a well-meaning or tempting one) and not feel like a bitch? You can say something like this:

Script for Declining a Bartering Request

It's great to hear from you, and I appreciate your offer. I have a no-bartering policy because I'm focused on growing my business with paying clients. But I'll be sure to check out your services!

Clients won't suddenly rain in because you've passed this test, but you'll feel an energetic shift because you're really in business now. Barter offers usually come because people see the value in what you do. That's the good news. The bad news is that, if you say yes, you're not respecting your own value. When you put a price on your time and energy, you're energetically aligned with paying clients. You're symbolically open for business.

If you keep saying no, people will stop asking and, eventually, nobody will ask again. It's been years since anybody asked me to make a barter arrangement because I'm no longer energetically aligned to that. But it started with me saying no and declaring myself open for business.

— *Lesson* —

**Saying no to bartering sends the right message –
both to potential clients and to the universe.**

'Can I Have a Friends-and-Family Discount?'

Should you offer what we call 'mates rates' in Australia to your friends and family? It depends. First of all, it's a natural thing to want to help your loved ones, and it's natural that they'll want to support your business. As usual, it only becomes a problem if it's causing you stress or keeping you from making money.

Offering discounts to friends and family can create a potentially awkward situation, but it doesn't *have* to be that way if you put a few boundaries in place. The biggest problem arises when your friends and family don't respect that your skills and talents are a commodity – especially if you're a service-based business. It doesn't appear to 'cost' you anything to do a 'quick' website for a friend or to proofread your sister's blog, but it does. It's time, energy, and expertise that you could be using for your own business, to put food on the table for your family, and to free you from your day job.

So, what should you charge them? It depends. What feels better: charging them full rates, discounted rates, or working for free? Check in with yourself and see how it feels. There's no right or wrong, but it's a useful exercise to see what objections come up in each of these scenarios.

Some of your friends will be amazing clients who will respect you, and even insist on paying your full rate. Or, if they are getting a discount, they'll be appreciative, pay you on time, and be a dream to work with. I have friends who I go to for products and services, and I have friends who've joined my courses, and it's entirely cool to pay each other's full rate. We respect each other as professionals, and there's no awkwardness.

That's the best-case scenario. I've even told some of my friends *not* to give me a discount because I just wanted to feel like a proper client who had their full attention. On the other hand, some of your loved ones should *never* be your clients, even at full rates. They might be demanding, disrespectful, and someone you'd never choose as a client, no matter how much they paid you! (I've heard the stories.)

We want our family and friends to succeed, but we aren't necessarily doing what's in their best interest by working with them. A perfect example of this is coaching loved ones. You just don't have the distance needed for that kind of relationship. They're better off working with someone who can keep them accountable, with a clean, professional relationship. Just tell them that you're too busy to help – which is true. Even if you don't have paying clients, you should be spending your time trying to find them!

— *Lesson* —

Friends and family aren't always the best clients!

If they make you feel bad (and seriously, the audacity!), remind them that this is how you earn your money, feed your family, and pay your bills. Then remind yourself that not charging them will impact your ability to make money with actual clients. Your time, energy, skills, and experience are valuable and worth paying for. Send them the name of one of your competitors, a valued peer, or even a book or course that was helpful to you. But remember, this is your business. You decide whether you work with them or not.

Script for a 'Mates Rates' Request

I'm booked out for the next six months with paid client work, so I'm not going to be able to help you this time.

Or: I'd love to help, but I just don't have the capacity right now.

Or: I have a strict 'no friends or family policy,' but I can highly recommend [name of someone else].

If you *do* decide to go ahead, here are some guidelines:

Tips for Offering 'Mates Rates'

- **Decide in advance what percentage discount would feel okay for you** and would still value your time.

- **Treat them like a client.** Keep to your regular processes and systems, no matter what: you're allowed to keep your boundaries, even with loved ones.

- **Send a proper invoice with your full price shown,** even if it has a highly discounted bottom line. Show them what it would really cost to work with you.

'I Want a Refund!'

Refund requests happen. There's nothing you can do about it, and aiming for a zero refund rate is just unrealistic. Please, please, *please* don't feel bad when you get asked for a refund. It's just one of those things that happens, no matter how awesome you are, and it's something to celebrate because it means you've reached a new achievement level!

Do you want a strong and steady business? Do you want a six-figure or million-dollar business? Then refund requests are going to happen, baby! Yes, it sucks and it's unfair. It reminds you of when that kid in the playground said they didn't want to play with you. But it's *not personal.*

In fact, one rite of passage is having a client ask for a refund when you *know* they loved working with you. They were your biggest fan, then one day they went AWOL or even did a chargeback through your bank without telling you. It's heartbreaking at first, until you realize it happens to *everyone*.

Before giving you a script, I want to make sure that you have terms and conditions in place to deal with these inevitable requests. If yours haven't been revisited for a while, you may want to refresh them. Without a robust refund policy, people can just demand their money back at any time, and for the most random reasons. It's hard to deal with a refund when you have nothing in writing, which means you don't really have much power. You'll need to check for any local, state, or national laws that govern refunds, or even consult a lawyer, but whatever you do, just go sort out your policies: it's one of those annoying, but essential, things you have to do.

The first few refund requests I received were like knives in my heart. How could they not like me? It seemed unfair when they'd participated in my course and then asked for a refund at the very last moment. I've come a long way since then. The reason I can be so chill about refunds now is that:

- **I know they're inevitable.** Plus, refund rates will follow a predictable percentage over time. Watch for your own pattern, so you can budget for it.

- **It's not personal.** I've had people *rave* about my course and then ask for a refund on the last day of my money-back guarantee (because they could).

- **I have policies in place.** I'm not making up rules on the fly or making exceptions because a client made me feel guilty.

- **My assistant deals with them.** We discuss refund requests only if the number seems unusually high (which rarely happens, but I'll talk about that in a bit).

When it comes to refunds, I highly recommend that you have a 'bad cop' on your team to deal with them. It's hard to be a supportive coach or the expert when you also have to be the Debbie Downer law enforcer. I find that people respect it more coming from someone else too, especially if they have a personal relationship with you.

Having a bad cop might sound like a cop-out (pun fully intended) but remember: being successful in business is finding your path of least resistance. If you need to have confronting conversations, you can try and get better at it, or you can act like a CEO and delegate it where possible!

My policies and my assistant are my 'bad cop,' so I don't have to be. What if you can't afford an assistant? Well, make one up! Set up another email address for your fictional assistant and answer as them. You might not feel comfortable doing this, but trust me, it will change the way you enforce boundaries in your business. My first 'assistant' was called Sabrina, and she saved me again and again with her very polite but no-nonsense style, so I could take refunds less personally.

Whatever you decide, here's a script for dealing with refund requests:

Script for a Refund Request

Thank you for your message. We acknowledge your refund request.

We're ready to honor our refund policy, but before we do, is there any way we can rectify the situation? We may be able to help if we know what the problem is.

Please let us know by [date]. If we don't hear from you by then, we'll start processing your refund in accordance with our refund policy.

It's worth asking whether there's a problem that can be solved. In some cases, it's something small, like their course password won't work, or there's been a simple mistake that can be solved just by asking. Every situation like this is a chance to save the client or tighten up your refund policy. Or you can simply follow your process and give them their money back. Making refunds easy and stress-free for people *won't* increase the amount of refund requests you get. It will, however, give people a good impression of you, and they may purchase again in the future.

I see entrepreneurs get defensive about refunds, want to argue back, or not give refunds out of spite. The simplest policy, in my opinion, is a no-questions-asked one, but with limits around time. Just refund it, bless them, and try not to obsess about it at 3 a.m. Be like Elsa and *let it go*.

Before we grant a refund, we ask people to fill in a very simple survey, and remind them to delete copyrighted course material from any storage devices and remove themselves from the student forum. We also ask for the reason why they requested the refund – but the honest truth is that I don't really read it. As I said earlier, feedback isn't that useful unless it's stuff you can actually fix. If you can, get someone else to read the survey, otherwise you'll probably feel really bad. If it's something like, 'Your voice is really annoying, and I didn't like it,' there's honestly not much you can do about it. But it could ruin your week. I once had someone say, 'You are teaching Satan's tools. You must be a witch!' *Alllllrighty then.*

I prefer to be chill around refunds and just grant them without requiring the student to jump through too many hoops. But give refunds a specific timeline – they can't be an option forever – and keep an eye on *when* people actually ask for refunds. We found most came in the first few days of the course – people often know if I'm their flavor pretty quickly – but then we noticed a lot coming right at the end, which really annoyed me.

We used to have a 60-day, 100 percent money-back guarantee but changed it after a really disheartening experience, which I *did* take personally. We had a big launch for my Money Bootcamp on

October 25th one year. On December 24th, which was the last day of the money-back period, we had a record number of refund requests, including people who had enthusiastically participated in live calls, got personalized advice from me in the private networking group, and raved that the Bootcamp had changed their lives.

Merry fucking Christmas to me!

It was obvious that some people deliberately set their calendar to get the very most juice out of the course and then, during the holiday season, needed some extra cash. It felt like they stole it right out of my pocket on Christmas Eve. That was the first time I felt my generous refund policy was taken advantage of, so we changed it to 14 days, which felt right and in integrity for both myself and my clients.

I also changed the structure of the course. We held back some lessons and bonuses until after the refund period ended. Why? I had someone buy the course, download everything, create a similar Money Bootcamp, and ask for a refund on the very same day as the purchase! Yes, people can be that brazen. Don't feel bad, just live and learn!

CASE STUDY: SAYING NO WITH EASE

Name: *Bonnie Gillespie, USA*
Business: *Business and mindset for showbiz creatives*

I'll never forget the feeling! I received a gut-punch email from a longtime client who had prepaid for lots of coaching but now wanted a huge chunk of that money back. Not because she wasn't happy with our service; she just needed money and knew she had some 'banked' with me. I started feeling all the old stomach-twisting feelings and hot-neck anxiety of trying to figure out how I was going to handle this when it hit me: 'Chill and Prosper has scripts for you, Bonnie!'

So, I flipped to the awkward conversations scripts section and found exactly what I needed to use in an email to maintain the boundary. It felt so good not to have to figure that out for myself, not to worry that I was coming off as a bitch, and not to feel used by someone treating me like a pawn shop instead of a treasured career guide.

Thanks to this incredible resource, I was able to get the email answered professionally and without stress, which is worth so much energetic money in the brain bank. Previously I would've spent days agonizing over how to answer and probably would've ended up giving money back just 'as a compromise.' Still, thanks to Denise, I know I'm running a business, and it's not 'mean' to uphold a policy.

— *Lesson* —

Policies can be the 'bitch' for you.

Refund Requests After the Money-Back Period

Your answer to refund requests that come in after the refund deadline has passed can be simply 'no.' Recently, a biz friend told me she had a refund request a *year* after a customer had bought her online program. Apparently, her former student was hunting around for cash, decided to take a chance, and asked for her money back. This is way more common than you'd think. Some people are *so cheeky* and situations like that are why you need specific deadlines outlined very clearly in your refund terms.

Here's a script you can use to deal with this kind of refund:

Script for a Post-Deadline Refund Request

Thanks for your email. In regard to your refund request, our policy is a no-questions-asked money-back guarantee for [number of days] days after a program is purchased.

Because you purchased the program [number] days ago, it falls outside the refund period, and we respectfully deny your request.

Since you still have access, we recommend that you go through the program again and hope that you get value out of it.

You'll only get a few of these outrageously unreasonable requests in your career, but trust me, they will come!

Dealing with Zombie Clients

Sometimes clients purchase a package of sessions with you, or a certain amount of work, then go AWOL. They might cancel a few meetings or decide they need a break. You may suspect that their money blocks or fear got in the way. Then, a year or two later, they contact you asking to resume work, as if they hadn't ghosted you. *'I'm baaaaack! And this time I'm really ready!'* How you respond is entirely your choice. If you have solid contracts and deadlines in place, you can decline their request or get 'Dave' or 'Sabrina' to do it.

Script for a Zombie Client

Thanks for the update on where you are with your life/health/ business.

Unfortunately, we won't be able to resume sessions under your old package because it expired on [date].

If you'd like to start a new package, I'd be delighted to work with you again. My new rates and packages are here: [link to website].

I look forward to hearing from you.

No need to get defensive or blamey. Keep it simple and direct. You can get more specific in follow-up emails if they question it. For example, you can point to the instances where they cancelled or failed to show up and prove that you sent follow-ups.

If You Screwed Up Your Refund Policy

If a refund request comes in and you didn't cover the circumstance in your policies, be honest and ask yourself:

- Did I have a clear (and written) expiration date?

- Did I provide clear instructions on how to work with me?

- Did I send reminders?

- Did I cancel sessions or otherwise hold up the process myself?

Whoever is to blame, sometimes you have to suck it up and fulfill the work, even if it's unprofitable for you. If you do, make sure you have a specific deadline in place. (Oh, and make sure it doesn't happen again by tightening up your procedures for future clients.)

It sucks to perform work at old prices when your prices have increased significantly, and it's even worse to have to provide a service that you no longer offer (or desire to offer), *especially* for people who were non-ideal clients to begin with. Here's a suggested script:

Script for a New Refund Policy

Thanks for the update on where you are with your life/health/ business.

Normally, the package you booked expires after 12 months, but in this case I'm willing to make an exception, as long as you book and complete all sessions by [date].

My updated terms and conditions are here [link], and here's the link for my online calendar, so you can book our final meetings [link].

After that date, my new rate will be [amount] per hour.

I look forward to working with you again.

Again, keep it simple and put the ball in their court. Send them one last reminder; tell them that your calendar is filling up quickly, and if they don't get their act together this time, their sessions will expire.

— *Lesson* —

Your refund policy doesn't have to be complicated, but you sure do need one!

When Your Client Defaults on a Payment

The last scenario is when (not if) clients default on a payment or decline to pay the remainder of their bill. This often happens when you offer a payment plan. In fact, we often have up to 20 percent of our monthly payment plans fail. It's a huge amount of work to recoup those costs, especially since we have hundreds of people on payment plans. This is why payment plans are more expensive. Don't feel bad about adding an additional charge to them, because payment plans *will* cost you more time, money, and potential stress.

Does that mean you shouldn't offer them? Not at all. It's still an awesome way to incentivize people who can't afford to pay the full price upfront. There's no shame in that (I've used payment plans many times to manage cash flow myself), but you have to be prepared. This is where 'Dave from accounts' comes in handy. Have you noticed that every single company in the world has a Dave in the accounts (or IT) department? When 'Dave' took over from 'Sabrina' to chase down late or default payments, we had more responses to follow-up emails. It's a gender bias that worked in our favor. Even though Dave said the same thing, for some reason, people took his requests for payment more seriously. Sad but true (test it for yourself)!

Defaults happen in every business, and it's nothing to be scared of. People's credit cards expire, they have their wallet stolen, or maybe they're short of cash one month. Don't assume that they won't or don't want to pay – they might not have even noticed. You need to follow up: in marketing or in collections, 'the fortune's in the follow-up.' Take action quickly. Send them an email right away, using very brief, non-emotive, and non-apologetic language.

Scripts for a Defaulting Client

Just letting you know that your recent payment was declined. Here's a link where you can fix that easily: [link].

Thanks for taking care of this quickly.

If you have questions or need assistance, please let us know.

(It's totally okay for you to simply ask for your money. They signed up to your product, service, or offering in good faith, and you provided it in good faith. Don't be afraid to follow up. Some people might be embarrassed and are ignoring your email. Others might not have seen it.)

Your follow-up email could be:

You might have missed the email we sent yesterday, in which we let you know that your most recent payment was declined.

Here's how you can fix that easily: [link].

If you have any questions or need help, please let us know by responding to this message as soon as you can.

Give them specific instructions. Can they click on a payment link and pay right away? Do they need to log in to a system and update their card? Be accommodating but firm. If they come back asking for more time or a longer payment plan, be understanding but very clear on what you expect. Ask them to commit to a specific plan, not some vague time in the future.

Let There Be Consequences!

If things escalate, and people aren't willing to pay you, you're within your rights to tell them what the consequences will be. Again, be firm, polite, and non-emotive. Remind them of your terms and conditions of sale. Will they be removed from your program on non-payment? Does service stop? Will you withhold something until payment is made? At what point would you send them to a collections agency?

You don't have to be horrible about it. In fact, my friend Marissa Roberts, one of the nicest people in the world, uses a 'when/then' approach instead of threats:

- **When** you get up to date with your payments, **then** we can schedule our next session.

- **When** you update your credit card on file, **then** you'll get access to the course again.

- **When** you take care of that payment, **then** we'll make your new website live.

You can even end with 'Does that sound fair enough?' Lastly, outsource this as much as possible, whether it's to 'Dave,' a real assistant, or a company that specializes in this kind of service. Play Rihanna's 'Bitch Better Have My Money' to psyche yourself up, and go get that money!

EXERCISE: GET PREPARED

1. Download the scripts from this book's bonus section and customize them, so you're ready to deal with awkward money conversations when they arise.

2. Train your team or set up your fake assistant's email address so you're ready. (Put those eighth-grade drama skills to use!)

3. Tighten up your terms and conditions so you don't have to deal with unclear policies.

In the book bonus section, you'll also find scripts around time boundaries, how to fire suppliers, and other awkward dilemmas. None of this has to be scary, but it will happen, so be prepared! Download these resources before you forget at, denisedt.com/chill.

— *Lesson* —
Charging appropriately is an act of self-care and self-love.

— PART IV —

Marketing

INTRODUCTION

Marketing

'The best marketing of all is happy clients.'
Susan Stripling

One summer, I worked for my stepdad selling second-hand fridges and washing machines. Each day, I walked around the store thinking about how much money I could make on commission and dreaming about what I'd spend it on (it was 1995, so I'm guessing it was new pointe shoes for ballet and a Tamagotchi).

But nobody ever came in. Not a *single* customer. It didn't help that it was the rainiest summer on record, or that it was a crappy store in front of my stepdad's repair shop with zero signage. So, it was just me, practicing my ballet moves on the concrete floors. I was ready to sell used white goods *like a boss*. I'd rehearsed my sales pitch. I'd prepared myself mentally for bargaining. But without customers, there's not much you can do, no matter how enthusiastic you are about the product.

I hear many entrepreneurs say they've put their heart and soul into their product, and they can't believe nobody has bought it. It's disheartening if you've overcome a lot of resistance to starting your business in the first place, only to find that it's all for nothing. Heart and soul are essential, for sure, but it's just one part of the equation.

Yes, it's important to love what you do and to love your customers. But you need people to shower your love *onto*. You need to make money to have a viable business. It doesn't matter how much love and care you put into the personalized packaging or how much emotional work went into your sales page. You need *customers*. Lighting an abundance candle isn't marketing – it's procrastination if it's your only strategy (though I do love woo-woo practices on top of actual marketing).

It's sad when nobody buys. It's sad when you've launched a new course and there are zero sign-ups. And it's sad when you have no clients, despite being ready to change people's lives. It's easy to internalize it, and we often do. We think a lack of sales means:

- Nobody likes us.

- We're not good (or popular) enough.

- We didn't put enough heart and soul into it.

- We need a new website or a sexier logo.

I get it. It's frustrating and might trigger old memories of rejection from your school days. But now it's magnified because your rent and your ability to feed your family are at stake – not to mention financial independence.

You've got to stop making up stories about yourself and get real about how important marketing is for your business. And you have to cease the endless tinkering on your website, logo, and brand colors (procrasti-branding), instead of reaching more people. Yeah, I see you. *Stop tinkering!* Your brand is fine – just *tell* more people about it.

> *'Pretend that every single person you meet has a sign around his or her neck that says, "Make me feel important." Not only will you succeed in sales, you will succeed in life.'*
>
> MARY KAY ASH

Marketing Is a Numbers Game

You might have heard this expression, and every part of you may want to rail against it. You might say things like, 'My customers are special to me, Denise: they aren't just a number!' or 'But I put heart and soul into my marketing.' I'm not saying that's untrue, but you have to be realistic about the amount of marketing needed before potential customers can *experience* your heart and soul for themselves. Was it my fault that nobody bought a second-hand fridge? No. I would have done a great job selling the crap out of it, if only someone, *anyone*, had come in the door.

You're talented and ambitious enough to make a success of your business. You're good enough to hit all your goals. You just don't have enough *eyeballs* on your work right now – simple as that. I have a prescription for you, and it's called *marketing*. Marketing is about connecting with your peeps, so you can love them and help them solve challenges in their lives through your life-changing products.

Here's what marketing is *not* about:

- Making money through people's misery or problems.

- Bothering or annoying people until they say yes.

- Using Neuro-Linguistic Programming (NLP) in an evil way.

- Conning people out of their money.

Some of the most beautiful, big-hearted people worry that marketing is some evil form of trickery, but it's not. I often hear entrepreneurs say they don't want or need to learn marketing; they'll 'manifest' the clients instead. Let's reframe marketing right now: marketing *is* manifesting! Manifesting means 'to make real,' and marketing is a pretty quick way of bringing in real clients who will pay you real, spendable money in return. Win-win.

> — *Lesson* —
>
> **Marketing is how you manifest clients.**

Chillpreneur marketing

Marketing doesn't have to be scary. Chillpreneur marketing is just:

1.   Sharing what you know.

2.   Making offers.

Did you know that I have an actual marketing degree? I nailed all my marketing subjects and failed everything else because, instead of going to economics and accounting classes, I was president of my campus business club and performing as a professional sports mascot on the side. But even though I have legit marketing credentials, they didn't help in my business until I embraced these two things: sharing and making offers. It's that simple. *Share* your knowledge, expertise, advice, tips, experience, horror stories, mistakes and successes with people. And then, *offer a solution*.

This straightforward, two-step marketing strategy has made me millions of dollars. It's empowered me to live a life of freedom, adventure, abundance and joy (our family values). I've been able to support family members financially, donate to important charities, and fund causes dear to my heart. It's helped me build my dream house, buy new cars, and supported my crystal, candle, and book addictions. Money is awesome. Making money by helping people is even awesomer.

Those two steps are honestly all you need to do, whether your goal is to make millions or just a few extra hundred bucks on the side to help pay the mortgage. It's the same process either way. Share and make offers. Can we make SHAMOFF a thing?

That's how I started my Lucky Bitch 'empire,' and that's what I continue to do. If you follow me on social media, you'll see that I regularly share what I know about success, money blocks, and other topics, and then I suggest you either buy my book or sign up for one of my courses. My marketing strategy hasn't changed in *years*, and it works incredibly well because I don't overthink it. Next book: *SHAMOFF and Prosper.*

Of course, there are nuances, but not as many as you think. You could get caught up in finding the 'perfect' marketing channel or stress about creating the 'perfect' offer, but my advice is just to get started and tweak as you go. Most entrepreneurs are actually great at sharing but terrible at making offers. They have no problem helping people for free. They write great blog posts, give tons of free advice, and will gladly respond to email inquiries that never lead to a sale. But they forget (or are too scared) to tell people they have a solution.

The truth is that people will take and take *and take* if you let them. Some will be thankful and praise you for your generosity, but that's not going to pay your bills. Lots of people will accept your free support and never even thank you. Applause is great, and helping people for free is noble, but you know what's also awesome? *Money in the bank.* You can give the best, most life-changing advice in the world but, without an offer, your potential customers will think 'that's nice' and move on with their lives.

There's no silver-bullet solution to growing your business. Just share what you know and make offers. I know you're scared to put yourself out there. Everyone is. That's not a good enough excuse. The world doesn't owe you a successful business (or life). It's up to you to decide that you're good enough exactly as you are and to show up and be counted.

In this section of the book, I'm going to share with you chill marketing techniques that will make your life easier and your bank account happier. But not one of them will be 'build it, and they will come.' I'm going to get straight with you: this is a skill you need to get moderately good at. Not perfect, just good enough. In most cases, you can even half-ass it and still get great results (honestly). I almost called this book *Lucky Bitch Slap*, because I want us to get real about the role that marketing plays in our businesses.

> **'A year from now,**
> **you'll wish you had started today.'**
> KAREN LAMB

In Oprah style, here's 'what I know for sure' about your business. You'll:

- Sabotage yourself (and it will cost you sales)

- Feel scared when you ask people for money

- Resist doing the work

Fear costs you money, time, and freedom — and it's keeping your dreams out of reach. *Hoping* that your potential will be fulfilled won't make it happen. *Hoping* for clients to (physically or metaphorically) walk through the door won't make them come. Blaming yourself for not being perfect isn't the answer. You have to show up and make yourself known to your potential customers.

I'm not going to slap you – this is just a gentle reminder that you don't have to overcomplicate it. Share what you know, and make offers. You can honestly create whatever size business you want with those two skills (however imperfect), and you can change your world for the better. You can make the money you need to fulfill your dreams, and you can help more people than you thought was possible!

Ready? Let's get started!

— **CHAPTER 10** —

Cat Charming and Internet Dating

'When you don't close a sale, open a relationship.'
PATRICIA FRIPP

*B*efore we get into the detail of my Chillpreneur marketing techniques, you have to change your mindset about yourself as a salesperson. Everyone wants sales (and money), but *nobody* wants to be a salesperson, especially those who see their work as art or who help people transform their lives. Selling might feel dirty, and others might accuse you of 'selling out' just by putting a price tag on your services. I don't consider myself a salesperson either, even though I've sold more than 20 million dollars' worth of online courses. I consider myself more of a cat charmer.

Let me explain. I love cats, but you know how cats are: they don't always love you back. Have you ever tried to coax your cat out from under the couch when it doesn't want to come? Impossible! But I have a foolproof way of getting any cat to fall in love with me. It's easy. I sit near it (but not too close), and then I pretend I'm petting an imaginary cat. I 'speak' to it in cat talk and scratch it behind its imaginary ears.

The real cat can't stand it and, within a minute, comes over and begs for the same attention. It works every time. Same with dogs. Have you ever tried to chase a dog that doesn't want to be caught? It's frustrating. But if you give up and lie down on the grass, it can't help itself: it'll run over and lick your face.

Reminder: find the path of least resistance.

My marketing philosophy is simple: 'I'm just going to do my thing over here, and I'm having a great time. Do you want to join me? Cool either way!' I'm not saying that clients will rush over and lick your face, but this is way more fun that trying too hard to make everyone like you.

Liking myself regardless of what other people think of me is honestly my only personal development tool these days. That and my simple marketing strategy – share and make offers – seem to be a lucrative combination! My customers figure that, if I'm that chill about my work, it must be *really* good!

Have you noticed that, when you feel really desperate, opportunities seem to dry up? They say the best time to look for a new job is when you already have one, rather than when you really *need* one. I'm sure the same goes for dating or anything else you want. Desperation isn't sexy. Being unattached doesn't mean doing nothing. *You* have to believe you have something to offer your clients before *they* will believe it.

When I had a small list for my newsletter, I wrote it as if thousands of people were reading it, and that eventually came true. When I hosted my first few webinars (with zero attendees), I pretended there were thousands listening, and eventually there were. Again, the reason I can be so chill about sales is because:

- I understand my sales conversion numbers.

- I know that some people want what I have to offer, and some people don't.

- I don't take rejection personally because I believe in what I do.

- I like myself either way.

> *'Some will, some won't. So what?*
> *Someone else is waiting.'*
>
> JACK CANFIELD

If you get enough people in a room, or on the telephone, and make an offer, you'll make sales eventually. But if you're shouting into the void or spending all your time tweaking your website instead of marketing your offers, you'll never hit your income targets.

CASE STUDY: MAKING MONEY IN MENOPAUSE

Name: *Sarah Leather, Australian living in Ireland*
Business: *Business and mindset mentoring for menopausal entrepreneurs*

Even though I taught marketing, I started struggling with my own sales processes and didn't know why. Instead of posting regularly on social media, I wanted to hide, and my fingers often froze over the keyboard. I gave myself such a hard time for not doing business 'properly' and not being consistently visible like all the other business coaches out there.

I realized a lot of my biggest challenges were linked to menopause. I was doing a lot of work behind the scenes dealing with how the symptoms impacted my business, but I wasn't talking about it.

I had to give myself permission first – to stay in my lane, not compare myself to others in 'hustle mode,' and be honest about this season of life. Then, to make peace with my inner people-pleaser, create new boundaries, and please myself more.

I started speaking honestly about money and menopause and the realities of showing up when you're 40+ (or 50+ in my case), when your confidence drops, health challenges appear, and fear runs the show. It's a taboo topic that we need to talk about!

Just like in pregnancy, when we get 'baby brain' hormones to focus on the new life we're creating, I believe that 'meno brain' is an essential time to self-reflect and go inward, not sit in the corner and retire.

'Cat Charming' wasn't about doing marketing like other people; it was about being kinder to myself. Something clicked when I read this. It felt so liberating.

Now I'm sharing my message without filtering. I'm helping women make millions of dollars in midlife because I'm giving myself permission to do it too. Menopausal brain and all.

— *Lesson* —

Honesty is attractive to your customers!

Why Marketing Is Like Internet Dating

I've always been a 'path of least resistance' girl, so when I wanted to find a partner, I figured that internet dating was the fastest way to meet a lot of people quickly. I decided to treat dating like a marketing campaign and even wrote my marketing thesis on internet dating (which my professors thought was super-dumb); I also had the short-lived 'Manifest Your Soul Mate' course and book called *Get Hitched, Lucky Bitch* (major shiny object).

The most significant mistake people make in both internet dating and marketing their business is being too passive. They wait for customers to walk in the door, like me at my stepdad's white goods store. Big mistake. Having a profile on a dating website doesn't mean you'll automatically find your soul mate – just like having an Etsy store doesn't mean your product will sell itself. You have to be proactive and sell yourself.

Another big mistake is believing in scarcity. If you compare yourself to others whom you perceive as 'better,' you'll let doubt creep in and think there's no place for you. Remember, there's enough pie for everyone. A third mistake is to get scared about rejection. Hearing no from potential customers sucks, but you have to put yourself out there to gain anything good in life.

Before I started my 'internet dating formula' experiment, I got really specific about my goals and target audience. I created a list of the traits I wanted in a partner and separated it into 'preferences' and 'deal-breakers' (for example, I didn't want a partner who smoked cigarettes, but I wasn't too bothered about height). My dating profile was like a mini-sales page to pre-screen my potential dates. I chose my photos carefully and experimented with my 'sales copy,' so I stood out and seemed interesting enough for a second look.

Once I got clear on my target, I put out some 'bait,' with an introductory private message to 100 suitable guys. I didn't sit and agonize over each profile, wondering what our future children would look like. I just scanned their profiles and, as long as they roughly fit my preferences and deal-breakers lists, they got a copy-and-pasted private message in which I introduced myself.

Reaching out to customers is where most entrepreneurs get stuck with marketing. You might need to get on the phone with 100 potential customers before you hear 'yes,' or it might be 10. But a lot of people get freaked out at the first 'no' and stop asking. In marketing speak, this is called a funnel: you might need to contact a lot of people before a few winners shake out at the bottom. It isn't callous or impersonal – it's just what it takes to find the right 'customers', and the sooner you can accept it, the quicker you'll become chill about it.

The 10,000-Hours Rule

Malcolm Gladwell's book *Outliers: The Story of Success* says that, once you get to 10,000 hours of practice in any field, you'll master it. If you want to be an elite-level violinist or an Olympic gold medalist, for example, you probably need at least 10,000 hours of practice.

But in the real world? Being able to run a business that supports yourself, your family, and your goals doesn't need that level of mastery. It also perpetuates the Wonder Woman/Smurfette/ Highlander theory I mentioned earlier. You don't have to be that special, or 'The One,' to be successful in business. Any number of entrepreneurs can be successful, there's lots of room at the top, and last I checked, there's no gold medal to compete for.

Because we're Chillpreneurs and want to follow an easier path, let's call it the '100-hours rule.' Contact 100 customers or film 100 videos, and you're going to see massive improvement and results. It probably doesn't even take that much effort. Host 10 webinars, and you'll be ahead of 99 percent of entrepreneurs who are too scared to do even one! Okay – let's call it the '1-hour rule,' because starting is better than nothing!

> *'New affirmation for work that I'm worried is beyond me:*
> *"Anything I come up with is literally better than nothing."'*
> Marsha Shandur

If you start out thinking that you'll have to contact thousands of people before you make any money, you'll probably talk yourself out of it! Start with one newsletter. Start with one sentence in your book: *just take action.*

Back to internet dating. I copy-and-pasted an identical introductory message to 100 guys, so I was casting my net quite wide. Yes, this takes work, but you don't get results by just showing up and doing the bare minimum. Nobody is going to visit your website if you don't market yourself a little. Nobody is going to know what you do if you hide yourself. I got about 25 responses, same as my newsletter open rate! The 75 guys who 'ignored' me? Maybe not interested, didn't like my photo, or didn't see my message that day. For whatever reason, there wasn't a match. Some people just won't be into you.

Here's another thing to look forward to: when you send out an email, some people will unsubscribe. Some will even write back and tell you why (in some cases in a nasty way). It's very, *very* predictable. Turn notifications off, so you don't get unsubscribe reports. It's not useful for you to fixate on that number. Unsubscribers aren't your people, and they've self-selected out. You want a 100 percent open rate and no unsubscribes? Great. Just delete everyone from your newsletter list and keep your biggest fan (who might be your mother)! You won't have any customers, but you'll never get hurt feelings.

I started conversations with the 25 guys who replied to my message, to see if we had anything in common. This is called 'nurturing your audience' and doesn't necessarily lead directly into a sale any more than a response on a dating site leads to a wedding the next day. For my business, I build up a 'know, like, and trust' factor by producing weekly content, giving out free tips on social media, and otherwise being of service to my audience. That's just like having a casual conversation; and again, people will self-select out.

Of those 25 guys, I eventually invited about 10 on a 'mini-date' for a casual game of pool and a beer. I even batched these meet-ups at 6 and 8 p.m. with different guys. That's dating Virgo style: practical, efficient, and unemotional! I'm a big fan of batching – grouping similar tasks together – in life and business. Batch all your marketing activities if you can; record several videos when you have good hair and makeup; spend a day writing articles for the month ahead; or make all your sales calls back to back when you're in the groove. Take advantage of energy bursts! (More on batching later.)

Pre-Screening Your Customers

In marketing, as in dating, pre-screening is essential. It's really uncomfortable being stuck on a sales call with someone you already know isn't going to be a good customer for you. It makes you both feel like losers and is a massive waste of time and energy. Don't be afraid to tell customers what you're looking for in a perfect match, so they can self-select out of your marketing funnel. If I were ever single again, I'd get my assistant to pre-screen potential dates for me.

A great example of elegant pre-screening is Kathryn Hocking's sales page for her VIP launch management services.[1] She helps people determine whether they are a match for what she offers by asking them these questions:

- Do you feel alone in your business, like you are the only one holding the reins?

- Have you got great team members and providers, but still feel like it's all down to you to make sure things happen?

- Do you want to be able to stay directly in your zone of genius – as the figurehead of your brand – engaging and serving your community?

- Are you ready for the next level of 'going pro' in your business – bringing on a project manager, launch manager, or new program development manager?

She then helps those who *aren't* a match for what she offers recognize themselves as such, saying 'my services aren't for you if':

- You are struggling to pay your bills, and you are hoping this will save you.

- You don't already have an established list, social media following, and proven success with online products, programs, or one-to-one services.

- You don't have any other support team members – I work best when I can maximize the team you already have and fill the gaps as needed.

- You are not willing to invest in a suitable budget for a launch or new product development. I can work with varying budgets, but generally we will need some web and graphic design, copywriting, and advertising budget in addition to my services.

If Kathryn didn't pre-qualify her audience, she'd spend time on the phone with people who have zero marketing budget, team, or customer list. That's stressful for both parties. This is why casting your net wide at the start is so important. You don't want to feel desperate for everyone to say yes, or sign up a non-ideal client despite very obvious red flags. Been there, done that, *never again*.

— *Lesson* —

Customers don't want to be caught: they want to be courted.

Now, you might be curious about how my dating story ends. Did I find the love of my life (my hubby Mark) through this process? Yes and no. First up, look at the statistics again: 100 dating messages, 25 potentials, 10 mini-dates. That follows, almost exactly, my marketing conversion statistics *(See The 1 Percent Conversion Rule on page 235)*.

Two of the mini-dates ended up being really great potential partners whom I dated casually, but then I met Mark through a work thing, and it was love at (almost) first sight. So, does that disprove the 1 percent conversion rule? No. From a Law of Attraction perspective, I was 'open for business' to find a partner. You'll never know where that 1 percent will come from unless you take action to put yourself out there. Knock on a dozen doors, and the universe will knock on 1,000 for you.

I can't resist stretching this analogy one step further. When you find your 'perfect match,' the work doesn't end there. Partnerships take work (customer service), you might decide to grow your family (hire staff), or need a bigger house and car (upgrade your systems). You might redefine your preferences and deal-breakers (your target market might change over time), and some partnerships might even end in divorce (refund requests). But my point is, whether it's business or love, you've got to get in the game!

EXERCISE: BECOMING
MORE ATTRACTIVE TO YOUR CLIENTS

In your journal, answer these questions:

- Am I cat charming my customers?
- How can I get more eyeballs on my business (or butts on seats)?
- Can I pre-screen my customers better? How?
- What can I learn for my business from Denise's dating formula?

— CHAPTER 11 —

The 1 Percent
Conversion Rule

'When you accept life as it is, you're free.'
RICHARD CARLSON

*H*ere's a marketing truth that will either be depressing as hell, or the most liberating thing you've ever heard. Don't start marketing anything until you 'get' this: *Not everyone is going to buy.*

Yeah, I know. Revolutionary right? Totally worth the cost of this book! But do you know, on average, how many people will actually buy from you during your next marketing campaign, or are you just hoping for the best?

When I see people depressed over their failed launch or crying because their event didn't sell out, I ask, 'What were your conversion statistics? How many people viewed your sales page?' Yeah, okay, I may have failed Statistics 101 in college, but in business I finally realized the power of knowing this stuff. It's helped me be incredibly chill about my results and, in most cases, to be able to predict exactly how many sales (and even refunds) we'll see during a launch.

Mark once asked me to guess the sales figures from our latest marketing campaign, and all I asked was how many people we'd emailed. Knowing that our average email open rate is around 25 percent, our average click-through rate is 10 percent, and the sales conversion is around 1 to 2 percent, I guessed it almost exactly. It's predictable, but Mark was amazed. It was like a party trick! I'm not psychic; I'm just realistic about my sales conversions stats!

This is probably a vast generalization, but I've found that many people have a *huge* mental block around learning about sales conversions. I don't know if it sounds scary, if they think it's too complicated, or something else. But sales conversions, like gravity, are a truth that you just can't ignore. Not everyone will buy, and your sales results will follow a regular statistical pattern. Don't believe me? Track your next marketing campaign and then read this section of the book again. Virgos are rarely wrong!

Once I overcame my own resistance to tracking statistics, it was simple: just calculate how many people visited the sales page versus how many people bought from you. Once you know, it's not scary, it's actually fun, because you can set goals that you can achieve and have actual data you can use (instead of a vague, unexplained feeling that you're a loser).

The 1 Percent Conversion Rule Explained

On average, only 1 to 2 percent of people who see your sales page will buy. So, if you get 100 visitors to your page and only one sale, you're actually right on track. The bigger your numbers get, the more that statistic will play out. You might get 100 visitors, no sales, and be like, 'Hey Denise, where's my money?' But that 1 percent conversion might not kick in until you've had at least 1,000 people view your sales page. Either way, it's not personal: it's just the numbers playing out.

Now, 1 percent conversion is a good rule of thumb for a regular marketing campaign, but you *can* get higher conversions depending on *how* you're selling. Using a more high-touch approach like selling over the phone (for example, converting prospective clients from a free consult to a paid package), you could convert anything from 25 to 75 percent, depending on your skill and how well you pre-screen your potential clients. Selling from the stage to a cold audience could lead to an average conversion rate of 5 to 15 percent of the room. I have friends who've achieved a 60 to 80 percent conversion rate because of how well they pre-screened their audience. Stay with me.

But for any mass marketing campaign such as advertising (online and in print), email marketing, or direct response (such as letters or postcards), you're looking at 1 to 2 percent of customers who will buy.

Is that sobering? Scary? Daunting? I'm sorry about that, but I honestly hope it feels empowering because it gives you actual information about what it will take to hit your sales targets. Even though it sounds like more work to be aware of it, having a realistic barometer of success helps you be more chill and accepting of reality (and to take that reality less personally).

I'm often asked: can you beat the stats by being better than your competitors – for example, by having a sexier sales page, killer bonuses, or launching when Mercury isn't retrograde? Yes and no. Look at these list-size/conversion-rate numbers for some of my first few launches:

List size	Sales	Conversion rate
2,466	14	0.57 percent
3,461	42	1.21 percent
4,436	44	0.99 percent
5,275	42	0.80 percent
7,236	76	1.05 percent

Remember: 1 percent is a *good* conversion rate. I didn't always make it. You might think that because I'm a fancy internet millionaire with a massive newsletter list, my statistics must be better, but they aren't. My last launch converted at 1.12 percent with a list of around 100,000 people. You could argue that I'm way smarter about marketing now than when I started out, but I can't beat the stats! In fact, my sales conversion rate actually went *down* when I made my sales page 'too sexy' and professional. Simple is best.

Why the 1 Percent Conversion Rule Is a Good Thing

Be thankful for the 1 percent conversion rule: the universe is giving you what you can handle right now. That's why only a handful of people tend to buy your first product, which is exactly what happened with my Raw Brides Transformation Plan wedding weight-loss course back in 2009. I had one customer.

Like most people starting out, you probably don't have robust procedures in place to deal with a massive influx of new customers who have a million questions, who inevitably lose their passwords (more than once), need hand-holding to access your materials, and find broken links or typos in them when they do (been there!)

As your potential customer base grows, so does your ability to handle volume. New things, like your first refund request or a customer who defaults on a payment, can send you into a tizzy because you don't have procedures in place to deal with them. And you make mistakes because you're learning on the job. I've seen unicorns (very rare outliers) somehow beat the statistics and smash their sales targets, then crash and burn because they don't have the capacity, team, or systems to realistically serve that many people.

Have you heard of the Passion Planners, founded by Angelia Trinidad? In 2014, Angelia was shipping and packing planners out of her garage, printing out labels, and driving to the post office herself.

That year, she shipped 2,147 planners, which was an incredible achievement. The following year, her crowdfunding campaign went viral and raised more than $650,000 from more than 23,000 customers (her goal was $10,000). That's suddenly a lot of planners for one person to fulfill.

Angelia just wasn't yet equipped to pack and ship 3,000 planners *a day* by herself, especially when port strikes that were entirely out of her control held up shipping, making her customers *furious*. Suddenly, she was handling thousands of customer service complaints, tweets, texts and bad nationwide P.R.,[1] not to mention dealing with suppliers, finding a new warehouse, hiring (and training) new staff to do the physical packing, and buying a van to deal with deliveries to the post office.

Talk about firefighting! She was making up procedures and policies minute by minute in response to all the problems and requests for refunds. She barely slept for months. Most people would crumble after such an experience, but Angelia survived and is still going strong. (I buy a planner whenever they issue one in turquoise!)

Here's the lesson: it's okay to build your company steadily and consciously, so don't feel bad if your first (or last) campaign wasn't as successful as you wanted. As you can see, growing too fast can bring trouble. Seriously, if you only got a couple of customers in your first marketing launch, *you are a huge success*. You overcame all that resistance, tech problems, and money blocks, and someone *paid you to do it*. Even if you had no customers, you still created something, and it can be refined and improved for next time.

Trust me: you don't always *want* a ton of customers when you're not ready to handle them. There will be times when you have to grow faster than others (like, for example, when Sara Blakely got a call saying that her new product, Spanx, was going to be on Oprah's Favorite Things List), but it's better to make your mistakes when there aren't too many people watching. Build a secure container, so you can handle more people in the future. I believe the 1 percent conversion rule saves us from massive stress by pacing our success so it's more manageable. Thanks, universe!

— *Lesson* —

Having a 1 percent conversion rate isn't failure. It's success, so celebrate!

CASE STUDY: THE 1.36 PERCENT CHILL LAUNCH

Name: *Zachary Spuckler, USA*
Business: *Marketing and business strategy*

I felt chained to my desk, and I was struggling to make things easier. I knew I needed to off-board more of my agency work, have a few choice clients, and not rely on a machine that required time, staffing, and countless client meetings.

I love Denise's 'all roads lead to Bootcamp' business model and decided that a membership model for marketers could be our version. But with a big cross-country move on the horizon, I needed a simple, chill launch strategy that wouldn't cost me my sanity.

I know that I can write marketing emails in real-time without much stress. I also knew the 1 percent rule from Chill and Prosper, and with a list of 7,400 people, we already had the numbers. We just needed to present the offer and do it well.

Goal: 100 paying members with ease.

We didn't overcomplicate the offer; we added easy ads and organic social media strategies and simply presented the new membership to our existing audience, with a stress-free launch aligned with my strengths.

Result: We surpassed our launch goal with 101 paying members, creating $10,000 upfront income and $3,000 per month recurring revenue. The conversion rate was 1.36 percent! So, not only did we protect the Golden Goose, but we also created and launched a product that feels good, takes a stand in our industry, and is specific to our niche of 'not so average' marketers.

— *Lesson* —

**It's allowed to be easy,
just make the offer!**

CASE STUDY: MY LAUNCHES DIDN'T SUCK AT ALL

Name: *Rayna Campbell, UK and USA*
Business: *Actress, director, screenwriter, and artist mindset coach*

The 1 percent conversion rule aligns entirely with my experience as an actress. You don't get every role you audition for; auditions are a numbers game as well!

I've achieved some significant acting accomplishments because I show up and audition consistently. I've worked with Chris Hemsworth in Extraction, *Michelle Pfeiffer and Elle Fanning in* Maleficent 2, *and Michael C. Hall in* Safe. *I directed the play* Broken Code Bird Switching *in Los Angeles and had* some big greenlit projects in movies and theatre. You have to keep showing up.

I saw a massive need for mindset coaching for fellow artists, but running an online business was new to me. Many of the coaches I followed seemed to be launching something different every five minutes. That looked exhausting.

My goal: to create a sustainable and profitable business model that didn't take away from my acting career. Everything has to be easy and keep moving even if I'm out on set.

Of course, I was doing everything myself and it was taking up so much time. So, I hired a copywriter, social media manager, and part-time assistant. Once I got my little team together, it freed me to focus on the parts of my business I really loved.

The 1 percent rule is such a boost to my confidence. I thought my launches were doing badly when I actually had above-average sales conversion! This made it easier to predict my income; I just had to add more of the ideal audience to my list.

I was floored after my first £10,000 launch. It was fun and easy, and the numbers made sense. Now I've got a profitable coaching business that provides me with a consistent income every month while pursuing my acting, directing, and producing dreams. It's a numbers game!

— *Lesson* —

Making offers can support your other dreams.

The 3 Percent Customer Service Rule

Statistics are fun, I promise, and this one will change your business. So we know 1 percent of people buy. But what then?

Not all money is equal or fun to earn. Once you put a price on something, it comes with a certain set of customer service expectations. If I'm asking for money, I'd rather it be worth my while.

In my experience, at least 3 percent of customers need a lot of extra help, or in worst-case scenarios, become 'nightmare' clients. Unless you want to deal with that yourself, you'll have to hire someone to manage the inevitable emails and social media messages. People will lose their login or password details (sometimes more than once), have software glitches, need help figuring out how to access things, and want refunds that need to be processed.

This is true whether you're charging $2 or $2,000. If 1,000 people bought my aforementioned app at $2, my revenue would be $2,000; and if 1,000 people bought my Money Bootcamp, my revenue would be more than $2,000,000. If 30 people needed significant customer service help in both scenarios (and were potentially annoying to deal with), which would you rather spend time on? Is it worth two bucks for me to deal with a disgruntled customer? Not really. That's not my model, and I'd rather have the two million bucks, thanks very much!

Get Real About Your Return on Investment

It takes as much time (often less) to create a more expensive product as a cheap one. *Read that again.*

Think of books – it can take nine months or more to write and publish a book, and the average cover price is between $5 and $30; your cut will be just a few dollars. Creating my app took several months and it cost more to produce than most of my courses that sell for *a thousand times more*. What's the obvious choice? More or less work?

Everything you do in your business and life is an energetic trade-off. Think about the implications of everything you launch. Does the product or service require more customer service, technical help, or physical work such as shipping?

If my courses and the app each convert to sales at 1 percent, which would you rather create? My preference is always to go for the most profitable business that causes the least amount of hassle. That's when you become a Chillpreneur.

EXERCISE: LEARN YOUR STATISTICS

In your journal, answer these questions:

- What's the average conversion statistic for my industry?

- What are my past results?

- What do I need to do to be able to handle more customers?

- How many potential customers do I need to achieve my next sales goal?

CHAPTER 12

Show Up, Be Seen, and Be Heard

'I have never worked a day in my life without selling.
If I believe in something, I sell it, and I sell it hard.'

Estée Lauder

Let's recap on my super-complicated, two-step millionaire marketing formula:

1. Share what you know.

2. Make offers.

Before we start, a reminder: the basics work, but only if you work them. Some people second-guess the basics because they're so damned unsexy. They want a silver-bullet solution instead. Others avoid them as a form of rebellion ('If *everyone* is doing it, I'll do the *opposite!*'), even if that sabotages their business.

Nobody wants to hear this, but the way I grew my business to six, and then seven, figures was consistency, *not* perfection. I'm not super-organized, I don't have superior planning skills, and I don't have a solid marketing strategy. Nope. I've half-assed my way to a successful business, but I've half-assed *consistently*! I show up even when I'm second-guessing it. Just get on with it.

In this chapter, we'll cover the 'sharing' part of your very simple marketing strategy; after all, what is marketing if not just sharing what you're passionate about? First, let's cover some frequently asked questions about marketing.

How Do I Build My Marketing List?

'Money doesn't grow on trees; it grows in your list!'

NATALIE SISSON

One of the truisms of marketing is that the money is in your list. In this case, your list is your customer database, your newsletter subscribers, and your social media following. These are people who are interested in your business and in how you can help them.

If 'list' feels too impersonal to you, give your community a name! Lady Gaga has 'Little Monsters.' Nicki Minaj has 'Barbz.' And I have 'Lucky Bees.' Or maybe we should call them the 'Chilluminati'? Whatever you call them, your people are your gold. They aren't just the source of your income – they're how you can create loyalty and a big movement.

You might be thinking, *If 1 percent is a good conversion rate, and I have fewer than 100 people in my community, I'm doomed.'* Not true! But building an audience should be a major marketing priority for you. I don't want to brag, but I have a *pretty* big list (wink, wink), and I can tell you from experience that it's easier to build a Chillpreneur business when you have a lot more people to market to. Size *does* matter if you want to do less work and make more money, especially with passive income products.

My Lucky Bee community has grown slowly and consistently over many years, and for a long time I didn't spend any money on advertising, just my time and energy. My best list-building tip is to give, give, and give some more, with a mindset of 'people want to hear from me' and 'I have something valuable to share.' Stop thinking you're bothering people by sharing your knowledge with them. Remember: you don't have to be the über-expert. People want to hear *your* perspective and experience, so give it to them! Give away free resources, show the results from your last marketing campaign, tell an embarrassing story about one of your biggest business or life mistakes, show how you create your artwork, give tips and tricks that you've learned along the way, or share internal resources that save you time. The only caveat is that it has to be relevant to your business and useful to your target market.

Then *ask*: ask for an email address in return, ask for a follow on social media, and (most importantly) ask for *permission* to contact them again! Nurture that community with regular material to develop your 'know, like, and trust' factor and then, when you have something for sale, ask for the sale! Remember my super-imperfect Money Blocks audio that made me hundreds of thousands of dollars simply because it was THERE?

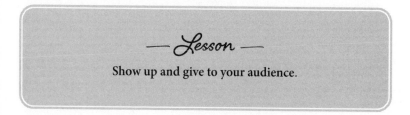

— Lesson —

Show up and give to your audience.

Don't overthink this. Your free content has to be useful enough for people to take the next step to becoming part of your community (either as a subscriber or follower). Always find the path of least resistance and create what's easiest for you, instead of procrastinating and waiting for the 'perfect' marketing idea.

Because I'm passionate about consistency, I've had the discipline of creating something new every week for years. And here's the thing: you never know what will resonate with your audience. I've spent hours agonizing over a blog post, only to hear... nothing... in return. Other weeks, I've dashed something out before my newsletter deadline, and people loved it! That's why you have to show up regularly if you want to build your audience consistently.

Tips for Creating Awesome Content

- **Remember the basics.** In my case that means 'What is a money block?' Don't forget that people are looking for the basics, so take them step by step, even if it feels obvious to you. The frequently asked questions you get via email or social media can give you ideas. Bonus: you can point new people to existing content instead of repeating yourself constantly!

- **Be useful.** Don't share for the sake of it. How does what you share help your audience? Does it solve a relevant problem? Point people toward resources, hacks, or shortcuts. It's okay to make these affiliate links and make some commission in the process (just disclose it). If you've created a tool for your business, share it with your audience.

- **Be inspirational.** People love to see transformations, so show before-and-afters of yourself and your clients. This works well for designers, weight-loss coaches, stylists, and even artists (show the progression, too). Remember: a picture is worth a thousand words.

- **Be real.** How do you make your artwork? Organize your cupboard? Make your kids' school lunches or create videos on the fly? People are curious (and nosy). You don't have to show your audience everything (keep it relevant), but in my experience, behind-the-scenes content builds trust and relationships with your audience more quickly than anything else.

- **Don't be afraid of giving all your best secrets away in your free content.** The more value you give, the more people will want to work with you! The point of sharing is to develop strong relationships so that, when the time is right, your customers will line up to give you money!

- **Search online for content ideas.** You'll find lots out there. That way, you'll never run out of things to talk about (and if you do, you might be in the wrong business!)

- **Build community.** If you can't find the place where your peeps gather in real life or online, create it. Become the leader you're looking for and create a community that gives people a sense of belonging. When you compare the words 'email list' or 'followers' to the word 'community,' which feels better – for you *and* the people you serve? People want to feel like they belong, not that they are a cash cow for you. I don't just send messages to my list or post for my followers – I built a community, and I watch with pride as members of that community *support each other.*

People resist consistency so much because it feels boring or it triggers their rebellious 'don't tell me what to do' side. But have you noticed that even 'un-marketers' who tell you to 'fuck marketing' still show up consistently? Remember, marketing IS manifesting.

You might wonder how creating consistency works with my ADHD? I'm surprisingly consistent and prolific, even when I don't feel like it. I use my hyper-focus as a superpower. Whenever I feel bored or distracted, I batch content for my social media and challenge myself to see how far in advance I can schedule. *(There's ideas and advice for batching on page 262).*

You need eyeballs on your work, otherwise you can't help people. But you can still honor your personality and who you are. If I redirect my procrastination to something useful and make it a fun game, I can create a lot of marketing in a short time. I only have one or two productive days a month, but I leverage the heck out of them.

— *Lesson* —

No excuses, find your flow.

CASE STUDY:
MY CONSISTENCY HONORS MY MENSTRUAL CYCLE

Name: Stasha Washburn, USA
Business: Period Coaching School

I always have eighty billion ideas going simultaneously: new books, podcasts, Kickstarter projects, etc. I love to create, but life can quickly become chaotic if I'm not mindful of my energy. Too many unfinished pots on the stove, and my painful endometriosis returns in force.

Chill and Prosper reminded me that I didn't go into business to work harder. I did it so I could take care of myself and get my endometriosis into remission. As a result, I can follow the path of least resistance without feeling lazy; I can focus on one thing at a time.

In my Period Coaching School, I teach how we can use our menstrual cycles to our advantage by using the shifts in hormones to make life easier. So, of course, when I read this book, it was a huge YES from me.

I plan much more realistically now, and I'm not afraid to say no to projects or delay them until I have the capacity. I pick only one big project per year, get clear on the support I need to succeed, and streamline and simplify. I delegate as much as I can and regularly check in to see where I'm the bottleneck.

I'm proud to be a good role model for my clients and communities. I'm regularly thanked for showing that you don't have to burn out to make it. I've had consistent growth across the board. Income, profit, clients, reach – everything has grown month to month, year to year.

I also never work an entire month! Instead, I average just under 100 hours a month (60 hours less than 'full time') by using my cycle productively to be a CHILLpreneur, not a workaholic!

— *Lesson* —

Consistency is still on YOUR terms.

EXERCISE: CONTENT IDEAS

In your journal, or in a conversation with an entrepreneurial friend, answer these questions:

- What knowledge can I share with my audience?

- What type of content would be the easiest for me to create?

- How would I like to turn my 'list' into a community? Is there a cool name we can call ourselves?

What's the Best Marketing Tool?

I'm not going to recommend a particular marketing tool, social media platform, or technology here, because they change so often. By the time you read this, we could be hologramming into each other's living rooms! The core of marketing is unchanging: get your message out there. Just choose the medium that works best for you and your audience.

Ignore coaches or marketing gurus who tell you that you can market only in one way. I once interviewed with a coach who told me that I had to go to every networking event within three hours of my house. When I told her I wanted a more online model because a) I'm an introvert, b) I have young children, and c) people, ew, she said, 'Online? But how would you get clients?' Needless to say, I didn't hire her. There are easier ways (for me) to make money.

You can choose the most comfortable and enjoyable marketing strategies for you. If you don't want to be on camera, you can write blogs or start a podcast. If you love spontaneity, you can do livestreams whenever you feel like it. If you're a former high-school thespian, you can confidently create silly or funny videos. But if you prefer face-to-face work, you can make networking and public speaking a major part of your marketing strategy. Respect your preferences and personality: you'll likely be more consistent than you would be if you followed the latest sexy marketing fad or forced yourself into doing something 'everyone else' is doing.

As an introvert, I like marketing in a way that requires minimal contact with other humans. I only speak on stages a few times a year; I hate traditional networking events; and I have to psych myself up to attend launch parties (even my own!) I like telling stories, so I love being interviewed on audio podcasts (because I don't have to wear a bra or makeup!) My videos and interviews can go out to thousands of people (who I don't have to meet in person), so I choose the most leveraged, easy way for me to reach as many people as possible. Remember: the key is knowing your personality.

> — *Lesson* —
> **Get your message out to more people in whatever way feels good to you.**

You don't have to do *all the things*. Some marketing platforms won't resonate with you, and that's okay. Start by focusing on the easiest medium for you – otherwise, you might never start! Give yourself permission to start something new and easy, and drop something hard or boring. Just because others are doing it, doesn't mean it's right for you!

CASE STUDY: I USE MY INTUITION TO SHOW UP AND SERVE

Name: Rebecca Gibson, Australia
Business: Psychic medium and mental health nurse

I hid my psychic medium abilities behind academia and overwork for 20 years until a near-miss car accident changed my life and I couldn't deny this part of myself any longer. But when I started my intuitive coaching business, I was confused at all the contradictory advice.

My background is in forensic mental health, working in prisons and emergency mental health services. Nurses are used to depleting themselves to serve others, so the 'charge what you're worth' message of the entrepreneurial world felt strange and, honestly, inauthentic.

I bought so many marketing courses, with advice like, 'Put a 7 at the end of your prices,' or, 'You need this EXACT funnel,' and it caused so much indecision. But with my background, I could see through the BS and decided to do things my way and use my intuition to make business decisions instead.

I now do my intuitive readings on the beach, and I rock up and do livestreams in my dressing gown! My marketing is authentic to me and not based on anyone else's made-up rules.

I know that it's okay to charge well for my intuitive gifts – people wouldn't expect me to nurse them for free – but I've also given myself permission to show up visibly as a spiritual healer and prosper from that skill too.

Showing up and sharing my knowledge helps other people be their authentic selves. When I show up, clients book. What bliss!

— *Lesson* —

The best marketing technique is authenticity.

EXERCISE: MARKETING IDEAS

Answer these questions in your journal:

- What's the most natural way for me to market (writing, audio, video, speaking, or networking)?

- What's something new I'd love to make for my audience?

- What would I like to drop from my marketing?

- If I had to choose just one marketing medium, what would it be?

How Often Should I Contact My Audience?

'People talk about perfect timing, but I think
everything is perfect in its moment.'

Eddie Huang

You know those 'friends' who pop back into your life every time they want something? Yeah, don't be that kind of marketer. You've got to show up consistently and give a lot of value between sales campaigns.

According to the Marketing Rule of 7 (which originated in the 1930s), people need to hear a message *at least* seven times before they act on it.[1] In some ways that's easier to do in the digital age, but also harder because there's *so much information*. I've heard that the number of contacts needed to lead people to action has increased, which wouldn't surprise me – we're bombarded with media that didn't exist in the 1930s.

A good rule of thumb for the frequency of contacting your audience could be:

- **A daily-ish presence on social media.** For example, a photo, inspirational quote, or a resource such as an article or book.

- **A weekly in-depth share.** For example, a helpful newsletter, article, podcast, resource, or video.

- **A monthly training.** For example, a live webinar to share your expertise and remind people how to work with you.

- **A quarterly launch.** For example, something new or a special offer on something that already exists.

A lot of woo-woo and spiritual entrepreneurs ask me about 'divine timing,' like, 'Is there a perfect time to launch my website or book?' or 'What's the best day of the week to send out my newsletter?' Here's my philosophy: *The day you do it is your lucky day.*

Yes, I'll admit that I look at my horoscope to get good launch dates, but not as an excuse to procrastinate or wait for the stars to align before I take action. If you can muster the energy only to launch on a particular day, go with that. Don't psych yourself out looking for the perfect time to send your newsletter. Pick a date and time, and send it out – you can always change it. I've met many entrepreneurs who have done nothing for years for fear of getting it wrong. Sometimes, you just have to launch and see what happens!

'Repetition makes reputation
and reputation makes customers.'

ELIZABETH ARDEN

More Timing Tips

- **Check for clashes.** Don't launch on the night of a presidential election or a major holiday weekend (ask me how I know). It takes only a few minutes to check dates, and there might be a festival or a national or international day that's actually better for sending promotions related to your business.

- **Respect your target market.** We used to close promotions at midnight, until I realized that my target market was probably in bed! The midnight deadline comes from the male-dominated internet marketing world, which is probably perfect if your target market is a 20-something childless, male entrepreneur. Ours meant that my team had to stay up late making sure everything was okay. If something doesn't work for your customers (or you), go against what the gurus tell you. You know your customers best.

- **Be kind to yourself.** Don't launch on your birthday, unless you want to ruin your day, and although life happens, think twice about launching if you know you won't have childcare or your partner is away (I've done both and it can be done, but isn't the easiest!)

Screw the rules. I've made so many timing mistakes and still made money; sometimes you've just got channel Richard Branson and say 'Screw it, let's do it' or you never will.

Consistency is so much more important than finding the perfect timing. Why? Social media is like a digital river. You never know if the people you want to reach will be standing on the bank when your tweet, email, or post flows by. Become a reliable presence in people's lives, and they'll get excited to buy from you when the time comes.

My Face Is My Fortune

How many times have you seen me popping up on your screen? That's because my marketing philosophy is: 'My face is my fortune.' I want you to think of my name when you hear 'money mindset' and 'money blocks,' or see a blue Kombi van. Some people read just one of my books and jump into my Money Bootcamp, others take years.

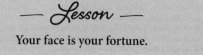

— *Lesson* —
Your face is your fortune.

Bonus Million-Dollar Marketing Tips

You want some *advanced* strategies? Okay, here they are: share *more* and make *more* offers. I'm only kinda kidding – it really is that basic. Stop overcomplicating everything.

Don't Reinvent the Wheel

Writer and comedian Judd Apatow recommends that stand-up comedians stick to 80 percent tried-and-true material that they *know* people will laugh at, and try out new content only 20 percent of the time. I saw Bette Midler's show in Vegas, during which she said, 'I've been telling the same jokes for 30 years. But you keep laughing, so I keep telling them!' And she was right – I laughed my ass off!

Listen to the superstars and chill out. You don't have to reinvent everything. I've been teaching money mindset for several years now, and let's be honest: I'm saying the same things over and over in slightly different ways from slightly different perspectives.

Most entrepreneurs assume that marketing has to be 100 percent new every single time or it doesn't count. But don't assume that everyone has seen *everything* you've created (remember the river). It's okay to repurpose older content because it will be new to a lot of your audience (especially if you've grown your business recently) and your loyal customers won't mind. I tell the same stories on stage all the time (just like Bette Midler)! But even my oldest clients tell me they loved hearing a message reinforced or appreciated finding a new nugget of wisdom in an old lesson. Stop saying 'Everyone has already heard this' – they probably haven't.

While your audience is small, you might develop content that few people will see, but consider it an apprenticeship. Every time you put something out there, you're becoming a better writer, podcaster, or video producer. Keep practicing! The blog posts, videos, and podcasts you create will accumulate and create a library of media that your growing audience can discover any time. Everybody starts with zero content, but you've got to start somewhere.

Not Everything Is Your Job

Remember: being everyone's 'go-to' for everything isn't super-fun or lucrative. It's tempting to solve everyone's problems, but knowing what's out of scope for your marketing is essential. Give yourself some 'content rules,' so you can catch yourself before you go too off-topic. I steer clear of the following: how-to advice – I don't usually give detailed information about *how* to make more money; instead, I stick to the mindset behind it; financial advice or accounting (I'm not qualified to give that, anyway); technical business advice – don't ask me about the best software to use for anything!

Narrowing your scope might mean killing some of your old or existing content. I had to delete all my old blog posts about random off-topic things. I unpublished some of my old books, including an e-book called *Planning a Green and Ethical Wedding*. Hardly anyone bought it, but it still came up in online searches, which diluted my message. Get focused, and watch your audience grow. Be everything to everyone, and you'll never stand out in a crowded market.

— *Lesson* —

Get focused about what you do and don't offer.

Batch and Schedule

If you follow me on social media, you might think I work 24/7. I really don't. The truth is that I work *way less* now than I did several years ago, and I make a ton more money. I seem way more 'on' than I actually am, even when I'm doing 'life stuff' like being on holidays or having my babies, because a lot of my marketing is batched and automated.

I once sat down at my computer and created 200 affirmation images for my website; I was inspired (and to be honest, procrastinating something else), but that was over a year's worth of content for my social media. When you're in a groove, keep going!

Each pregnancy I batched video content ahead of time, so I wasn't missed during my maternity leave. I once even hired a studio for three days and created a year's worth of videos because I knew I had a new book to write and wanted to conserve my energy that year but still serve my community with fresh weekly content. Batching will change your life and free up so much time for you. It also really focuses your marketing on what's important. When you're clear on your audience and your topic (and on what's out of scope), it's really easy to brainstorm a lot of potential marketing ideas.

Batching also saves you a lot of money if you're outsourcing because it gives you economy of scale. It's cheaper to give your graphic designer 20 similar jobs to do at the same time than it is to send the work out piecemeal over several months. Then, when you have a lot of content, you can schedule it using free or low-cost software, so your marketing is consistent without you having to think about it. You can schedule things to go out automatically on a daily, weekly, or monthly basis.

— *Lesson* —

You don't have to be 'on' 24/7. Embrace batching and automation, so you can chill a bit and not have to work so hard.

The concept is simple but mindset around batching is fascinating. You may resist it because it feels inauthentic to you. Shouldn't you just share when you *feel* like it? My answer is: if I'd waited until I 'felt like it,' I wouldn't have a business, let alone a financially successful one. The idea of a regular marketing schedule might sound exhausting, but not if you embrace the power of technology for scheduling and batching.

Plus, here's the thing: it's not about you. As long as your marketing was authentic when you *created* it, it's none of your business when your audience *consumes it*. It might actually come at the perfect time for them, even if it's 'old news' to you.

My only caveat is that, in my experience, it's best not to batch more than six months in advance. Any more than that and your branding or message might feel a bit stale. I once lost a ton of weight and cut my hair after filming 60 videos, and they annoyed me every time I saw them because they felt so out of date. Find your happy medium!

CASE STUDY:
I BATCH SO I CAN TRAIN FOR A TRIATHLON

Name: *Braden Drake, USA*
Business: *Tax, legal, and business development*

One of my biggest takeaways from this book is how Denise runs her business. While I'm not an introvert, and I personally love doing student calls, I want to build a business that allows me to create content, be on camera, do live calls with my students, and do little else. I can batch most of my work. Knowing Denise operates a successful business this way gives me confidence that I can build something similar myself.

I particularly resonated with the quote: 'Not everything has to be my business.' As an Enneagram 7 who likely has ADHD, I want to do it all, but that doesn't support my specific business and lifestyle goals. Thanks to this realization, I phased out most of my one-on-one services, hired another virtual assistant, said no to different content channels, and I'm streamlining my online offers into one signature program.

I now work around five hours per day, averaging $8,000 in monthly revenue with a 70 percent profit margin. My goal is to get to $30,000 months at 75 percent profit within the next two years on a three-hour workday. Reducing my daily work hours has allowed me to train three hours a day for my fourth Ironman Triathlon.

— *Lesson* —

Batching gives you MORE freedom, not less.

Ideas for Batching

- Instead of responding to emails all day, set aside time in the morning and afternoon.

- If you're creating graphics for your website, create a template and create multiple graphics at the same time.

- If you're going to do your hair and makeup, record four videos instead of just one. Or, if you're going to set up your audio equipment, interview multiple podcast guests on the same day.

- Batch your client-facing days instead of spreading them out through the week, so you have more time for marketing or for coming up with new ideas.

- Write all your newsletter content for the month ahead.

Make People Feel Less Alone

The best thing about the internet now is realizing that you're not alone. Sharing helps people feel understood and assures them that you have similar problems in common – or that you did until you solved those problems in a way that enables you to help them. Entrepreneurs have a huge advantage over big companies because we can be more personal in our marketing and create intimate relationships with our clients.

When I started my business, I realized the blog posts that had the most traction were ones in which I simply told the truth. *My* truth. When I did that, without shame or embellishment, people *loved* it. For example, I posted a picture of me using hair-removal crème on my mustache. People said, 'Oh Denise, you're so funny!' I wasn't trying to be funny, and it had nothing to do with money, but I wanted to be honest and show that my life isn't all hammocks on the beach, *because it's not.*

Nobody has a perfect life but, for some reason, we all fear that we're not perfect enough and that, if our audience saw the 'real us,' they wouldn't like us anymore. The way to overcome this is what I call my 'Hairy Toes Strategy' (HTS). When I was younger, I honestly thought I was the only person in the world to have 'unladylike' hair on my toes. It didn't help that I had lots of friends who only seemed to wax the peach fuzz off their legs once a year.

If I'd had a mentor who mentioned that she had hairy toes too, or even had a stray pimple occasionally, I wouldn't have felt like there was something wrong with me all the time. I love working with people who show me their real lives, warts and all. There's something so compelling about showing up and being who you are. Maybe you feel that your accent disqualifies you for success in the business world, or you're worried that, if you disclosed your infertility journey, a physical disability or mental illness, your audience would reject you or think you're 'unprofessional.'

Show people they're not alone. There are people waiting for a leader who looks exactly like *you*. Someone who has your background and has experienced the challenges you've faced. If you're sick of being the only person like you in your industry, talk about it! Have you faced challenges and discrimination? Share it openly. I guarantee you won't be the only one.

I'm not saying that you should turn your whole life into a business. It's okay to take space and privacy for yourself and not share everything, but your very existence might be challenging the norms of your industry. Showing full-length photos of yourself or making videos might be an act of bravery that inspires others to do the same. Being honest about your challenges might be revolutionary for your audience to hear.

There's so much power in talking about taboo topics. Your voice might be the one that tips a whole industry into a new phase! The maker of Icon pee-proof undies (for light bladder leakage) has changed an industry from an embarrassing secret to a fact of life for a lot of people. One of the first things you see on its website is, 'Yup, it happens to 1 in 3 people, from spring chickens to silver foxes.'[2] My first thought was, *Wow, thank you! I kind of felt like I was the only one.*

Icon doesn't wrap the problem up in vague, flowery language (tampon companies, I'm looking at you). It injects some humor into its marketing – you can join its 'VIPee list,' and there's a 'Dribble Diaries' feature on its blog. It's not crude or crass, it's honest, and it's so freaking reassuring! Icon created a movement because it was unafraid to tell the truth about a very common problem. And the company's marketing shows people of all shapes, ages, sizes, and colors, too.

I'm not saying you need to quit your business and start a hairy toes blog, and you don't have to share anything you're not comfortable with. All I'm saying is: don't be afraid to be genuinely yourself. Will you get criticism for it? Yes, probably. There could be someone who says, 'I can't believe you're talking about this!' Or someone who thinks you're tacky, bragging, or even being crude. But the overwhelming majority of people will thank you. And that little piece of your heart that's terrified of being rejected, shunned, or unlovable if people saw the 'real you' will be comforted and reassured. That's how you become a leader.

— *Lesson* —

There's no secret, and there are no silver bullets.
Show up, be consistent, and share.

— CHAPTER 13 —

Make Offers, Make Money

**'Success is not an accident; it's something
we have to create on purpose.'**

CARRIE GREEN

The reason I'm so passionate about helping you make more money is independence. Making money for yourself will change your life and start a ripple effect throughout your world.

Nobody is responsible for making money in your business except *you*. It sounds obvious, but to make more money, you have to *ask* for it. You need something for people to buy and an easy way for them to give you money. But I'll admit that asking for money (especially in exchange for something that you love) is going to feel scary, and this is when your money blocks will probably have to be revisited.

Even if you feel you've cleared your money blocks, there are times when they (or entirely new ones) will come up. When people tell me they don't have any money blocks, I often say, 'Oh, you don't? Then launch something in your business. You'll see them soon enough!' But don't worry. This is about finding the path of least resistance and making it easy for your customers to buy from you. Don't overcomplicate it. You don't need everyone in the world to be your client – just some people!

CASE STUDY:
I WAS SCARED MARKETING WOULD RUIN MY 'VIBE'

Name: *Annick Ina, Mauritius*
Business: *Book doula*

Denise's fridge shop story made so much sense. I always got clients from referrals, but I knew I wanted to go to the next level and fill up ALL my one-on-one spaces. But I couldn't love those clients unless I got them in the door first.

I had so many fears about marketing; it felt like I was brand-new to business all over again! I was worried people would be annoyed at my promotions and think that I only cared about selling, or that talking about my writing and editing packages would ruin the 'vibe' of my feed.

I was listening to the Chill and Prosper audiobook at the nail salon when the penny dropped. Hearing that Denise helps people make more money by focusing on mindset, rather than how-to, was a huge moment for me. This distinction gave me so much clarity and, importantly, permission to own what I do. It made me feel like I was standing there with all my fridges but no business because I hadn't let the world know that I exist and that my services are available for them to hire. I didn't have to write about the technical aspects of writing; I could focus on the mindset and my zone of genius.

I sat down to write some short posts that would bring value to potential clients. Then, I just did what Chill and Prosper said: Share what you know and make offers. It took me only one hour to write five posts. The next day, I posted my content and, within a few hours, got a sales call booked to discuss my six-month package. It was a woman who'd been following me for years, and she'd finally read my post as her nudge to take action.

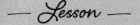

— *Lesson* —

People can't buy if you don't know what you do!

Understand Why People Buy

> *'People don't buy for logical reasons.*
> *They buy for emotional reasons.'*
>
> ZIG ZIGLAR

I'm with Zig on that one. Think of some of your biggest purchases – were they logical, or emotional? Heck, I've bought entire *houses* for emotional reasons (and once because I was nine months pregnant and nesting). And I bought an unrenovated 1974 VW Kombi van because it was pretty. Actually, my vintage car collection has grown a lot recently: I also have a 1955 Chevy, a 1990 Japanese S-Cargo (it looks like a little snail), an old truck, and a derelict VW Bug.

What if your business isn't the 'impulse purchase' kind? What makes people buy things for their business or themselves when they don't 'need' them? People are motivated by a very clear answer to the question 'What's in it for me?' For your customers to see the value in what you do, your offer has to tap into specific universal desires. Otherwise, you'll get frustrated when people keep saying no to you. It's not *you* (or your product) that's the problem; you just haven't shown them the value.

I see way too much wishy-washy marketing because some entrepreneurs feel uncomfortable tapping into these universal desires. I get it. I've prided myself on very chill, non-pushy marketing techniques over the years, but I can't deny the power of knowing what customers want (and giving it to them). Even the words 'marketing strategy' might make you feel like there's an ulterior motive, and asking for the sale might feel pushy. But when you tap into specific desires ethically, you're just telling people exactly how you can help them. Give them what they want!

You might feel it's unethical or exploitative to 'trigger' other people with sales techniques. But there's a difference between negative and positive triggering. I hate marketing that preys on people's fears or desperation. Tapping into people's desires is the opposite: it reminds them of their goals and gets them excited and optimistic about changing their lives. It's important to use your power of persuasion for good. I see so many entrepreneurs get frustrated when a client doesn't see the value of what they offer. But, unless you really believe in your results, you probably won't believe people will pay for them either.

Think about what most people want in life; they want to:

- Make (or save) more money

- Look good and feel better

- Find or maintain better relationships (including love)

- Protect themselves, their families, and their business from loss or harm

- Improve, upgrade, or transform their lives

- Impress other people

Now, don't freak out if your business doesn't immediately fit into an obvious category in the list above: you don't have to change your marketing completely. But you'll see how, by tapping into some of these desires, you can help your clients justify working with you, and it will immeasurably improve your offer. Here's my biggest tip:

Use Money Language in Your Marketing

You don't have to be a financial advisor, accountant, or bookkeeper to help people make more money, and you don't have to be richer than all of your clients to be able to tap into that desire. Does your business help people make or save money, even indirectly? You might not think so, but lots of different businesses can be tweaked to become more explicitly linked to money. See if you can answer this question:

'I help people to ...., so they can make more money.'

You don't have to put this on your sales pages if you don't want to, but if you can put any monetary figure on your results, you'll feel much better charging money for what you do because you can see a direct return on your customers' investment.

Here are a few examples:

- **A graphic designer**: 'I help people create amazing websites that attract more customers, which brings in more money.'

- **An energy healer**: 'I help entrepreneurs eliminate blocks and an energetic resistance to success, so they can be more confident and make more money.'

- **A book coach**: 'I help people write the best book they can, so they can reach more people and make more money.'

- **A photographer**: 'I help people show themselves, their products, and services in the best possible light, so their brand is magnetic and they can make more money.'

- **A stylist**: 'I help women feel attractive and confident, so they can make more money in their businesses.'

You might feel adamant that your business is decidedly *not* about helping people make money. But does it save people time? Remember, 'time is money,' and for some customers, time is actually more valuable than money. How do you save people stress, time, or energy? Even if your business doesn't feel connected to money, you can still use money language to express the value of what you do. For example, *cost, spend, invest,* and *save*: 'I help you *save* time and energy, so you can *spend* more *priceless* time with your family.'

If your business is about the business of transformation, either in a wellness sense (health coach, weight loss), medical-based healing, or beauty, you can still use this language. Look at L'Oreal: they've used variations on 'I'm worth it' *for years.*

- Your health is *priceless.* You're *worth* spending *money* on.

- What is your health problem *costing* you right now?

- Health is *wealth.*

- Look and feel like a *million bucks.*

- *Invest* in your health, so you can *spend* more time with your loved ones.

You get the idea, right? What's the payoff for them working with you? What is it costing them not to work with you (in terms of time, energy, money, or peace of mind)?

— *Lesson* —

Money language is powerful. It helps you and your customers see the value in what you do.

What if you help people with their relationships – anything from dating advice, marriage counseling, and parenting advice to matchmaking and networking services?

- *Save* your marriage.
- *Invest* in your child's self-esteem.
- Good relationships are *priceless*.

You can use this money language in subtle ways, or you can be explicit about how you can help people in any of these areas. This is especially important if you want to charge premium prices: your clients need to see the value in working with you.

EXERCISE: MONEY LANGUAGE

Answer these questions in your journal:

- How do I help clients make or save money?
- What is a priceless result I offer?
- What does it cost my clients not to work with me?
- How can I use money language in my marketing?

Make It Easy for People to Give You Money

If I see people I like or read an article about them that resonates with me, I often look for the next step to take with them, like buying their book or scheduling a private consultation. But most of the time, I find that there *is* no next step. There's no offer and no obvious way to give that person money, so I forget about it. Some entrepreneurs will do anything to avoid asking for the sale, including getting awkward at the very idea of money changing hands.

My best sales technique has been to say, 'I have this thing that could help. Here's how you can get this thing.' For example, 'I have a Money Bootcamp that could help you with your money blocks; here's where you sign up.' It's chill, it's straightforward, and it's non-sleazy.

Tell people what to do. I often use the words 'next step' in my marketing. I freely give information, and then I say, 'If you want to take this further, the next step is to sign up for my Money Bootcamp,' and I point them to the website. Easy. It's totally okay for you to make an offer, and it's okay for people to say no. But some people want and need exactly what you have, right now. Stop hoarding your talents. Help them give you money!

Sales really can be this easy! Chill and prosper. Just make the offer!

Business mentor Fabienne Fredrickson calls this 'sharing your brownies.' Imagine yourself hosting an informal dinner party for friends and spending the whole evening talking about the delicious brownies you just made. After dinner, you head off to the kitchen to get them but never return. Or you come back empty-handed and never mention them again. This awkward behavior is precisely what happens when entrepreneurs chicken out of asking for the sale. They build up all this anticipation for what they can do, and then they ghost! They don't follow through with the goods, and don't share their brownies! It's selfish.

Now, imagine that you do offer the brownies to your guests. Most people will *love* them. But, inevitably, there will be guests who are too full, on a diet, or just don't *like* brownies. Would you be offended (maybe) or cry (doubtful)? Would you be so disappointed that you refuse ever to hold a dinner party again? Probably not. Why? It's just brownies – some people like them, and some don't.

Someone once asked me, 'Denise, how do I buy your Money Bootcamp? Is there a special hidden password or something?' I thought, *What is she talking about? It's right there on my website!*

But it wasn't. It was hidden behind pages of digital breadcrumbs. I thought it was obvious, but it required detective work to find. I was actively *hiding* my brownies! All the marketing techniques in the world aren't enough if you make your customers work to give you money. Make it an easy *yes* for them. Have an obvious 'Work with me' or 'Hire me' button on your website. At the bottom of every page, have a 'next step' call to action.

A comedian I follow has a plug for his book at the bottom of *every single blog post*. Eventually, I bought it because he kept reminding me! I see lots of entrepreneurs put out amazing content every week, but they don't give concrete solutions as a follow-up. They write thoughtful, useful newsletters and always provide value. Yet they ask *nothing* in return. If you don't ask, you don't get. Even toddlers know this. It's okay to say, 'Here's some free info, and if you want to take this further, here's how you can work with me.' Or 'Here's how you do XYZ, but if you want to outsource it, I can do it for you! Book here.' It honestly doesn't have to be more complicated than that.

Here are some examples:

- 'Here's your free weekly horoscope. If you want a more personalized, in-depth horoscope, you can buy it here.'

- 'Here's my DIY guide for making your own website in a weekend. If you'd rather have me do it for you, you can buy my website package here.'

- 'Here are three things I did to improve my own fertility. If you want even more tips on getting pregnant, you can buy my fertility book here.'

If you have a solution, why not just give it to people who need it, and just assume that people who want your help are willing to pay you for it. To those who write back and say, 'Oh, I was hoping you'd help me for free' (and they will), you can simply say, 'I can't help with that. Good luck with your search,' or just repeat the message, 'I do exactly what you're after for my paying clients. Here's the link again.' If you have free or low-cost offerings, you could point people who are looking for free services to those.

You don't have to work with people for free. Offering them a different solution is okay. (There's advice on how to deal with persistent brain-pickers in Part III: Money.)

What to Offer When You're Starting Out

When in doubt about which products or services you should create first, offer your time. It can take months to write a book, create a course, or develop a product, but you can start making money right away through coaching, mentoring, consulting, training, or offering personal support.

When I started out as a life coach, all I had to sell was coaching sessions with me. I didn't have any books, courses, or events for people to buy. It was basic: an hour with me cost $75. I didn't even really specify what they'd get for that – I just promised an hour of 'coaching.' I didn't have a sales page or testimonials – just a payment link at the end of every blog post that basically went like this: *'Here's how to make a dream board. If you need help setting and achieving your goals, book a coaching session with me here.'*

In a world of carefully curated social media accounts, it's easy to forget that some people have a business at all! I often see 'empowering' posts with no indication whatsoever of what the poster actually does. Don't forget to tell people how you can help them. Making their day a bit brighter isn't enough (if there's nothing for them to buy, you've got a hobby, not a business). Remember this affirmation: *I serve, I deserve.*

It's okay to give to your audience, and it's okay to receive money in return. Making offers is just telling people how you can help them; it's the next logical step. And people will thank you for it!

EXERCISE: PROVIDING CLARITY FOR YOUR CUSTOMERS

Go through your website, blog posts, and social media accounts (or get someone else to) and evaluate the following:

- Is it really clear how people can work with me?
- Am I giving them a next step?
- Am I making it really easy for people to give me money?
- Can I make it even *more* obvious?

How to Get People to Commit

I go to a local nail salon that *never* turns away a potential customer. Even if they're busy, they'll put your feet in warm water and give you a magazine. At that point, you're *committed*. Even if you sit there for 20 minutes, you feel like you're a customer, so you're not going to dry off your own feet and leave.

Contrast this to another salon I went to recently. I just needed a quick pedicure but they turned me away, even though the place was *totally empty*. They offered to fit me in, in three days' time; but if they had asked me what I wanted, I could have been out of there in 10 minutes.

As a family, the same thing often happens to us at restaurants. With young kids, you eat early and quickly; you're not lingering over dessert! But we get turned away all the time, even when the place is completely empty. We've since learned to say, 'We promise we'll be quick!' Or they could hand us a take-out menu and some free breadsticks while we wait. A bird in the hand is worth two in the bush!

I'm a *huge* fan of any restaurant that gives free food while I'm waiting, because I get hangry. Giving waiting customers a few nuts, olives, or chips and salsa (my favorite) is equivalent to putting my feet in warm water and bringing me a magazine. It inspires commitment, generates loyalty, and costs very little. I've walked out of restaurants after being ignored for ages, but had I been given free food, I would have happily waited for service. This has *huge* applications for any business. Do you see the theme? Micro-commitments! When you have available clients, ask them to commit to you in very small ways.

This is exactly what I did with 'mini-dates' when I conducted my internet dating research. What's the marketing equivalent of a mini-date? An offer to work with you. Most marketing gurus advocate giving a low-cost, low-commitment offer, like an e-book, a cheap course, or an inexpensive taster of your work, with the idea that this will be the 'gateway drug' to working with you further. You might have also heard this called a 'tripwire.' Basically, it's a tasty little snack that people can enjoy while they decide if they want to continue working with you.

The mini-date might be a free consultation to see if there's a fit on both sides – a casual 'try before you buy.' Your best customers are the ones who have already made a commitment to you, so give them the opportunity to buy *more*.

Don't be afraid to upsell. For example, one of my most popular freebies is my Manifesting Formula Workshop – there's no commitment other than providing an email address. At the end, I offer my Advanced Manifesting Course for $197, and if someone buys *that*, I casually suggest they join my Money Bootcamp; if they do that, I credit them for their Manifesting Course purchase. Not everyone takes me up on this offer, but enough people do to make it worthwhile. If you're interested in the statistics, the normal 1 percent of people buy the Manifesting Course, but a whopping 20 percent of those people upgrade to the Money Bootcamp at $2,000. Trust me: it's worth making the offer!

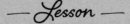

— Lesson —

Get people to commit to you – even in small ways.

Practice Your 'Closing' Technique

It's obvious to say, but you don't have a client until they've paid you some money.

When I was a teenager, I was a children's performer at a summer fair. Every day, I noticed that the most popular food stall was the corncob-on-a-stick. When the queue got out of control, the owners of the business did the most genius thing: they walked the length of it and collected everyone's money in advance. It was a pretty simple set-up: each corncob was $4, and you could pick any flavoring you wanted once you got to the counter. So, they collected the right amount of money and gave each person a ticket for pre-purchased corncobs. After a customer had paid, they were *not* going to leave that queue: they were committed.

I've had 'discovery' calls with potential suppliers who go round and round about their service until I finally say, 'Okay, how can we work together? Tell me the options.' I often have to sell myself to *them*! Then, even when they tell me the price, I have to say, 'Okay, how do you want me to pay? Do you take credit cards?' because they never ask! I'm very reluctant to get on the phone with anyone unless I'm interested in their service. Assume the same is true for your customers. Let them pay you money!

When I was offering coaching packages, I'd often give potential clients a free 'taster' session to see if there was a fit. At the end of the session, I'd pitch my services, and if a client was interested, I'd be ready to take a deposit over the phone to 'secure their spot,' otherwise they would inevitably chicken out or feel scared about taking action. Remember the corn stand? People who pay a deposit are *committed*.

Your fear of sales might come from watching movies like *Wall Street* or experiencing a pushy salesperson in real life. You might even have sat through an excruciating sales pitch and vowed never to be a sleazy salesperson *ever*. Well, it doesn't have to be that way. You're just making people an offer to work with you – not asking for a kidney!

If you practice your closing technique, you'll naturally find the best fit, won't sound like a robot, and won't forget to ask for the sale. With practice, you can be relaxed about asking for it without sounding vague or chickening out. Write your favorite closing technique on a Post-it and put it where you can see it while you're on sales calls. Here are some examples:

- Here are my three solutions – which one sounds best to you?

- How would you like to pay your deposit?

- Are you ready to book your first session?

- Seeing now what I offer, would you like my help?

Be prepared to get that money! Don't make people wait for the invoice – have payment options ready to go (especially over the phone), and don't chicken out of receiving that money, honey!

I asked some of my Money Bootcamp students for their 'chill-closing' tips:

- **Jodie Thornton**: 'Every time I had a sales conversation, I used to panic! Now I give myself permission to be imperfect; the conversation goes how it goes, good or bad. Afterward, I debrief with myself to get better for next time. It's just practice!'

- **Anthea Cutler:** 'I used to overthink how the sales conversation was going to go. Now I take a few moments to connect to my potential client and their struggles, and figure out how I might be able to help. Then I jump on the call to first listen and then simply let them know how I can help. It takes practice, but it's powerful.'

- **Romina Cavagnola:** 'I would get so caught up in the pressure of 'having a sales conversation' that I would often not even pitch my offer (then stew over it for days afterward). Now I trust that whatever needs to be said will come to me, and I have closed more clients in this way because it's quickly obvious if we're a match.'

- **Ali Bengough:** 'It's crucial in my business that I create and maintain a safe space for my clients. So, I practiced letting go of the need to make sales, and it became okay for people to ask questions and say no. And that freed me up to relax and be myself. Sales conversations became natural and fun.'

- **Tiffany Souhrada:** 'Sales conversations used to be a major stressor for me; I would overthink every little part of the conversation for days before the actual call. Now I realize sales conversations are just another way to connect with people. It's just as much about me working with the potential client as it is the potential client being able to work with me.'

- **Ashley Winning:** 'Closing is one of the hardest parts of my business. But I like to think that if I can have the courage to put myself out there, be vulnerable, and push through that block, I know that it will soon become a natural process that I no longer have to push through. It will become as natural as brushing my teeth.'

- **Camila Sunshine:** 'I used to feel like a fraud in sales calls, and my mind would assume that clients weren't interested in working together. Now I approach calls as being a deep conversation with a new friend I'm excited to meet.'

> — *Lesson* —
>
> **Practice asking for the sale!**

Sweeten the Deal

I love offering incentives for people to work with me, mainly because I know it works for me as a customer! I like an extra nudge to get off the fence, and if I get a sweet deal out of it, even better (especially if I was ready to buy anyway). For phone or webinar sales pitches, I often give a special price that's only valid for 24 hours or, if I'm selling on stage, it's for 'today only.' Your sales incentive could be a limited-time discount or an added bonus that's valid only for the first few customers.

Again, this doesn't have to be pushy or salesy. There's a way to do it that's open, transparent, and kind. I openly tell customers that the reason I offer an incentive is that I know some people need a nudge to do something they want to anyway. And I remind them that, if they sign up later, they'll just have to pay full price, so no big deal either way. I'm giving them an option and a choice to take it. I've seen this done in sleazy ways, like, *'Run to the back of the room now and sign up or you're a loser!'* but it's all in the delivery. Make it a reward, rather than a penalty.

> — *Lesson* —
>
> **People won't have an opportunity to work with you unless you ask.**

Overcoming the Fear of Rejection

Let's reframe 'selling' into 'service.' You're not taking people's money: you're making a fair exchange. They're investing in themselves, and you're providing a valuable service in return.

The idea of hearing no might be terrifying to you, but you're going to hear it a lot more than you'll hear yes. Remember the 1 percent conversion rule. If you focus on the fact that 99 percent of people will say no, you might never get started, so you have to focus on the *yeses*. Sometimes no means a 'not now.' Sometimes what you're offering isn't a good fit for a prospective client (or you). Sometimes customers would genuinely work with you if they had the money. It's tough when you know they need you, but their inability to afford you is honestly none of your business. Move on to the next person you can help.

You might even have had old clients stop working with you. It will happen, and you'll want to grab their ankles as they walk away and scream: *'Why are you leaving meeeeeeee?'* But the best thing for you (and your dignity) is to let them go. It's not personal. There are many reasons why someone says no (that have nothing to do with your talent), for example:

- They don't need what you're offering right now.

- They are *shocked, disappointed,* and even *angry* that you're selling them something. (These people are not your customers.)

- They're just not that into you or your style of doing business. (These people are not your customers.)

- They don't have the money (right now).

- They think they can do it themselves.

- They don't understand what it takes to get the results you offer.

Either way, it's none of your business. It's okay for someone to say no, and there are plenty more fish in the sea. Not everyone has to be your client. Here's the truth: if you can't handle even the tiniest bit of rejection, you're going to struggle in business. If you're too scared to ask for the sale because people might say no (and they will), then you won't have the opportunity to serve the people who *want* to work with you.

That's not to say rejection is fun. I'm not like, 'Bye, bitch!' every time someone says no. I've never been rude back or said: 'Well, you're doomed to fail, then.' I try to be gracious about it. It's not personal and I just move on. Sometimes those 'no' clients are ready to work with you in the future, so don't burn those bridges. Your business won't be successful in a day. Your community won't be built in a week. It's going to take time, so show up and be consistent. Every no will get you closer to *yes*.

The original *Chicken Soup for the Soul* book was rejected 144 times; today, that series has sold more than 100 million books. The novel *The Help* received 60 rejections, but eventually it was on the *New York Times* best-seller list for more than 100 weeks and was made into a movie that received more than 40 awards.[1] Author Kathryn Stockett says '… letter number 61 was the one that accepted me. What if I had given up at 15? Or 40? Or even 60?'[2]

I've been rejected so many times on the path to a million-dollar business. But I don't focus on that. Rejection is just inevitable, and I'm not willing to let it stand in the way of my dream life. Neither should you.

— *Lesson* —

If you never ask, the answer is always no.

How to Reject 'Wrong Fit' Clients

You want to create more ease and flow in your work? At some point during the sales process, you'll realize that you can't, don't want to, or *shouldn't* work with some potential clients. Maybe you're seeing red flags about their temperament; perhaps they're at the wrong stage of life and business for your expertise, or they see you as a silver-bullet solution to their problems. Pretty much every entrepreneur I know has taken clients when they should have known better, but you'll learn that through trial and error (and it's a rite of passage anyway!)

Some businesses even use rejection in their marketing, like the canned seafood brand John West. Their slogan 'It's what John West rejects that makes John West the best' recently got changed to a simple 'It's a No from John West.' Are you exclusive? Do people have to jump through hoops to work with you? Make that really clear in your marketing – not only to pre-screen clients but to get them excited about working with you.

I once asked my friend for a recommendation for an accountant, and before she gave me a name, she said, 'He doesn't work with *everyone*. He only works with people he really believes in.' I was nervous and went into the introductory meeting trying to sell myself to *him*! Like, 'Please sir, can I give you some money?'

You'll start to realize who you can and can't help, and it's okay to say no. You're not rejecting abundance from the universe – you're being really smart and discerning. No amount of money is worth accepting for a situation you know is going to cause you stress. Over time, you'll get better at pre-screening your potential clients, but some will slip through your net, so you have to be able to skillfully say no to them. How? Make it about *you*, not *them*, by saying:

- 'That's not my area of expertise.'

- 'I don't think I'm the best person for you.'

- 'I'd love to help, but I can recommend someone who's a better fit.'
- 'I'm booked out right now.' (White lies are okay sometimes).

The most gracious way I've handled it is to say, 'Look, I'd gladly take your money, but from my experience with this particular situation, I know I'm not the best person to help you. It just won't be a good use of your investment.' Then I recommend a different solution – in the form of a book, resource, course, or another provider who's a better fit.

Ignore your gut at your peril. I've had friends who ignored the signs because they needed the money and ended up in litigation with disgruntled clients, turned off other customers (in retreat or group coaching settings), or just ended up in a miserable experience all round. *Listen to your gut!*

— *Lesson* —

You don't have to work with everyone.

How to Prevent Buyer's Remorse

Have you ever had a client who was enthusiastic to work with you and then ghosted when you sent an invoice? Or worse, paid and then, days later, asked for a refund? Yeah, me too. It sucks, but you can avoid it with a few more micro-commitments post-purchase.

Your after-sales service is incredibly important. One of my pet peeves is when you buy something online and then hear nothing. You feel like the sale was the most important thing, and now you're an actual paying client, you're at the bottom of their priority list. Remember, getting the sale is half the battle – now you have to deliver the goods to ensure a happy customer!

Don't make people guess or wonder what happens next. On your online thank-you pages, tell them what to do next in really simple language. I usually make a simple video, saying something like, 'Thanks for your purchase. Here's *exactly* what to do next.' If you need people to fill in a form or schedule time with you, make it incredibly obvious. I've even seen screenshots of what the email the customer will get looks like, and a reminder to check their spam folder. Show your customer service email address, so they know how and where to get help.

Embrace the Keyless Life philosophy and set up autoresponders and automated receipts, so you don't have to do any of this manually. Use an online scheduling system, so you don't have to chase people down to find a mutually convenient time to talk. Make your life and theirs as easy as possible. Good follow-up helps clients avoid buyer's remorse and makes them feel committed. Yes, they just gave you their money, but you want them to feel safe and secure about it, even after clicking the 'Buy now' button. You don't want them to worry whether they've made the wrong decision. Trust me: that's when you'll get refund requests, even from people who literally *just* bought from you.

On my Money Bootcamp thank-you page, I have a little video of current members giving advice about how to get the most out of the course, and even about how nervous they were to join at first. This assures new members that they've made the right decision. I also provide the link to the member's group right away. Joining a group and introducing themselves is a micro-commitment that's a lot easier than diving straight into a course. We've done the research, and members who join the group are way less likely to ask for a refund, especially if they had tech problems getting in or their introductory email went into spam (things that make them think they made the wrong decision).

Another way to delight your clients and inspire loyalty is to add unexpected surprises after they buy. For example, you could

send them some of your favorite resources or tools to help them –
something they can access right away (like a metaphorical free chips
and salsa) that will solidify their commitment to working with you.

Now, a *huge* mistake that entrepreneurs make is over-delivering
in ways that cause stress, cost money, and lead to unnecessary waste.
There's nothing wrong with being generous to your clients, but do it
appropriately, and don't create extra work for yourself unless it's in
line with what you're offering. For example, my web designer, Ellissa
Jayne, sent me a cinema gift card when I signed with her and flowers
when we wrapped up the new site. It wasn't a cheap project – it was
a significant investment in my website – and Ellissa treated me like a
VIP. That's appropriate.

Over-delivering for someone who has bought a cheap course
or e-book? No: that's not sustainable for your business. Instead of
mailing presents to every single client, consider freebies that don't
cost you much but are valuable to them. For example, my Money
Bootcamp students get free access to many of my other courses
and programs, which don't 'cost' me anything and are completely
automated to deliver. Keep physical gifts to a minimum and save the
high-end items for your high-end clients.

CASE STUDY: LETTING GO OF CLIENT OUTCOMES

Name: *Michelle Gyimah, Spain*
Business: *Organizational pay gaps consultant*

*I was working hard and doing all the things I 'should' do, yet I
still wasn't earning much money.*

*It was so powerful to read in Chill and Prosper that it's my
business and my rules. We live in an age where my mother,
grandmother, great-grandmother, and so on would have
loved my choices today. I realized that if my measurements
of success are a mixture of good money, enjoying my work,*

helping others, and creating a new and innovative family legacy, I don't have to follow the conventional rules.

For me, this meant letting go of the need to say yes to things I didn't want to do. It also meant detaching myself from feeling responsible for client outcomes and doing everything they want from A–Z.

For years, this has been a real stumbling block. However, letting this obligation go allows me to stay in my zone of genius, which, in turn, makes me happier and more productive. Plus, the types of inquiries coming into my business now are much more aligned with what I enjoy doing.

So now, I focus on providing insights and strategies to my clients and nothing else. This is where I shine.

— *Lesson* —

Your client is ultimately responsible for their results.

CASE STUDY: SIMPLICITY IS GENEROUS TOO

Name: Leonie Dawson, Queensland, Australia
Business: Author, podcaster, and course creator

Even after two decades of doing business online and taking over $11 million in revenue, I was worried about whether I was enough as a teacher. Should I be more polished and professional? Should I swear less? Should I hide that I'm neurodiverse, have ADD and ADHD, and have experienced anxiety and depression?

I wanted to try out a different model of teaching, with shorter workshops instead of longer courses, but I was feeling anxious about it. This book reminded me I don'' need to know everything; I can just share what I know.

I've started experimenting with selling online workshops (with 1–2 hours of videos) rather than 4–6 week-long e-courses. They take so much less of my energy, and my students adore them. My first one, 'Marketing Without Social Media,' made over $165,000 in the first launch.

I'm creating courses at a prolific rate without getting paralyzed or over-delivering with too much content. I make sure my head stays firmly out of my butthole!

— *Lesson* —

You can be simple and generous. It's not one or the other.

EXERCISE: RETHINKING CLIENT CARE

Go through your after-sale process and evaluate:

- Do my clients know *exactly* what to do after they purchase?
- What else can I put on my 'thank you' page?
- What processes can I automate post-sale?
- What bonuses can I offer to surprise and delight my customers?

Your Simple Marketing Plan

Remember, marketing boils down to two things: share and make offers. Your marketing plan doesn't have to be complicated.

Something is better than nothing, and you'll be surprised by how much progress you can make even if you half-ass it. Keep it simple, tweak as you go, but above all, take action!

I've compiled all the marketing questions in this section into a simple marketing plan that you can customize, and I've also included my own marketing plan. (You can download both at denisedt.com/chill) You don't have to answer every question. Choose the ones that will move your business forward, and take action. If you improve just one thing a month, it will make a huge difference in your business. Remember, SHAMOFF and prosper.

The 1 Percent Conversion Rule

Remember, for a mass-market campaign, your results will be 1 to 2 percent. If you're selling from the stage, it could be 5 to 15 percent, and if you're selling over the phone, it could be 25 to 75 percent.

- How many clients could I realistically handle right now (considering time, energy, systems, and customer service)?
- To hit my sales targets, how many potential customers do I need to reach?

Show Up, Be Seen, and Be Heard

- What free content do I want to create?
- What incentives do I have for people to join my email list or subscribe to my updates on social media?
- What Hairy Toes Strategy would work best for my audience?
- Which topics are in scope and out of scope for my business?
- Can I stop some of my marketing efforts? If so, which ones?
- Which marketing medium works best for me?

- How often do I want to contact my audience?

- Which marketing tasks could I batch?

Make Offers

- What do my customers really want? What's their biggest desire?

- How can I bring money language into my marketing?

- What micro-commitments would work for my audience?

- Am I being clear about the benefits of working with me?

- What red flags should I look out for in potential clients?

- How could I be clearer in asking for a sale?

- How can I avoid buyer's remorse?

 **THE BIG IDEA**

If you remember nothing else from Part IV of the book, remember this: *Marketing is simply manifesting the clients you need to create a successful business!*

Your Mission and Legacy

> *'Carve your name on hearts, not tombstones.*
> *A legacy is etched into the minds of others*
> *and the stories they share about you.'*
>
> SHANNON L. ALDER

Oprah Winfrey told her mentor, the late writer and activist Maya Angelou, 'This girls' school I'm building in South Africa will be my greatest legacy. It will change the trajectory of the girls' lives. It will impact generations to come.'

Maya interrupted Oprah: 'You have no idea what your legacy will be! Your legacy is every life you touch! It's every person who watched your show and was moved to do something: go back to school, leave an abusive marriage, stop hitting their kids, no longer remain silent, not be a victim. It's not one thing – it's everything!'[1]

When I met Oprah on her Sydney tour, she asked me what I learned from her show. I said, 'To break the cycle.' She said, 'Ah, I raised you.' It's true. I can't underestimate the impact Oprah has had on my life. I'm a multimillionaire today because of that lesson.

Millions of other people have broken cycles because one Black woman born in 1954 in Kosciusko, Mississippi, dared to dream that she could grow up differently than her grandmother did: 'I remember a specific moment, watching my grandmother hang the clothes on the line, and her saying to me, "You are going to have to learn to do this," and me *knowing* that my life would not be the same as her life.'[2]

I'm not descended from slaves, and I acknowledge my privilege as a white woman – my family have always been working-class people, but with dysfunction, addiction, and problems like many others. My life without that lesson would have been okay. But I want my business to honor my mother and grandmother too.

My mum, Vicki, had me at 17, and I've seen first-hand what a lack of money does to a woman's choices, especially when she has kids. Now I get to support my mum financially, so she can travel and relax. I'm so thankful she was able to retire from her healthcare job.

My nan, Judy Hannah Thomas, worked hard, raised four kids, and would have had a completely different life if she'd had my financial independence. Instead, she did what she could, and her side hustles paid for holidays. She sold cosmetics, bartended at her local bowling club, and took in sewing for extra money (and apparently once spilled a cup of tea on a wedding dress that had to be completely unpicked). If born in my generation, I'm sure Judy Hannah Thomas would have a thriving Etsy store or be an artist. Before she died, I saw all these half-finished oil paintings in her bedroom. My grandfather had a whole room for his hobbies and trophies; she hid hers away in a closet.

The year before she died, we went on a long road trip together. I was really into personal development tapes, and we listened to six hours of guys like Zig Ziglar and Dr. Wayne W. Dyer. At the end of the trip, she turned to me and said, 'You could do this.'

I wish she was here to see my life and what I've built for our family. I'm sure she'd be proud – not of the trappings of success but of my financial independence, because for women of her generation, their only backup was hiding 'running away' money at the bottom of the sewing box.

Think of all the ancestors who lived so you could be here today. Some were trailblazers, but many died with unpublished books, ideas unmanifested, and burning ambitions unrealized just because of when or who they were born. Because they didn't have any power and they didn't have their own money. It wasn't that long ago that our mothers couldn't have a credit card or a bank loan.

We live in an incredibly privileged time. Yes, it's tumultuous, yes, there's still a lot of inequality to dismantle, but we have all the freedom and opportunity that our ancestors didn't. You can start a business without asking for a bank loan. You can write and publish a book without a single pitch to a publisher. You can choose yourself. You can start today.

> *'You don't have to get it right;*
> *you just have to get it going.'*
> Barbara Corcoran

Yes, I know it's scary marketing yourself and having awkward money conversations, but come on! Our grandmothers would be astounded by our opportunities. We can take an idea and, with a few clicks of a button and this magical thing called the internet, sell something to the whole world? Without our own factory or delivery vans?

We can get paid to help, coach, teach, or counsel someone online? What? It's magical! Next time you're scared, imagine your great-great-great-grandmother standing behind you saying, 'You've got this!' Imagine saying, 'But Gram, what if someone is mean to me on the internet?' Don't let your fear of a one-star review derail your legacy before it has even started.

Breaking cycles is thirsty, scary, and sometimes lonely work, but you don't have to do it alone. If it was easy all the time, everyone would do it, and they don't. But you can. And you will.

You don't need to implement everything in this book to succeed. I'm just one person with one perspective, and you can find other courses and tools to help you shortcut your success. Just make a plan and follow it step by step. But you have to want it.

I used to resent my husband when he didn't see my vision for our life and family. I wanted him to hold the space and make it happen. And he's a massive, integral piece of the puzzle, but I had to find the courage to be the keeper of the flame. I stepped into being the matriarch of our family and did the work to break cycles of poverty, chastity, and silence. He supports it all, but I'm the one who leads it. As Glennon Doyle says, 'We can do hard things.'

A Final Message

> *'You are here for a reason...*
> *you are here to shine your light.'*
> KAREN GUNTON

This isn't goodbye. I hope we'll see each other at an event or at my rose farm one day.

I'm rooting for your success, and I'm here to help. If you'd like to work with me further, remember, I'm just a click away. You can join my Money Bootcamp today, attend our next live monthly call, and be surrounded by incredible fellow Chillpreneurs in our community support group. Join us at denisedt.com/bootcamp.

Remember, being in business can be simple if you let it. Reread this chapter when you need a boost of inspiration. You only have to remember a few things anyway:

- Business is just a game, and you can choose to roll the dice anytime you like.

- Everyone is scared, and everyone feels like an imposter.

- The Witch Wound feels real, but it's safe to visit No Man's Land.

- You're allowed to make money easily and by helping people.

- You're the Golden Goose (and Mickey Mouse too!)

- Create a keyless life – it's allowed to be easy.

- You're allowed to charge whatever price you like.

- Awkward money conversations won't kill you.

- Marketing is manifesting, so share what you know and make offers.

And if you remember nothing else, remember this: you have no idea what your legacy will be. You have no idea how many people will be touched by your business, your leadership example, your messages, and the sheer audacity of you showing up.

It's your time. Why not you?

xx Denise

P.S. If you liked this book, please share it with your business besties or in business groups. I'd love to see a picture of yourself reading this book – it honestly makes my day. Keep in touch!

Instagram: @denisedt
Facebook: facebook.com/denisedt
Twitter: @denisedt
Download your book bonuses here: www.denisedt.com/chill

References

Chapter 1: Playing the Game of Business

1. Katha Pollitt, 'Hers; The Smurfette Principle': www.nytimes.com/1991/04/07/magazine/hers-the-smurfette-principle.html
2. Rachel Rodgers, *We Should All Be Millionaires: A Woman's Guide to Earning More, Building Wealth, and Gaining Economic Power*, p.126; HarperCollins Leadership, 2021.
3. Kimberley Jones, 'What is the Witch Wound?': www.kimberleyjones.com/witch-wound/#sthash.KuH71lym.dpbs
4. ibid.
5. Ewen Callaway, 'Fearful Memories Passed Down to Mice Descendants': www.scientificamerican.com/article/fearful-memories-passed-down
6. Natalie Ann Taggart, 'Healing the Witch Wound': www.huffingtonpost.com/entry/healing-the-witch-wound_us_5a259f77e4b05072e8b56b70
7. ibid.
8. Seren Bertrand, 'Wound of the Witches': www.thefountainoflife.org/wound-of-the-witches
9. Sheryl Sandberg, *Lean In: Women, Work, and the Will to Lead*, p.28; Knopf, 2013.
10. Valerie Young, *The Secret Thoughts of Successful Women: Why Capable People Suffer from the Impostor Syndrome and How to Thrive in Spite of It*, p.40; Crown Business, 2011.

Chapter 2: Three Money Mindset Blocks That Will Derail Your Business Success

1. Marianne Schnall, 'The Rising Activism in Women's Philanthropy': www.forbes.com/sites/marianneschnall/2018/02/02/the-rising-activism-in-womens-philanthropy/#1035b58e44a9

Chapter 3: Millionaire Mindset Lessons

1. Dictionary.com
2. Thomas J. Stanley, William D. Danko, *The Millionaire Next Door: The Surprising Secrets of America's Wealthy*, p.1; Taylor Trade Publishing, 2010.

Chapter 4: Designing a Chillpreneur Business

1. Gary Chapman, *The Five Love Languages: How to Express Heartfelt Commitment to Your Mate*, Northfield Publishing, 1995.

Chapter 5: Protecting the Golden Goose

1. Paul F. Boller Jr., *Hollywood Anecdotes*, p.262; Ballantine Books, 1988.
2. Ruthanne Reid, 'How to kill your "darlings" and survive the process': https://thewritepractice.com/kill-your-darlings
3. Sarah Wilson, 'A long letter about my business': www.sarahwilson.com/2018/02/long-letter-business
4. Amber McCue, 'My cloning secret': www.ambermccue.com/get-efficient-prioritization-matrix/

Chapter 7: Big Pricing Mistakes

1. Carly Findlay, 'Why I won't provide disability advice for free': http://carlyfindlay.com.au/2014/11/09/why-i-wont-provide-disability-advice-for-free
2. ibid.

Chapter 10: Cat Charming and Internet Dating

1. www.kathrynhocking.com

Chapter 11: The 1 Percent Conversion Rule

1. ABC 10 News, 'Customers upset with Passion Planner delays': www.youtube.com/watch?v=klzd8UWXSqw

Chapter 12: Show Up, Be Seen, and Be Heard

1. Kruse Control Inc: 'The Rule of 7': www.krusecontrolinc.com/rule-of-7-how-social-media-crushes-old-school-marketing
2. https://www.iconundies.com

Chapter 13: Make Offers, Make Money

1. https://en.wikipedia.org/wiki/List_of_accolades_received_by_The_Help_(film)
2. Susan Gabriel, 'The Help Turned Down 60 Times': www.susangabriel.com/writers-and-writing/kathryn-stockett

Your Mission and Your Legacy

1. Oprah.com, 'What Oprah Knows for Sure About Being a Supportive Friend': www.oprah.com/inspiration/what-oprah-knows-for-sure-about-being-a-supportive-friend
2. Oprah Winfrey, Quotes from Oprah Winfrey: www.brainyquote.com/quotes/oprah_winfrey_417336

Michelle Swan

ABOUT THE AUTHOR

Denise Duffield-Thomas is a lazy self-made millionaire and unbusy mother of three children. Her best-selling books give a fresh and funny road map to creating an outrageously successful life and business.

As a money mindset mentor, Denise helps women release their fear of money, set premium prices for their services, and take back control of their finances.

She is an award-winning speaker, author, and entrepreneur who helps women transform their Economy-Class mindset into a First-Class life.

Denise lives with her family by the beach in sunny Australia. Find her at www.DeniseDT.com

 DeniseDT

 DeniseDT

 DeniseDT

 www.DeniseDT.com

We hope you enjoyed this Hay House book. If you'd like to receive our online catalog featuring additional information on Hay House books and products, or if you'd like to find out more about the Hay Foundation, please contact:

Hay House, Inc., P.O. Box 5100, Carlsbad, CA 92018-5100
(760) 431-7695 or (800) 654-5126
(760) 431-6948 (fax) or (800) 650-5115 (fax)
www.hayhouse.com® • www.hayfoundation.org

———

Published in Australia by: Hay House Australia Pty. Ltd.,
18/36 Ralph St., Alexandria NSW 2015
Phone: 612-9669-4299 • *Fax:* 612-9669-4144
www.hayhouse.com.au

Published in the United Kingdom by: Hay House UK, Ltd.,
The Sixth Floor, Watson House, 54 Baker Street, London W1U 7BU
Phone: +44 (0)20 3927 7290 • *Fax:* +44 (0)20 3927 7291
www.hayhouse.co.uk

Published in India by: Hay House Publishers India,
Muskaan Complex, Plot No. 3, B-2, Vasant Kunj, New Delhi 110 070
Phone: 91-11-4176-1620 • *Fax:* 91-11-4176-1630
www.hayhouse.co.in

———

Access New Knowledge.
Anytime. Anywhere.

Learn and evolve at your own pace
with the world's leading experts.

www.hayhouseU.com

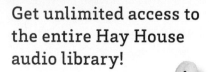

FREE WEEKLY BUSINESS INSIGHTS
from a MASTER IN THE FIELD

Over the past 30+ years, Reid Tracy, President and CEO of Hay House, Inc., has developed an independent upstart company with a single book into the world leader of transformational publishing with thousands of titles in print and products ranging from books to audio programs to online courses and more.

◆ Reid has dedicated himself to **helping authors create successful businesses around their books and vice versa**, and now he's here to help you achieve success by guiding you to examine and grow the business best suited to you.

◆ The Hay House Business newsletter isn't just about book publishing or becoming an author. It is about **creating and succeeding with your business and brand.**

◆ Whether you are already established or are just getting your business off the ground, the **practical tips delivered to your inbox every week** are invaluable and insightful.

*Sign up for the **Hay House Business newsletter**, and you'll be the first to know which authors are sharing their wisdom and market-tested experience with self-starters and small business owners like yourself!*

Hay House Podcasts
Bring Fresh, Free Inspiration Each Week!

Hay House proudly offers a selection of life-changing audio content via our most popular podcasts!

Hay House Meditations Podcast

Features your favorite Hay House authors guiding you through meditations designed to help you relax and rejuvenate. Take their words into your soul and cruise through the week!

Dr. Wayne W. Dyer Podcast

Discover the timeless wisdom of Dr. Wayne W. Dyer, world-renowned spiritual teacher and affectionately known as "the father of motivation." Each week brings some of the best selections from the 10-year span of Dr. Dyer's talk show on Hay House Radio.

Hay House Podcast

Enjoy a selection of insightful and inspiring lectures from Hay House Live events, listen to some of the best moments from previous Hay House Radio episodes, and tune in for exclusive interviews and behind-the-scenes audio segments featuring leading experts in the fields of alternative health, self-development, intuitive medicine, success, and more! Get motivated to live your best life possible by subscribing to the free Hay House Podcast.

Find Hay House podcasts on iTunes, or visit
www.HayHouse.com/podcasts for more info.

HAY HOUSE
Look within

Join the conversation about latest products,
events, exclusive offers and more.

 Hay House

 @HayHouseUK

 @hayhouseuk

We'd love to hear from you!